PRAISE FOR *THE GREAT SUCCESSOR*

"There is, quite simply, no journalist in any language who has done more to unearth and tell the astounding story of Kim Jong Un than Anna Fifield. *The Great Successor* slashes through myths to yield the first essential and vivid biography of the man and his era."

—Evan Osnos, author of *Age of Ambition: Chasing Fortune, Truth, and Faith in the New China*

"Intelligent, insightful, sometimes comic, and also worrying: Anna Fifield has written a vivid, compelling, and, above all, illuminating portrait of a rogue family's rule over the world's most reclusive nation."

—General David Petraeus (US Army, Ret.), director of the CIA when Kim Jong Un became leader

"Anna Fifield owns the North Korea story today in a way that few other journalists, myself included, have ever been able to do. She claims mastery over this most elusive subject."

—Barbara Demick, author of the best-selling *Nothing to Envy*

"With a journalist's eye for detail and with the gift of a storyteller, Anna Fifield has written the quintessential bible on Kim Jong Un. No one working to solve the North Korean puzzle should let *The Great Successor* sit on a bookshelf; it's a must-read."

—Ambassador Wendy R. Sherman, former undersecretary of state for political affairs and author of *Not for the Faint of Heart: Lessons in Courage, Power, and Persistence*

"An important, riveting, and detailed account of the rise of Kim Jong Un. Anna Fifield, who is an intrepid reporter and a lively writer, breaks important new ground in *The Great Successor*. Drawing on a broad array of sources, including remarkable defector accounts, she paints a disturbing portrait of a country fueled by heady delusions of military strength; a potent, bizarre ideology; an unflinching devotion to nuclear weapons; and a disturbing addiction to crystal methamphetamine. Spoiler alert: be prepared for a lot of gore."

—Evans J. R. Revere, senior advisor with the Albright Stonebridge Group and former senior state department official with fifty years of experience working on Korea

"I loved reading Anna Fifield when she had the Korea beat for the *Post*, and now she has outdone herself with the first English-language biography of the most opaque and mysterious leader in the world. Carefully crafted from her reporting with additional research, fieldwork, and exclusive interviews with those close to and in the Kim family, *The Great Successor* peels back the layers to reveal Kim Jong Un's psyche and the ominous future of the country over which he presides. A must-read for the general and expert reader!"

—Victor Cha, Korea chair at the Center for International and Strategic Studies and author of *The Impossible State: North Korea, Past and Future*

"*The Great Successor* shows how a pudgy young heir to tyranny—using fratricide, nuclear terror, crony capitalism, and strategic flattery of a vain American president—has become a sure-footed Machiavelli for the twenty-first century. In this devastating portrait of the latest dictator named Kim, Anna Fifield expertly dissects North Korea's first family of despotism."

—Blaine Harden, author of *Escape from Camp 14: One Man's Remarkable Odyssey from North Korea to Freedom in the West*

"*The Great Success*or is a tour de force of reporting. Anna Fifield has penetrated the secrecy and myths surrounding Kim Jong Un to provide a remarkable, multilayered portrait of North Korea's youthful and enigmatic leader. The ruler depicted in this book, which is based on Fifield's interviews with an impressive range of people who have had contact with Kim or experience inside his system, plus insights gleaned from her own travel as a journalist in North Korea, is not the bomb-throwing 'rocket man' so often mocked and caricatured. Instead, Kim Jong Un comes across as smart, ruthless, diplomatically savvy, and determined to survive at all costs. An essential guide to understanding the man who could well be in charge of North Korea for decades."

—Mike Chinoy, former CNN senior Asia correspondent
and author of *Meltdown: The Inside Story of
the North Korean Nuclear Crisis*

THE
GREAT SUCCESSOR

THE
GREAT SUCCESSOR

The Divinely Perfect Destiny
of Brilliant Comrade Kim Jong Un

ANNA FIFIELD

JOHN MURRAY

First published in Great Britain in 2019 by John Murray (Publishers)
An Hachette UK company

1

Copyright © Anna Fifield 2019

A CIP catalogue record for this title is available from the British Library

Hardback ISBN 9781529387216
Paperback ISBN 9781529387254
Trade Paperback ISBN 9781529387230
eBook ISBN 9781529387247

Printed and bound in Great Britain by Clays Ltd, Elcograf S.p.A.

John Murray policy is to use papers that are natural, renewable
and recyclable products and made from wood grown in sustainable forests.
The logging and manufacturing processes are expected to conform to
the environmental regulations of the country of origin.

John Murray (Publishers)
Carmelite House
50 Victoria Embankment
London EC4Y 0DZ

www.johnmurray.co.uk

To the twenty-five million people of North Korea.
May you soon be free to follow your dreams.

Why, I can smile, and murder whiles I smile,
And cry "Content" to that which grieves my heart,
And wet my cheeks with artificial tears,
And frame my face to all occasions . . .
I can add colors to the chameleon,
Change shapes with Proteus for advantages,
And set the murderous Machiavel to school.
Can I do this, and cannot get a crown?

—Richard, in *Henry VI, Part 3*, Act III, Scene II

CONTENTS

AUTHOR'S NOTE

MANY OF THE ESCAPEES FROM NORTH KOREA WHO APPEAR IN this book asked me not to use their real names. They are afraid that doing so would endanger family members still in North Korea. In those cases, I used pseudonyms or no names at all.

I have used North Korean romanization and style for North Korean places and names. So Kim Jong Un not Kim Jeong-un, Ri not Lee, Paektu not Baekdu, Rodong not Nodong, and Sinmun not Shinmun.

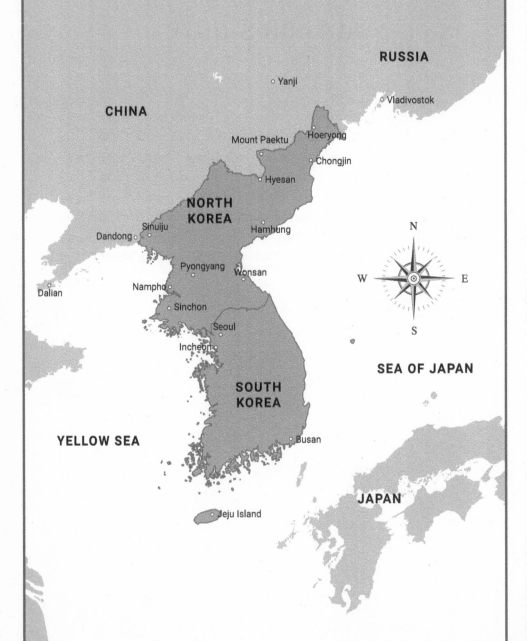

KOREAN PENINSULA

RUSSIA

CHINA

Yanji

Vladivostok

Hoeryong

Mount Paektu

Chongjin

Hyesan

NORTH KOREA

Hamhung

Sinuiju

Dandong

Pyongyang

Wonsan

Dalian

Nampho

Sinchon

Seoul

Incheon

SOUTH KOREA

SEA OF JAPAN

N

W   E

S

YELLOW SEA

Busan

JAPAN

Jeju Island

KIM FAMILY TREE

(Selected members)

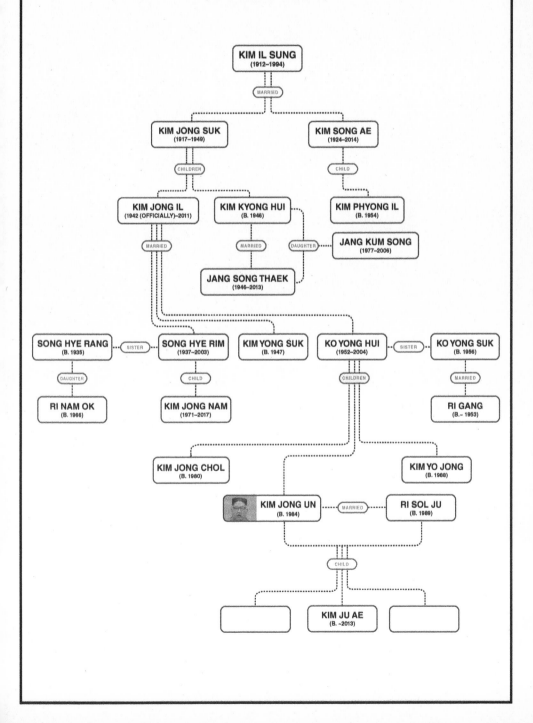

PROLOGUE

I WAS SITTING ON AIR KORYO FLIGHT 152 TO PYONGYANG, READY to make my sixth trip to the North Korean capital but my first since the third-generation leader, Kim Jong Un, had taken over. It was August 28, 2014.

Going to North Korea as a journalist is always a bizarre and fascinating and frustrating experience, but this trip would reach a new level of surrealness.

For one, I was sitting next to Jon Andersen, a three-hundred-pound professional wrestler from San Francisco who goes by the ring name of Strong Man and is known for moves including the diving neckbreaker and gorilla press drop.

I ended up next to Andersen in business class (yes, the Communist state airline has classes) because a passenger wanted my economy seat so he could sit next to his friend. We settled into the red seats of the aging Ilyushin jetliner, which, with their white-doily-covered head-rests and gold brocade cushions, looked like armchairs from Grandma's front room.

Andersen was one of three American wrestlers who, their best days behind them, had washed up in Japan, where their size had helped make them the top attractions they no longer were at home. They enjoyed modest levels of fame and income there. But they were still in the market for new opportunities, so the three were on their way to a gig like no other: the first-ever Pyongyang International Pro Wrestling Games, a weekend of martial arts–related events organized by Antonio Inoki, a lantern-jawed Japanese wrestler who was promoting peace through sports.

As we took off, Andersen told me he was curious to see what North Korea was really like, to get past the clichés of the American media. I didn't have the heart to tell him that he was flying into a charade crafted over decades specifically to make sure no visitor could see what North Korea was really like, that he would not have one unplanned encounter or one ordinary meal.

The next time I saw Andersen, he was wearing tiny black Lycra shorts—some might call them underwear—with STRONGMAN emblazoned across his butt. He came romping into the Ryugyong Chung Ju-yung Gymnasium in Pyongyang in front of thirteen thousand carefully selected North Koreans as the sound system blared: "He's a macho man."

He seemed so much bigger without his clothes on. I gasped at his bicep and thigh muscles, which seemed to be straining to escape his skin like sausage meat from its casing. I could only imagine the shock that went through the North Koreans, many of whom had experienced a famine that killed hundreds of thousands of their compatriots.

Moments later, an even bigger wrestler, Bob Sapp, emerged in a white sequin-and-feather cape. He was dressed for Mardi Gras, not the Hermit Kingdom.

"Kill 'em!" Andersen yelled to Sapp as the two Americans charged at two much smaller Japanese wrestlers.

It was as foreign and as mind-bending as anything I'd ever seen in North Korea: American farce in the home of the world's most malevolent propagandists. It soon dawned on the North Koreans in the audience, no strangers to deception, that it was all highly choreographed, more entertainment than sport. With that realization, they laughed at the theatrics.

I, however, had trouble discerning what was real and what was not.

It was six years since I'd last been to North Korea. My previous visit was with the New York Philharmonic in the winter of 2008. It was a trip that had, at the time, felt to me like a turning point in history.

The United States' most prestigious orchestra was performing in a country founded on hatred of America. The American and North Korean flags stood like bookends at either side of the stage, while the orchestra played George Gershwin's *An American in Paris*.

"Someday a composer might write a work entitled *Americans in Pyongyang*," conductor Lorin Maazel told the North Koreans in the theater. They later played "Arirang," the heartrending Korean folk song about separation, which visibly affected even these carefully selected Pyongyang residents.

But the turning point never came.

That same year, North Korea's "Dear Leader," Kim Jong Il, suffered a debilitating stroke that almost claimed his life. From that point on, the regime was focused on one thing and one thing only: ensuring that the Kim dynasty remained intact.

Behind the scenes, plans were taking shape to install Kim Jong Il's youngest son, a man who was at that time still only twenty-four, as the next leader of North Korea.

It would be two more years until his coronation was announced to the outside world. When it was, a few analysts hoped that Kim Jong Un would prove to be a reformer. After all, the young man had been educated in Switzerland, traveled in the West, and been exposed to capitalism. Surely he would try to bring some of that to North Korea?

Similar hopes had greeted the ascension of London-educated eye doctor Bashar al-Assad in Syria in 2000 and would later await Crown Prince Mohammed bin Salman, who toured Silicon Valley and let women drive after taking power in Saudi Arabia in 2017.

In the case of Kim Jong Un, too, the initial signs were positive, thought John Delury, an expert on China at Yonsei University in Seoul. He was looking for signs that the young leader would bring reforms and prosperity to North Korea, just as Deng Xiaoping did to China in 1978.

But mostly, there was a different kind of optimism—an optimism that the end was nigh.

From nearby Seoul to faraway Washington, DC, many government officials and analysts boldly predicted—sometime in whispers, sometimes in shouts—widespread instability, a mass exodus into China, a military coup, imminent collapse. Behind all the doom mongering was one shared thought: surely this regime couldn't survive the transition to a third totalitarian leader called Kim, much less to a twentysomething who'd been educated at fancy European schools and had an obsession about the Chicago Bulls—a young man with no known military or government background.

Victor Cha, who served as a top negotiator with North Korea in the George W. Bush administration, boldly predicted in the pages of the *New York Times* that the regime would collapse within months, if not weeks.

Cha was maybe the most unequivocal in his predictions, but he was hardly alone. Most North Korea watchers thought the end was near. There was widespread skepticism that Kim Jong Un was up to the task.

I, too, was doubtful. I couldn't imagine North Korea under a third generation of Kim family leadership. I had been following North Korea, up close and from afar, for years. In 2004, the *Financial Times* newspaper posted me to Seoul to cover both Koreas. It was the start of an enduring obsession.

Over the next four years, I traveled to North Korea ten times, including five reporting trips to Pyongyang. I toured the monuments to the Kims and interviewed government officials, business managers, and university professors—all in the company of my ever-present regime minders. They were there to make sure I didn't see anything that called into question the carefully arranged tableau before me.

All the time, I was looking for glimmers of truth. Despite the regime's best efforts, it was easy to see that the country was broken, that nothing was as it appeared. The economy was barely functioning. The fear in the eyes of the people was inescapable. The applause I heard for Kim Jong Il, when I stood just fifty yards from him at a Pyongyang stadium in 2005, seemed canned.

This system could not continue existing into a third generation. Could it?

The experts who predicted widespread reforms were wrong. Those who predicted imminent collapse were wrong. I was wrong.

In 2014, after six years away from the Korean Peninsula, I returned to the region as a correspondent for the *Washington Post*.

A few months into my posting, and almost three years into Kim Jong Un's tenure, I went to cover the pro-wrestling tournament in Pyongyang. The things journalists do to get a visa for North Korea.

I was stunned.

I knew there had been a construction boom in the capital, but I had no idea how widespread it was. It seemed like a new high-rise apartment block or theater was going up on every second block in the center of the city. Previously, it had been unusual to see even a tractor, but suddenly there were trucks and cranes helping the men in olive-green military uniforms put up buildings.

When I'd walked on the streets before, no one as much as glanced at me, even though the sight of a foreigner was a rare thing. They would look down and keep walking. Now, there was an easier air in the city. People were better dressed, kids Rollerbladed in new rinks, and the atmosphere was altogether more relaxed.

There was no doubt that life was still grim in the showcase capital: the lines for the broken-down trolley buses were still long, there were still plenty of hunched-over old ladies carrying huge sacks on their backs, and there was still not a fat person in sight. Not even a remotely chubby one. Apart from the One. But it was clear that Pyongyang, home to the elite who kept Kim Jong Un in power, was not a city on the ropes.

Seven decades after the establishment of the Democratic People's Republic of Korea, I saw no signs of cracks in the communist façade.

Over those seven decades, the world had seen plenty of other brutal dictators rise and reign, tormenting their people while advancing their own interests. Adolf Hitler. Joseph Stalin. Pol Pot. Idi Amin. Saddam Hussein. Muammar Gaddafi. Ferdinand Marcos. Mobutu Sese-Sekou. Manuel Noriega. Some were ideologues, some kleptocrats. Many were both.

There were even cases of family dictatorships. In Haiti, "Papa Doc" Duvalier passed power to his son, "Baby Doc," and Syrian president Hafez al-Assad handed the leadership to his son Bashar. Cuba's Fidel Castro arranged for his brother Raul to take over.

But what sets the three Kims apart is the durability of their family's hold on the country. During Kim Il Sung's reign, the United States went through nine presidents, starting with Harry S. Truman and ending with Bill Clinton. Japan cycled through twenty-one prime ministers. Kim Il Sung outlived Mao Zedong by almost two decades and Joseph

Stalin by four. North Korea has now existed for longer than the Soviet Union.

I wanted to figure out how this young man and the regime he inherited had defied the odds. I wanted to find out everything there was to know about Kim Jong Un.

So I set out to talk to everyone who'd ever met him, searching for clues about this most enigmatic of leaders. It was tough: so few people had met him, and even among that select group, the number of people who've spent any meaningful time with him was tiny. But I went in search of any insight I could get.

I found Kim Jong Un's aunt and uncle, who had been his guardians while he was at school in Switzerland. I went to the Swiss capital of Bern to look for clues about his formative teenage years, sitting outside his old apartment and walking around his former school.

I twice had lunch in a grimy restaurant in the Japanese Alps with Kenji Fujimoto, a down-and-out cook who made sushi for Kim's father and who became something of a playmate to the future leader. I talked to people who had gone to North Korea as part of basketballer Dennis Rodman's entourage and heard tales of drunkenness and questionable behavior.

As soon as I heard Kim Jong Un's older half brother, Kim Jong Nam, had been killed in Kuala Lumpur, I immediately got on a plane and went to the spot where he had been assassinated just a few hours before. I waited outside the morgue where his body was held, watching angry North Korean officials coming and going. I went to the North Korean embassy and discovered they were so annoyed with reporters that they'd actually removed the button on the doorbell at the gate.

I found Kim Jong Nam's cousin, the woman who essentially became his sister and stayed in touch with him long after her defection and his exile. She had been living an entirely new life under an entirely new identity for the previous quarter century.

Then, amid the frenzy of diplomacy in 2018, it suddenly became a lot easier to find people who'd met the North Korean leader.

South Koreans and Americans had arranged and attended Kim Jong Un's summits with presidents Moon Jae-in and Donald Trump. I talked to people who'd talked with him in Pyongyang, from a South Korean singer to a German sports official. I watched his motorcade zoom past me in Singapore. I searched for any understanding to be gleaned from any encounter with this puzzling potentate.

I also repeatedly asked the North Korean diplomats assigned to the mission at the United Nations—a collection of urbane officials who lived together on Roosevelt Island in the East River, sometimes jokingly referred to as a socialist republic in New York City—if I could have an interview with Kim Jong Un. It was a long shot but not a completely crazy idea. After all, Kim Il Sung had lunch with a group of foreign journalists shortly before his death in 1994.

So every time we met—always over lunch at a steakhouse in midtown Manhattan, where they always ordered the forty-eight-dollar filet mignon rather than the daily special—I would ask. Each time, I was met with guffaws.

On the most recent occasion, a month after Kim Jong Un's summit with Donald Trump in the middle of 2018, the suave diplomat responsible for American media, Ambassador Ri Yong Phil, laughed at me and said, "You can dream."

Rather than dreaming, I set out to hear about the reality outside the fake capital, in the places that the regime wouldn't let me visit. I found North Koreans who knew Kim Jong Un, not personally but through his policies: North Koreans who'd lived through his reign and had managed to escape it.

Over my years covering North Korea, I've met scores, perhaps even hundreds, of people who've escaped from the Kimist state. They're often called "defectors," but I don't like that word. It implies that they've done something wrong by fleeing the regime. I prefer to call them "escapees" or "refugees."

It is becoming increasingly difficult to find people willing to talk. This is partly because the flow of escapees has slowed to a trickle during the Kim Jong Un years, the result of stronger border security and rising living standards inside the country. It is also because of a growing expectation that escapees will be paid for their testimony, an ethical no-no for me.

But through groups that help North Koreans to escape or settle down in South Korea, I managed to find dozens of people who would talk to me without payment. They were from all walks of life: officials and traders who'd thrived in Pyongyang, people in the border regions who were earning their livings through the markets, those who'd ended up in brutal regime prisons for the most frivolous of offenses.

There were also people who had also been optimistic that this young leader would bring about positive change, and there were those who remained proud that he'd built a nuclear program that North Korea's richer neighbors had not.

I met some in South Korea, often at down-market barbecue restaurants in their satellite suburbs after they'd finished work for the day. I talked to others near the banks of the Mekong River as they stopped for a pause in their perilous escape, sitting on the floor with them in dingy hotel rooms in Laos and Thailand.

And most dangerous of all, I met some in northern China. China treats escapees from North Korea as economic migrants, meaning they would be repatriated to North Korea and to severe punishment if they were caught. But hiding out in borrowed apartments, they bravely told me their stories.

Over hundreds of hours of interviews across eight countries, I managed to piece together a jigsaw puzzle called Kim Jong Un.

What I learned did not bode well for the twenty-five million people still trapped inside North Korea.

PART ONE

THE APPRENTICESHIP

CHAPTER 1

THE BEGINNING

"The Majestic Comrade Kim Jong Un, descended from heaven and conceived by Mt. Paektu."

—*Rodong Sinmun*, December 20, 2011

WONSAN IS A PARADISE ON EARTH. OR AT LEAST A PARADISE IN North Korea.

In a country of jagged mountains and rocky soil, of Siberian freezes and flash floods, the east coast area of Wonsan is one of the few spots of natural beauty. It has white sandy beaches and a sheltered harbor dotted with little islands. Wonsan is where North Korea's 0.1 percent spend their summers. It's their Martha's Vineyard, their Monte Carlo.

They swim in the sea or relax in the pools at their beachfront villas. They suck the delectable meat from fur-covered claws of the prized local hairy crab and scoop the rich roe from inside it. They repair to nearby Lake Sijung, where the 107-degree mud pool is said to relieve fatigue and erase wrinkles, making a tired old cadre feel instantly refreshed.

This area is especially beloved by the most elite of the elites: the Kim family, which has controlled North Korea for more than seven decades.

It was here that a young anti-imperialist fighter with the nom de guerre of Kim Il Sung landed when he returned home to Korea in 1945, after Japan had been defeated in World War II and ejected from the peninsula.

It was here that Kim Jong Il, just four years old when the war ended, hid out while his father maneuvered to become the leader of the newly created North Korea. This half of the peninsula would be backed by communist Soviet Union and China, while the southern half would be supported by the democratic United States.

And it was here that a little boy called Kim Jong Un spent the long, lazy summers of his childhood, frolicking on the beaches and zooming over the waves on a banana boat.

When he was born on January 8, 1984—a year forever associated in the outside world with oppression and dystopia, thanks to the novelist George Orwell—the little boy's grandfather had ruled the Democratic People's Republic of Korea for thirty-six years. He was the Great Leader, the Sun of the Nation, and Ever-Victorious Brilliant Commander Kim Il Sung.

The little boy's father, an odd little man who was obsessed with films and who was about to turn forty-two, had been designated heir to the regime, ready to give it the dubious honor of becoming the world's first Communist dynasty. He was preparing to become the Dear Leader, the Glorious General Who Descended from Heaven, and the Guiding Star of the Twenty-First Century.

They both loved to spend time in Wonsan. And so, too, did the little boy who would one day follow in their footsteps.

As he was growing up, he would come east from Pyongyang or very far east from his school in Switzerland to spend his summers here. Much later, when he wanted to show off this funfair made for one, he would bring an idiosyncratic American basketballer here for boating and partying—lots of partying. Even later still, an unconventional American real estate developer turned president would praise Wonsan's "great beaches" and describe it as an ideal place to build condos.

The Kim regime shared Wonsan's natural beauty with selected outsiders to propagate the myth that North Korea was a "socialist paradise." The city itself wasn't particularly attractive. Wonsan was entirely destroyed in the sustained American bombing campaign of the Korean War and had been rebuilt in drab Soviet style. Red signs exhorting "Long Live Great Leader Comrade Kim Il Sung" and billboards advertising totalitarianism to a population that had no choice but to buy it sat atop the gray concrete buildings in the city center.

The pristine white beach at Songdowon was always the main attraction. Throughout the 1980s, when Kim Jong Un began playing on the beach, Wonsan was a focal point for communist get-togethers. A Boy Scout camp there in 1985 attracted children from the Soviet Union and East Germany, and the state media published photos of happy children flocking from across the world to spend their summers in Wonsan.[1]

The reality—even then in the 1980s, when the Soviet Union still existed and still propped up its Asian client state—was very different.

When Lee U Hong, an agricultural engineer who lived in Japan but was ethnically Korean, arrived in Wonsan to teach at the agricultural college in 1983, he watched as a class of young women learned about a famous tree called the golden pine. Lee thought they were visiting junior high school students. They turned out to be college students—but because they were so malnourished, they looked years younger.[2]

The following year, when he went to the beach to look for Wonsan's famed sweetbriar flower, he couldn't find any. A local told him that North Korean kids were so hungry that they picked the flowers so they could eat their seeds.

Lee saw none of the advanced agricultural methods or the mechanized farms that the government and its representatives liked to crow about. Instead, he saw thousands of people harvesting rice and corn by hand.[3]

But the Kim regime had a myth to perpetuate. When floods caused devastation in South Korea in 1984, the North sent food aid on ships that departed from the port in Wonsan, which sits just 80 miles north of the Demilitarized Zone, the 2.5-mile-wide no-man's land that has divided the peninsula since the end of the Korean War in 1953.

Eight months after Kim Jong Un was born, even as ordinary North Koreans were suffering from severe food shortages, sacks marked "Relief Goods for South Korean Flood Victims" and bearing the symbol of the North Korean Red Cross were being shipped from Wonsan.

"As it was the first happy event in our 40 year history of separation, the wharf was full of passion," the *Rodong Sinmun*, the mouthpiece of the ruling Workers' Party of Korea, reported in 1984. "The wide wharf echoed with cheerful farewells . . . The whole port was full of love for family."

Of course, Kim Jong Un would know none of this. He was living a blissful, cloistered life in one of the family's compounds in Pyongyang or at the beachfront residence in Wonsan, where the house was so huge that the Kim children rode a battery-powered golf cart to get around.[4]

In the 1990s, while North Korean children were eating seeds for nourishment, Kim Jong Un was enjoying sushi and watching action movies. He was developing a passion for basketball and was flying off to Paris to visit Euro Disney.

He lived behind the curtain of the world's most secretive regime until 2009, when he reached the age of twenty-five. Then, when he was formally introduced to the North Korean elite as his father's successor, his first commemorative photo was taken in Wonsan. It was broadcast on North Korean television only once or twice and is very grainy, but it shows Kim Jong Un, dressed in a black Mao suit, standing under a tree with his father, his brother and sister, and two other men.

Wonsan remained an extremely important place to Kim Jong Un. After he became leader, perhaps to re-create the carefree fun of his youth, he sponsored the creation of a huge amusement park in Wonsan. The city is now home to an aquarium with a tunnel through the tanks, a funfair-style mirror house, and the Songdowon Water Park, a sprawling complex with both indoor and outdoor pools. There is a twirling waterslide that empties into a series of round pools. It is a socialist paradise recast for a theme park era.

Kim Jong Un inspected the development not long after he became "Beloved and Respected Supreme Leader" at the end of 2011. In a white summer shirt with a red pin placed over his heart that featured the faces of his father and grandfather, he leaned over the waterslides and peered along them. He smiled broadly, declaring himself "very pleased" that North Korea had been able to build a waterpark all by itself.

From the high diving boards, kids could see the colorful umbrellas on the beach and the pedal boats in the bay. Summer in Wonsan brought "the unusual sight of students standing on the sandy beach with beautifully colored tubes slung over their shoulders, and laughing grandparents, hand-in-hand with grandsons and granddaughters jumping from foot to foot as they look out at the sea," state media reported.

These facilities are for the proletariat. The royals have their own.

The Kim family's huge compound includes luxurious beachfront residences for the family members, as well as spacious guesthouses for visitors, situated far enough apart from each other and shielded by trees to ensure privacy. Even among the elite, discretion is key. There's a large indoor swimming pool at the compound and pools set into barges that float offshore, allowing the Kims to swim in the water without the perils of the open sea. A covered dock houses the Kim family yachts and more than a dozen Jet Skis. There's a basketball court and a helipad. Not far away is a new airstrip so Kim Jong Un can fly himself into the resort on his personal plane.

The family shares their playground with the other elite who help keep them in power. The Ministry for the Protection of the State, the brutal security agency that runs political prison camps, has a beachfront summer retreat here. So, too, does Office 39, the department charged with raising money specifically for the Kim family coffers. Since their toil funds this playground, it's only fair they should enjoy the spoils.[5]

An unusual feature of the coast at Wonsan—one not yet found in any Western Disneylands, which make do with much tamer firework displays—is the missile launching sites. Kim Jong Un has launched dozens of rockets from the Wonsan area since he became leader and has supervised large-scale artillery exercises there.

On one occasion, he watched as his munitions chiefs used new 300mm guns to turn an island just offshore to dust. On another, he didn't even have to leave the comfort of his beachfront residence. His rocket scientists simply rolled a missile on a mobile launcher to a spot across from the house, and Kim sat at a desk at the window, smiling broadly as he watched it blast off into the atmosphere in the direction of Japan.

And it was here, on his private beach, that Kim Jong Un ran a swimming exercise for the navy's top commanders in 2014. The commanders,

who all looked like they should be collecting their pensions, stripped off
their white dress uniform and hats and changed into swimsuits before
running into the sea and swimming three miles, as if they were on "a
battlefield without gunfire."

It was quite a sight. The new leader, just turned thirty, sat at a desk on
the beach, watching through binoculars as men twice his age and half his
size crawled through the sea on his instruction. The man with no military
experience or qualifications was showing them who was boss. And there
was no better place to do it than on his home turf and surf at Wonsan.

The Kim family's claim on the leadership of North Korea has its origins
in the 1930s, when Kim Il Sung was making a name for himself in
the northern Chinese region of Manchuria as an anti-Japanese guerilla
fighter.

Kim Il Sung was born Kim Song Ju on the outskirts of Pyongyang
on April 15, 1912, the same day that the *Titanic* hit an iceberg and sank.
At that time, Pyongyang was a center for Christianity, so much so that
it was called the Jerusalem of the East. He was born into a Protestant
family, and one of his grandfathers served as a minister.

Imperial Japan had annexed Korea, still one country back then,
two years before he was born. It was the start of a brutal occupation.
To escape the Japanese colonizers, the Kim family fled in the 1920s to
Manchuria. This area had become the focal point for Koreans railing
against the Japanese occupation, and Kim—who took the name Il Sung,
meaning "become the sun," in the early 1930s—emerged as an anti-
imperialist leader.

In his official memoirs, Kim talked up the power of the anti-Japanese
forces. "The enemy likened us to 'a drop in the ocean,' but we had an
ocean of people with inexhaustible strength behind us," he wrote. "We
could defeat the strong enemy who was armed to the teeth . . . because
we had a mighty fortress called the people and the boundless ocean
called the masses."[6]

North Korea's official history exaggerates Kim's efforts. It portrays
him as the heart of the resistance at a time when he still had Chinese

and Korean generals above him and claims that the guerrilla movement would have collapsed without him. Though he was just one cog in the resistance machine, Kim even claimed the credit for Japan's defeat in World War II.

At some stage, contrary to the official narrative, Kim Il Sung shifted from his base in Manchuria to the Soviet Union with the woman who, in 1940, became his wife, in common law at least. Kim Jong Suk was probably only fifteen years old and working as a seamstress when Kim Il Sung met her in 1935.

In 1942—again, according to the official history, but in reality it was 1941—she gave birth to their first son, Kim Jong Il, in an army camp near Khabarovsk, in the far east of the Soviet Union.

When the war in the Pacific came to an end and Korea was liberated from Japan, the fate of the peninsula was uncertain. It had existed as one country for almost fourteen centuries. But the United States and the Soviet Union, the victors in the Pacific War, decided to divide the peninsula between them—without bothering to ask the Koreans what they might want.

A young US Army colonel named Dean Rusk, who would later go on to become the American secretary of state, and another officer, future four-star general Charles Bonesteel, found a *National Geographic* map. They simply drew a line across the Korean Peninsula at the 38th parallel, proposing a temporary solution in which the Americans would control the southern half of the peninsula and the Soviets would take care of the northern part. To their surprise, Moscow agreed.

This "temporary" solution lasted much longer than Rusk and Bonesteel ever anticipated or intended. It was cemented into the Demilitarized Zone after the bloody Korean War of 1950 to 1953. It has endured for six decades—and counting.

The Soviets needed to install a leader in their northern half of the new country, a mountainous territory that covered about 46,500 square miles of land. The country is the same size as Mississippi, a bit smaller than England.

Kim Il Sung wanted the job.

While he was in the camp near Khabarovsk, he had impressed his Soviet benefactors enough to earn himself a role in the new North Korean regime. But the Soviets had not envisaged Kim as the leader of North Korea. They were wary of his ambition. Stalin didn't want Kim to build his own power base independent of the Soviet occupation forces.[7]

So there was little fanfare when Kim Il Sung returned to Korea, wearing a Soviet military uniform as the *Pugachyov*, a naval ship, docked at Wonsan on September 19, 1945. He wasn't even allowed to join the Soviet troops who had expelled the last remaining Japanese occupiers and marched victorious into Pyongyang.

Moscow's preferred leader of their new client state was a nationalist called Cho Man Sik, a sixty-two-year-old Presbyterian convert who had headed a nonviolent reformist movement inspired by Gandhi and Tolstoy. He wasn't ideal—the Soviets were suspicious of his ties to the Japanese—but he was promoting education and economic development as the way to ensure a bright and independent future for Korea.[8]

Kim Il Sung wasn't having it. He soon began positioning himself for the role of leader of the new North Korea, a process that involved, among other things, hosting his Soviet patrons at alcohol-fueled banquets and providing them with prostitutes.

It helped improve Kim Il Sung's standing in the eyes of the Soviet generals. Less than a month after his return, Kim Il Sung appeared at a rally in Pyongyang and delivered a speech written for him by Soviet officials. As he took to the stage, cries of "Long live Commander Kim Il Sung" rang out. The people had heard awe-inspiring tales through the grapevine about this outstanding guerrilla leader and his daring feats in Manchuria.

But the man on the stage did not match the picture in their minds. They'd expected a gray-haired veteran, an electrifying figure. Instead, they saw a man who looked much younger than his thirty-three years and was wearing a navy-blue suit that was a size too small and clearly borrowed.

To make matters worse, Kim Il Sung wasn't even very proficient in the Korean language, having spent twenty-six of his thirty-three years in exile. What little education he'd received had been in Chinese. He stumbled through the turgid speech the Soviet occupation forces had written for him, full of Communist terminology awkwardly rendered into Korean. Undermining himself even further, he spoke, as Cho's secretary would later write, in a "duck-like voice."[9]

One onlooker said he had "a haircut like a Chinese waiter" or that he looked like "a fat delivery boy from a neighborhood Chinese food stall." Others called him a fraud or a Soviet stooge.[10]

Kim Il Sung was a flop.

But he got a lucky break when Stalin's team discovered that peacenik Cho was neither Communist nor a pushover. Cho started making irritating demands about running the country as an independent entity. Suddenly, the lackluster Kim Il Sung looked like a useful, pliant alternative.

Cho was quickly arrested and disappeared, and Moscow settled on the ambitious young hopeful as their man. They elevated him through a series of roles until the Soviet occupation officially came to an end. The Democratic People's Republic of Korea was declared founded on September 9, 1948, and Kim Il Sung was installed as its leader.

No sooner had he been appointed than Kim began a personality cult so pervasive it would soon make Stalin look like an amateur. Within a year, Kim started going by the title "the Great Leader." Statues of him started to appear, and history began to be rewritten.

The 1945 speech that bombed was described in his official biography as an electrifying moment. People "could not take their eyes from [his] gallant figure" and cheered out of "boundless love and respect for their great leader."[11]

Kim Il Sung also quickly established a Korean People's Army, led by fellow veterans of the anti-Japanese struggle. He formulated a plan to take control of South Korea, and at a meeting in Moscow in March of 1949, he tried to convince Stalin to support a military invasion with reunification in mind. Stalin turned him down—he did not want to begin a war against nuclear-armed America—and told Kim that the North should respond only if it was attacked.

But Kim and his generals watched enviously as the Chinese Communists ousted Nationalist leader Chiang Kai-shek and his Kuomintang later in 1949. He continued to badger Stalin about making a play for the South, especially after the United States withdrew all of its combat troops from South Korea that year, leaving the lower half of the peninsula vulnerable.

A year after Kim Il Sung first started making the case for war, Stalin finally gave in and approved the invasion in principle—as long as Mao Zedong in China also agreed. Kim went to Beijing in May 1950 and tried to convince Mao, but the Chinese leader was more concerned with Chiang and his Nationalists in Taiwan. He eventually came around to the idea after Stalin leaned on him.[12]

Kim Il Sung seized his opportunity. In the early hours of June 25, 1950, soldiers of the North Korean People's Army drove 150 Soviet-made T-34 tanks over the military demarcation line and into the South. Seven army divisions thundered toward Seoul, followed by North Korean troops on foot.

The North Koreans overtook the entire country except for an area around the southern city of Busan. It looked like it was going to be an easy victory.

General Douglas MacArthur, the commander of the American military in Japan, was caught by surprise, but he reacted swiftly. His troops landed on the mudflats at Incheon, west of Seoul, in September and pushed the northern army back. China, sensing that things had taken a wrong turn, then sent in troops to help North Korea.

After six months, the northern army was back where it started, at the 38th parallel. For the next two and a half years, both sides remained bogged down, unable to make any headway.

It wasn't that the United States didn't try hard to break the deadlock. Just five years after the unfathomable devastation of Hiroshima and Nagasaki, MacArthur, in all seriousness, raised the idea of dropping a nuclear bomb on North Korea.

The nuclear option was quickly discarded. But the United States went for a literal scorched-earth approach with conventional bombs, dropping 635,000 tons' worth on the northern half of the peninsula, more than the 503,000 tons used in the whole Pacific theater during World War II.[13] That included 200,000 bombs unleashed on Pyongyang—one for every citizen in the capital.

Curtis LeMay, the head of the United States' strategic air command, said they "burned down every town in North Korea." After running low on urban targets, US bombers destroyed hydroelectric and irrigation dams, flooding farmland and destroying crops. The air force complained it had run out of things to bomb.[14] A Soviet assessment after the war found that 85 percent of all structures in the North had been destroyed.

By the end of the war, almost three million Koreans—10 percent of the peninsula's population—were dead, injured, or missing, according to historians. LeMay estimated that some two million of the dead were in the North.[15] Some thirty-seven thousand American soldiers were killed during the fighting.

After all this destruction and long after it became apparent that neither the Chinese- and Soviet-backed North nor the American-backed South could win outright, the two sides agreed to an armistice. On July 27, 1953, the fighting stopped. But because a peace treaty was never signed, the war never officially ended.

In the North, Kim Il Sung's regime blamed the conflict on an American-supported invasion from the South, a lie that is propagated in North Korea to this day. The regime pronounced itself the victor.

North Korea still refers to the conflict as the Victorious Fatherland Liberation War. There's a museum devoted to this in Pyongyang, where the wreckages of captured American warplanes are perfectly preserved. It is part of an effort to keep alive the memories of that ferocious war, a way to keep the population on perpetual alert, to make citizens coalesce around the Kim family.

In the immediate aftermath of the war, Kim Il Sung cemented his leadership of the shattered country by overseeing a massive rebuilding program funded by North Korea's allies. He also purged a number of senior military leaders and Workers' Party officials, to whom he assigned blame for the destruction of property and life, and he put down rival factions.

Meanwhile, his propagandists accelerated their efforts to build up admiration around him. Soviet officials—themselves no strangers to personality cults—began voicing concern about the way Kim Il Sung was forcing the North Korean people to revere him.

In a Soviet cable from 1955, officials based in North Korea noted there was "an unhealthy atmosphere of sycophancy and servility toward Kim Il Sung" among senior officials in the Workers' Party.[16] By this time, even the Soviet Union was going off this kind of idolatry. Stalin had died, and Khrushchev had secretly given a speech denouncing the adoration that his predecessor encouraged.

The new leader also set about showing he was no Chinese or Soviet puppet. He began positioning himself as a great thinker who was leading an independent, nonaligned nation.[17]

He espoused a spurious concept called *juche*, pronounced "joo-chay" and usually translated as "self-reliance."

The central idea was that North Korea was entirely self-sufficient and that its achievements had been earned "by our nation itself," conveniently overlooking the state's total dependence on its communist benefactors. But in other ways, North Korea had achieved a level of autarky, crafting relatively independent foreign and defense policies.

Juche was enshrined as policy in the constitution in the 1970s. But the scholar Brian Myers likes to point out that this idea is so thin that the entry in a North Korean encyclopedia for the Juche Tower, a Pyongyang monument, is twice as long as the entry for the ideology itself.

Still, North Korea's economy remained larger than the South's until the mid-1970s. This was partly because the North had all the natural resources, so all Kim Il Sung had to do was rebuild heavy industry and the mining sector that had been developed by the Japanese occupiers. Plus, he had the Soviet Union's provisions to its client state and the benefits of socialist-style labor mobilization. South Korea had to start from scratch after the war.

Now in his sixties, Kim Il Sung was beginning to think about his legacy—and about making sure that the dictatorship he'd established would endure. While the Soviet Union and China were using Communist Party apparatuses to elevate new leaders, Kim Il Sung wanted to keep it in the family. He toyed with passing the crown to his younger brother. To the dismay of some, he instead decided on his eldest son as his successor.

First, however, the system needed a few tweaks.

The 1970 edition of North Korea's *Dictionary of Political Terminologies* stated that hereditary succession is "a reactionary custom of exploitive societies." That was quietly dropped from future publications.[18] State media started referring to "the party center," a phrase used to obliquely refer to Kim Jong Il's activities without explicitly stating his name, and Kim Jong Il began to be promoted up the Workers' Party hierarchy.

The North's allies picked up on Kim Il Sung's plans early on. The East German ambassador to Pyongyang cabled the foreign ministry in 1974 to say that North Koreans were being asked to "swear loyalty to Kim Jong Il" at Workers' Party meetings across the country "in case something grave might happen to Kim Il Sung." Portraits of Kim Jong Il started to appear on the walls of government offices, along with slogans of statements he had made on reunification or socialist construction, the ambassador said.

Official publications began portraying Kim Il Sung as a benevolent, fatherly figure. Photos and paintings showed him lavishing affection on happy North Koreans or laughing with children. This kind emperor façade would make a comeback some fifty years later, when Kim Jong Un would channel his grandfather and adopt the same smiling dictator persona.

Kim Il Sung's first wife and his oldest son were featured prominently for the first time, forming a North Korean holy trinity. Some photos showed Kim Jong Il instructing propagandists and film producers. "He already displays the pose usually reserved for Kim Il Sung in his talks with DPRK citizens," the ambassador wrote. "This visual observation confirms in fact our assumption we have made earlier: Kim Il Sung's eldest son is systematically groomed to become his successor."[19]

At the sixth Workers' Party Congress in Pyongyang in 1980, it was made official. The younger Kim was elevated to high positions in the three main organs of the Workers' Party—the Politburo Presidium, the Central Military Commission, and the party secretariat—in one fell swoop. Only Kim Il Sung and Kim Jong Il held concurrent leadership of all three of the main Workers' Party organs.[20]

Presenting Kim Jong Il as his chosen heir, Kim Il Sung said that his son would ensure the revolutionary task was continued "generation after generation."

Kim Jong Il took on more and more responsibility within the Workers' Party and accompanied his father on his "on-the-spot guidance" tours around the country—the practice where North Korea's supposedly benevolent and omniscient leaders show up unannounced and tell farmers how best to grow their crops or factory managers how best to produce steel. Photos show the recipients of this knowledge dutifully taking everything down in little notebooks.

In 1983, Kim Jong Il made his first known foreign trip without his father, a visit to factories in emerging China. The visit, one of a handful the Dear Leader made over the years, was part of Beijing's efforts to encourage North Korea to embark on a journey of economic transformation without democratizing, just as China had done.

"Through tireless revolutionary activities spanning over 30 years, he ushered in a new era of prosperity," according to an official North Korean history of Kim Jong Il's life that was published soon after he became leader.[21]

But the reticent Kim Jong Il could hardly have been more different from his gregarious father. Kim Il Sung was lionized as a fearless guerilla fighter who led the charge against the imperialist Japanese. Kim Jong Il had next to no military experience. He was a film lover, a heavy-drinking playboy with a bouffant hairdo whose main contribution to the state was the movies he directed.

Still, in 1991, he was pronounced Supreme Commander of the Korean People's Army. It was hardly an auspicious time to cement the succession. The Berlin Wall had come down. Just two days after his promotion, the Soviet Union collapsed. The Communist Bloc that had supported the North Korean regime, both economically and ideologically, was no more.

To bolster the case for hereditary succession in these challenging circumstances, the regime created a fantastical story about Kim Jong Il's provenance that borrowed heavily from both Korean mythology and Christianity. He would be leader not simply because he had been appointed by his father but because he had some divine right.

His birthplace became not a guerrilla camp in Khabarovsk but Mount Paektu, the volcano on North Korea's border with China that has legendary status in Korean culture. It is said to be the birthplace of Tangun, the mythical half-bear, half-deity father of the Korean people. The creature conferred a heavenly origin on the Korean people, and, thanks to this story, Kim Jong Il appeared to come from heaven too.

North Korea's propagandists didn't stop there. They said that Kim Jong Il was born in a wooden cabin and that a single bright star shone in the sky at his birth. They stopped short of making the building a manger or his mother a virgin. But, for good measure, they added a double rainbow spontaneously appearing over the mountain. The myth of the holy Paektu bloodline was created.

Kim Jong Il had been busy perpetuating that Paektu bloodline over the previous two decades. He had racked up quite a cast of wives and consorts—and children.

First, in 1966, Kim Jong Il had married a woman with an appropriate revolutionary pedigree chosen by his father. They reportedly had a daughter in 1968. But the marriage didn't last, and they divorced in 1969. Still, the woman remained in good standing for years afterward, serving in the Supreme People's Assembly for fifteen years and then as principal of the main education college for almost twenty years, taking her into the Kim Jong Un era.

Kim Jong Il then took up with a famous actress called Song Hye Rim, whom he had spotted while he was directing movies. She was older than him and married with at least one child at the time, but he insisted she divorce her husband to be with him. He installed her in one of his mansions in Pyongyang, and in 1971 she gave birth to their son, Kim Jong Nam. Kim Jong Il was overjoyed. In deeply traditional, Confucian Korea, males are prized as heirs to carry on the family name and the family line. But both the relationship and the love child were kept secret from Kim Il Sung until about 1975.

When that child, Kim Jong Nam, was only three years old, the Great Leader told Kim Jong Il that he needed to marry again. Unable to reveal the existence of his mistress and their child, he followed his father's orders and wed the woman who was considered his only "official" wife. They had two daughters.

It wasn't long before a beautiful young dancer called Ko Yong Hui, who was ethnically Korean but had been born in Japan, caught Kim Jong Il's eye. They had three children together: boys called Jong Chol and Jong Un, born in 1981 and 1984 respectively, followed in 1988 by a girl they named Yo Jong.

There was some debate over Kim Jong Un's true birth year, with some sources saying it was 1983. There were suggestions his official birthdate had been moved to 1982 to provide symmetry with his grandfather, born in 1912, and his father, whose birthdate was officially moved from 1941 to 1942.

But Kim Jong Un's aunt, Ko Yong Suk, laughed when I asked about her nephew's birthdate. It had been almost two decades since she had fled the North Korean regime, but she knew for sure that Kim Jong Un was born in 1984. She'd given birth to a son of her own the month before, and she'd changed both babies' diapers at the same time.

The aunt had been looking after all the children. Her sister, Kim Jong Il's concubine, was occupied tending to the designated next leader of North Korea as he worked his way up through a series of Workers' Party and military positions.

Ko and her husband lived in Pyongyang in a compound of several houses—including one for them and one for Kim Jong Il—with a heavily guarded outer wall around the whole compound and another wall around Kim Jong Il's house, which was huge, they said, with a home theater and a big playroom for the kids.

Despite the luxurious surroundings, the children lived a relatively secluded life. They played with their cousins or stayed with their father when he was at home in the compound.

There were no other kids around. The intensely paranoid Kim Jong Il kept all his families separate from each other, meaning that the children grew up without knowing their half siblings or really anyone their own age. Even when he sent them to Switzerland for school, he kept them separate: Jong Nam went to Geneva, while the other three went to Bern.

All the while, Kim Jong Il carried on running the propaganda and agitation department, directing movies, and writing six operas, according to his official biography. He continued to appear alongside his father, dispensing pearls of wisdom on everything from agricultural methods to military tactics during the on-the-spot guidance sessions.

Then came the day for which all the preparation had been put in place: on July 8, 1994, Kim Il Sung died after suffering a massive heart attack. His death was kept secret for thirty-four hours while the regime made the final arrangements to confirm the succession.[22] Then Radio Pyongyang announced the news: "The Great Heart has stopped beating."

In a seven-page announcement, the Korean Central News Agency said Kim would be remembered as a man capable of "creating something from nothing. . . . He turned our country, where age-old backwardness and poverty had prevailed, into a powerful Socialist country, independent, self-supporting and self-reliant."[23]

Although the regime had been readying itself for this moment for a quarter century, Kim Il Sung's death was an earth-shattering event. The system built around a personality cult had lost its personality. It now had to do what no other Communist regime had done before: pass the leadership down from father to son.

Kim Jong Il embarked on a three-year mourning period, not because he was especially grief stricken but because he had been bequeathed a catastrophe and was anxious to avoid the blame for it.

A devastating famine had just begun to ravage the country, the result of decades of mismanagement by the Kim regime. During the Cold War, there hadn't been much incentive to encourage food production in the country's inhospitable soil because the Soviet Union and China had been sending in food supplies. When those shipments stopped, North Korea had to fend for itself. But it didn't have enough arable land, and it didn't have enough energy to produce the chemical fertilizer needed to boost crops.

This political catastrophe coincided with a series of natural disasters: floods and droughts in the mid-1990s that wiped out what little food North Korea could produce. No one knows exactly how many people died during those years. Some experts say it was half a million; others say it could have been as high as two million.

There was an explosion in the number of street urchins whose parents had died or abandoned them during this period. They were rather whimsically called "flower swallows," as if they flitted about looking for nectar. Instead, they were fending for themselves by stealing everything from manhole covers to scraps of wire during these years.

Many of those who survived were skeletons who'd picked single kernels of corn from cow pats and eaten rats to survive. Some did unconscionable things, including resorting to cannibalism, to make it through a period known euphemistically in North Korea as "the arduous march." This was the name that had been given to Kim Il Sung's struggle in Manchuria, and it was resurrected during the famine to create a sense that this was another epic battle for the nation.

The famine loosened the regime's grip on the populace in a way no other event had before. Food rations stopped being distributed; people had to rely only on themselves. Citizens of a Communist state became quasi-capitalists out of necessity—and the authorities had to tolerate it because they knew the state had nothing to give.

Pak Hyon Yong, who was a young man living in Hamhung, north of Wonsan, at the time of the famine, watched his younger brother starve to death. Then his older sister's children. Then his sister too. Realizing he would be next, Pak started making noodles from "corn rice," North Korea's measly substitute staple involving grains of "rice" made out of dried corn kernels. He would eat a little but sell the rest, using the pitiful profits to buy more corn rice for the next day's batch.

"The police would come by and try to persuade me not to sell the noodles, saying that I should not succumb to capitalism and that the Dear Leader would resolve our food shortages," Pak told me in the northern Chinese city of Yanji, where he was living in hiding after he'd escaped from North Korea.[24] But the Dear Leader did no such thing.

The famine in North Korea coincided almost exactly with Kim Jong Il's ascent to power, forever associating him with a time of extreme hardship. Even today, people who have escaped from North Korea tend to remember Kim Il Sung fondly and recall a time when North Korea was strong and prosperous in reality and not just in the state media's version of events.

There was no such love for Kim Jong Il. North Koreans wondered, *If he cares for us so much, why are we starving?*

After the famine passed and North Korea returned to a state of mere gnawing hunger and malnutrition, Kim Jong Il began pouring his energies into the military. He had promoted a "military first" policy and elevated the military to pole position within the regime's hierarchy. The Workers' Party of Korea, the political arm of the regime, adopted the slogan "The Military Is the Party, the People and the Nation."[25] For a cash-strapped regime intent on strengthening its army, no weapon offers more bang for the buck than a nuclear bomb. The regime had been pouring all its energy and resources into a covert nuclear program over the years. Then Kim Jong Il blew the lid off it when his regime conducted its first nuclear test in 2006.

By then, the leader, who was sixty-four, had started to look noticeably unwell. Once plump, his frame was gaunt, and his skin was pallid. In the middle of August 2008, he suffered a stroke.

He recovered, but when he finally appeared in public again, he seemed diminished. He looked smaller and thinner and appeared to have some paralysis on his left side that affected his leg and the use of his left arm.

Speculation mounted about who would succeed the Dear Leader.

According to the rules of traditional Korean hierarchy, it should have been the oldest son, Kim Jong Nam.

Over the years, many people have contended that the First Son lost the crown because of an embarrassing incident that happened in 2001.

That year, Kim Jong Nam was caught sneaking into Japan with a fake Dominican Republic passport bearing the name Pang Xiong—"Fat Bear" in Chinese. Kim Jong Nam, who was with his wife and young son, told Japanese authorities he was just trying to take his family to Tokyo Disney. After that, he went into exile in Macau, a Chinese territory near Hong Kong, and remained based there for the rest of his life. It was never clear if the exile was forced or voluntary.

In fact, he had fallen out of favor many years before.

The succession question had much more to do with the ambitions of the mothers than the suitability of the sons.

Kim Jong Nam's mother had been living in Moscow more or less continuously since 1974, when Kim Jong Il had taken up with his next "wife." When she did return to Pyongyang, she was often temperamental, suffering from migraines or volatile episodes that cast a black mood over the entire house. Plus, she had been raised to have ambitions and a career rather than become a traditional homemaker. Subservient, dutiful wife was a part the actress never reconciled herself with playing.

Kim Jong Un's mother, on the other hand, became a consistent presence in Kim Jong Il's life. As his favored consort, she planted the seeds of change from behind the scenes. Her influence came to be seen everywhere, such as in the way *Donald Duck* and *Tom and Jerry* cartoons suddenly appeared on television, dubbed into Korean, right around the time her children would have been watching them.[26]

Around the same time, Kim Jong Il had flown into a rage when he discovered that Kim Jong Nam, who was then about twenty, had been going out and drinking in Pyongyang. For disobeying his orders, Kim Jong Il put Kim Jong Nam's household under house arrest for a month, cutting off their food supplies and making them clean up after themselves. He even threatened to send them to work in the mines in the labor camps where political prisoners were held.

Plus, Kim Jong Nam has been judged illegitimate because his mother had been married before and she had had at least one child by that man.

Kim Jong Nam's cousin, who lived with him, saw the "other woman's" fingerprints all over this. She imagined Kim Jong Un's mother setting up the situation, encouraging Kim Jong Il to allow his oldest son more freedom—then ratting on the young man when he enjoyed that freedom.[27]

There was also speculation in Seoul, a capital perpetually abuzz with theories about North Korea, that Kim Jong Un's ambitious and calculating mother had deliberately leaked Kim Jong Nam's travel schedule to the Japanese authorities so he would be caught and discredited.[28]

That would put her children next in line as long as some inconvenient facts were overlooked: she hadn't legally married Kim Jong Il either, technically making their sons illegitimate too; she had been born in Japan, the country of "imperialist aggressors"; and her sister had defected.

Their oldest son, Kim Jong Chol, was quiet and introverted, according to his classmates in Switzerland. Kenji Fujimoto, the Japanese sushi chef who'd spent years cutting up fish for the royal family, said that Kim Jong Chol never showed any ambition. Anyway, he seemed to have some kind of hormonal imbalance that made Kim Jong Il think he was "like a little girl" and unsuitable for leadership.[29]

Fujimoto had reported that Kim Jong Il anointed his third son, Kim Jong Un, as his successor. He turned out to be right.

CHAPTER 2

LIVING WITH THE IMPERIALISTS

*"Comrade Kim Il Sung told his neighbors: Japs are the bastards who
take away Koreans. Their spawn are bastards of the same color. We shall
play amongst themselves and if they say something, will attack them
together and beat them down."*

—From a biography of Kim Il Sung's father, published 1968[1]

THE SIX-YEAR-OLD KIM JONG UN STOOD BY THE BILLIARD TABLE
in the games room of the royal family's residence at Sinchon, south of
Pyongyang. He and his older brother were waiting for their father to
come out of a meeting with some officials, including their uncle Jang
Song Thaek.

The boys were dressed in child-sized military uniforms, olive green
suits complete with gold buttons and red piping. They had moon-shaped
hats on their heads and gold stars on their shoulders. They were little
generals.

When their father entered the room, they stood to attention like
soldiers and saluted him, serious expressions on their chubby faces. Kim
Jong Il was delighted and wanted to introduce the boys to the officials
and the household staff before they went into the dining room next door.
Everyone lined up to meet the little princes.

Kenji Fujimoto, who had moved from Japan to North Korea to
make sushi in the royal households, was at the end of the line. He grew

more and more nervous as the princes got closer, his heart beating faster with every step they took.

Kim Jong Chol was first. Fujimoto extended his hand, and the eight-year-old reciprocated with a firm shake. Then Fujimoto put out his hand to the younger child. This one was not so well mannered.

Instead of shaking Fujimoto's hand, Kim Jong Un glared at him with "sharp eyes" that seemed to say, "You abhorrent Japanese." The chef was shocked and embarrassed that a child would stare down a forty-year-old man. After a few seconds that stretched out painfully for Fujimoto, Kim Jong Il intervened to save the situation.

"This is Mr. Fujimoto," Kim Jong Il said, prompting "Prince Jong Un" to finally agree to shake hands, although without much enthusiasm. The chef thought there may have been some name recognition. Perhaps the boys had eaten the sushi he had prepared and heard that it had been made by "Fujimoto from Japan."

The boy's reaction made the chef wonder if he had taken on the "anti-imperialist" mind-set that is a key part of North Korea's narrative, but he may simply have been struck by the oddity of Fujimoto, who could charitably be called idiosyncratic.

In 1982, down on his luck and unhappy in his marriage, Fujimoto responded to an ad in a Japanese newspaper for a sushi chef in North Korea. It was an unusual career choice, given that Japan was entering its boom years, when bankers in Lamborghinis thought nothing of paying hundreds of dollars for a raw fish dinner. Meanwhile, North Korea was, well, North Korea.

But Fujimoto got the job, and off he went. He ended up slicing fish for Kim Jong Il for some fifteen years and regularly saw Kim Jong Un throughout his childhood and teenage years.

When it emerged in 2010 that Kim Jong Un was going to be the next leader of North Korea, Fujimoto instantly became an unlikely source of intelligence on the North Korean leadership, perhaps the most unlikely source until a pierced, tattooed bad-boy American basketballer came along.

Fujimoto lived in North Korea for a year from 1982—before Kim Jong Un was born—and then returned in 1987 and stayed until 2001.

He lived in the Secretariat Residential Block in a compound in Pyong-yang that also contained the Workers' Party of Korea offices and one of Kim Jong Il's residences.

The meals prepared for Kim Jong Il by a team of chefs were lavish. There was grilled pheasant, shark fin soup, Russian-style barbecued goat meat, steamed turtle, roast chicken and pork, and Swiss-style raclette cheese melted on potatoes. The royal family ate only rice produced in a special area of the country. Female workers handpicked each grain one by one, making sure to choose flawless grains of equal size.[2]

Sushi was on the menu once a week. Fujimoto made lobster sashimi with wasabi soy sauce and nigiri sushi with fatty tuna, yellow tail, eel, and caviar. Seabass was Kim Jong Il's favorite.

Because of his role within the inner circle, Fujimoto frequently visited the other royal compounds around the country, including the beachfront palace in Wonsan. He went jet-skiing with Kim Jong Il, rode motorbikes with him—a powerful Honda for Kim Jong Il, a lesser-powered Yamaha for Fujimoto—near the western border with China, and joined him on duck-shooting expeditions in the countryside. They traveled on Kim's luxury train or in a convoy of Mercedes-Benzes.

And Fujimoto spent lots of time with the children.

Shut into compounds in Pyongyang, being schooled at home by tutors, spending the summers alone on the beach in Wonsan, Kim Jong Un had a solitary childhood. He and Jong Chol had no friends—they didn't even play with their older half brother, Jong Nam, who lived his own entirely separate sequestered life—and their little sister was too many years younger than them to make her a good playmate.

This seems to have led them to seize on any opportunity for outside company. Even a princeling who wanted for nothing wanted friends.

To find out what Kim Jong Un was like as a boy, I got on the bullet train from Tokyo and zipped out to Sakudaira, a small town in the Jap-anese Alps where Fujimoto—a pseudonym, which he says is needed for his protection—was living.

"He was a bit lonely when he was little," Fujimoto told me over lunch in the sleepy town. "I became a kind of playmate to him; we became like friends."

I had seen photos of Fujimoto, so I knew he wore a kind of disguise to obscure his identity a little. Still, it was jarring when I emerged from the station to find him waiting for me: a black bandanna with a white skull motif on his head, purple-tinted glasses, a huge watch and diamond-encrusted square ring that were more rapper bling than low-profile witness protection scheme.

On my first trip to see him, when we had gone upstairs to a private room in the Chinese restaurant, Fujimoto gave me his business card. It featured a photo of Kim Jong Un embracing Fujimoto on one side, and on the other it read, "If you want to talk about North Korea, call me." He carried a clipboard holding Japanese newspaper clippings from his most recent trip to Pyongyang and some photos that he'd had printed out in A4 size. With so few outsiders having met the young North Korean leader, Fujimoto had become something of a Kim-Jong-Un-ologist.

The presence of Fujimoto in the royal household was a contradiction in the regime. While North Korea's existence was based on its rejection of the United States and its vision for a democratic world order, it was also built on a hatred of Japan.

Korea had suffered greatly during its colonization by imperial Japan in the first half of the twentieth century. In the previous decades, Japan had embarked on an aggressive expansion in Asia, defeating both China and Russia militarily and taking control of the entire Korean Peninsula. Japan made Korea its protectorate in 1905 and then formally annexed the peninsula in 1910, starting thirty-five years of often-brutal colonial rule.

Toward the end of this period, Koreans were forced to take Japanese names and speak Japanese at school and work. Once World War II started, men were forced to work in Japanese factories and mines to help the war effort and were conscripted as soldiers into the Imperial Japanese Army. Tens of thousands of Korean girls and women were forced to become sex slaves for Japanese soldiers in "comfort stations."

When Japan was defeated in 1945, it had to give up control of the peninsula to the victors. In both halves of the Korean Peninsula, the memories of this period run deep, even to this day.

The Kim family had built its regime on Kim Il Sung's anti-imperialist, anti-Japanese credentials: the Japanese "hated General Kim Il Sung the most among thirty million Koreans," a biography published in 1948 noted approvingly.[3]

For decades after Japan's defeat, the North Korean regime found it helpful to keep the hatred burning strong. It also took provocative acts of revenge. Starting in the late 1970s and continuing through the 1980s, North Korean spies abducted dozens of Japanese citizens, snatching them from beaches and parks on Japan's west coast and bundling them into boats.

Once the Japanese abductees were in North Korea, the regime's agents worked to break them psychologically and then, once under control, put them to use as spies or language teachers.[4]

The Japanese government officially says that seventeen of its citizens were taken to North Korea, which has acknowledged thirteen of them. The most famous of the abductees is Megumi Yokota, a thirteen-year-old who was taken on her way home from school in 1977. North Korea allowed five of the abductees to return in 2002 but says eight of the others—including Megumi—died in North Korea.

To this day, North Korea still regularly demonizes Japan in its state media, denouncing "Japanese reactionaries" and threatening to turn the country into a "nuclear sea of fire."

But there's one important detail that state propaganda never reported: Kim Jong Un has a strong personal connection to Japan. His beloved mother was born there.

In 1929, when the Korean Peninsula was under Japanese colonial rule, a man called Ko Kyon Taek, the twenty-six-year-old son of a boatman, moved from the southern Korean island of Jeju to Osaka, a Japanese city that was becoming home to an increasingly large Korean community.

He settled in the area of Ikuno, a part of central Osaka that is still a strongly Korean neighborhood. There, he worked at a factory called Hirota Saihojo Sewing Plant, which had stopped making business shirts and started making military uniforms and tents.

After the end of the war, as Japan was rapidly trying to rebuild itself into a modern and democratic nation, Ko and his wife built a family: first, a son and then, on June 26, 1952, a daughter that they named Yong Hui.

Yong Hui went by the Japanese name of Hime Takada at her public elementary school in Osaka. She loved to perform and sang hymns in a church choir every Sunday. Four years later, a sister arrived. Her name was Yong Suk.

After the war, their father got in trouble with the police. He was rumored to be operating an illegal boat connecting Osaka and Jeju and was reportedly ordered to be deported. There were rumors that Ko was also a womanizer and had multiple children by different mistresses. To cut ties with these other women and get himself out of hot water, Ko decided to hightail it out of Japan.[5]

Conveniently, North Korea had begun encouraging ethnic Koreans to return from Japan at the end of the 1950s. Never mind that almost all the Koreans in Japan hailed from the South. The Japanese government had supported the idea, seeing it as a way to shrink the ethnic Korean population in their country.

North Korea, the potential migrants were told, was a socialist paradise on earth—a country that offered free housing, education, and healthcare, where jobs were guaranteed, where Koreans would suffer none of the prejudice that they endured in Japan.

What's more, North Korea's economy was in better shape than the South's at that time, and the South was led by Syngman Rhee, a ferocious conservative who was viewed as a puppet of the United States.

Between 1959 and 1965, more than ninety-three thousand people fell for the Kim regime's sales pitch and moved from Japan to North Korea.

The Ko family joined the tide. When Yong Hui was ten, they boarded the ninety-ninth repatriation ship setting out to make the 560-mile journey to North Korea. They disembarked in Chongjin, the port city on the east coast and the farthest place on the Korean Peninsula from the Ko family's ancestral home on Jeju Island.

For many ethnic Koreans who had left a country that was rapidly turning itself into a world economic power after the war, coming "home" was a huge disappointment. Some killed themselves on arrival when they realized they'd been duped.

Pyongyang's version of the life that the returnees led in North Korea was, of course, very different. The North Korean magazine *Korean Pictorial* featured the Ko family in its December 1972 issue, under the headline "My Happiness-Filled Family."[6]

The photo shows the family gathered around a table in a picture of domestic bliss. Ko stands looking over his wife and the two girls, all cheery at the table, while a grandmother holds a baby boy. Everyone is well dressed and smiling. The room is stuffed with furniture, including a large radio that must have been cutting edge at the time.

In the accompanying story, Ko Kyon Taek says that when he went to Japan in 1929, he faced hardship and discrimination. Moving to North Korea put an end to that. "There's no happier family than mine now," the magazine quotes him as saying. The story also mentions that the eldest girl, a certain Ko Yong Hui who had joined the prestigious Mansudae Art Troupe, had been awarded a medal by Kim Il Sung.

The following year, that same Ko Yong Hui took the ferry back to Japan. In the summer of 1973, she and thirty-five other dancers from the Mansudae troupe went on a two-month-long, sixty-performance tour through Tokyo, Nagoya, Hiroshima, and Fukuoka—as well as to her birthplace of Osaka.

But Ko's identity was already being obscured. During the trip to Japan, the pro-North Korean newspaper *Choson Sinbo* called her Ryu Il Suk and said she was the main dancer during the performance of a song called "Azaleas of the Motherland." The newsletter's writer said that she was the star of the group, but he couldn't get close to interview her because her fellow dancers guarded her too closely.

Back in North Korea, the beautiful dancers from the Mansudae troupe were often asked to attend the boozy parties that Kim Jong Il held and to perform for the men in his court.

Kim Jong Il was smitten with Ko Yong Hui, asking her to sit with him at the parties, another dancer in the troupe later recalled. "Kim Jong Il took such a fancy that he came often into rehearsal rooms to watch her practice," the dancer wrote in a memoir after defecting from the regime.[7] Ko was absent from practice more and more often, and rumors started flying around among the other dancers that she was living with Kim Jong Il or that she had given birth to his baby.

Ko Yong Hui "married" Kim Jong Il—their union doesn't appear to have been official, but this is how her sister later described it—in 1975. Their relationship led to a rapid improvement in her family's status in North Korea. Her father became the manager of Mangyongdae Souvenir Factory in Pyongyang and remained in the capital until 1999, when he died at the age of eighty-six.

Fujimoto remembers meeting Ko Yong Hui and remarking that she was as beautiful as Sayuri Yoshinaga and Setsuko Hara, two Japanese actresses famous for their good looks. The comparison would doubtless have pleased the movie-mad North Korean leader.

But Ko Yong Hui was more than a trophy wife. She was often up late at night, poring over paperwork with Kim and offering her opinions. Once, when a bodyguard was drunk and waved his gun at Kim Jong Il, Ko is said to have thrown herself between the men. She may have been born in Japan, but she had proven herself a true patriot, loyal not just to North Korea but to her powerful husband.

Chef Fujimoto's second encounter with the boys was a happier one. They were still at the compound in Sinchon, and everyone was in the huge garden. Fujimoto was flying a kite. The boys were enthralled.

"That's good. Thanks to Fujimoto, the kite is flying," Ko Yong Hui said to her sons. Kim Jong Un was excited, and the episode seemed to help break the ice a bit. About a month later, Fujimoto said, he was asked to become the boys' "playmate."

He was very surprised. He was a grown man, and they were little boys. But it was impossible for him to say no. He wondered if it was because he was a foreigner and therefore somewhat exotic to the boys. They had admired his shoes: a pair of Nike Air Max sneakers, the height of cool in the early 1990s. Kim Jong Un asked if they were genuine, showing that he was used to people with counterfeit goods. Fujimoto assured him that he didn't wear fakes.

But perhaps Fujimoto just seemed to offer a bit of fun. After all, the boys had few other options in their isolated royal court.

Whenever he could, Fujimoto took Ko Yong Hui and the two "princes" angling for seabass on Kim Jong Il's private boat. Every time Fujimoto caught a fish, the young Kim Jong Un, still in elementary school, would demand to hold the fishing rod and then cry out happily, "I caught it!"

The boys developed a fascination with Japan after traveling there with their mother in 1991. With fake Brazilian passports in hand, Ko Yong Hui took her sons with her on a trip to Tokyo. Although Japan was North Korea's avowed enemy, there was still a sizable community of ethnic Koreans there.

So while the regime spurted forth anti-Japanese hate, Ko Yong Hui went shopping in Ginza, the upmarket district in central Tokyo that was world famous for luxury, and got her hair done by people known at home as "imperialist aggressors." She took the boys to Tokyo Disneyland, where they were drawn to a 3-D attraction with a moving chair. The boys loved it so much that Ko had her staff inquire about its cost.

She wanted to get one to take back to North Korea for her children, Fujimoto told me. But even for the North Korean royal family, the price was prohibitive. Still, for years after, they talked about their trip to Tokyo Disneyland and all the rides they had been on, trying to decide which one was the most fun.

The boys also appeared to be learning some Japanese. Kim Jong Un remarked to Fujimoto that it was strange that Japanese people had greetings for different times of the day—good morning, good day, good evening—while Koreans used only one no matter the time.

Kim Jong Un one day asked Fujimoto to write "wave" in Japanese. The boy had been learning the Chinese characters that are the basis of both Japanese and Korean, and he wanted to see if they stayed the same in both languages. Fujimoto wondered who was teaching the boys Japanese.

Once, when the royal entourage was at the seaside residence in Wonsan, Kim Jong Un asked two young women on the compound to sing two specific Japanese songs to Fujimoto. They were famous songs about feelings of longing—one about a girl who was taken from the city of Yokohama by foreigners and the other about a mother crow crying while waiting for her child.

Fujimoto would later wonder if those two women had been victims of abduction. Had the royal children been taught by Megumi

Yokota, the Japanese teenager abducted on her way home from school? She would have been in her late twenties at the time, and those songs were just the kind that a girl taken from her home might sing.

Another time, Kim Jong Un was drawing the Juche Tower, an obelisk with a red flame on top in central Pyongyang that is the monument to North Korea's philosophy of "self-reliance." While he was drawing, Kim Jong Un asked Fujimoto about Tokyo Tower, a red-and-white structure reminiscent of the Eiffel Tower that was built in the 1950s and quickly became a symbol of Japan's postwar revival.

Kim Jong Un asked Fujimoto to draw Tokyo Tower for him and declared the picture to be cool. He carefully put the drawing into the box where he kept his own. Fujimoto felt pleased. He was getting closer to the boy—and being in the child's good graces increased the chef's stature in the Kim household.

As Kim Jong Un warmed to his unlikely buddy, he became more overtly friendly. The boy was mad about basketball, and Fujimoto once brought back heavy-duty tape from Japan so he could make a court with it. One day, Kim Jong Un gave Fujimoto a photo of Ri Myong Hun, North Korea's most famous basketball player. Ri was an astonishing seven feet, eight and a half inches tall and played center for North Korea's national basketball team. In the 1990s, there were rumors that Ri—nicknamed Michael Ri because he idolized Michael Jordan—was going to play in the National Basketball Association. He went to Canada and was scouted by numerous teams, but it went no further. Ri joining the NBA was deemed a violation of the United States' Trading with the Enemy Act.

Back in North Korea, the basketballer loomed large in the young Kim's life. At Kim Jong Il's funeral in 2011, Ri's giant figure could be seen towering over the other mourners. He was also there a few years later when Dennis Rodman arrived for some basketball diplomacy.

Still, even as Fujimoto became a fixture in the royal household, Kim Jong Un reminded the sushi chef of his place. While Jong Chol addressed him with an honorific Korean suffix that loosely translates to "Mr.," Jong Un continued to refer to him by the disrespectful "Fujimoto."

If Kim Jong Un had been any other child or, rather, any other rich kid, these episodes would be considered normal spoiled-brat behavior. But because there is so little other information about him, these stories have taken on an outsized significance. Analysts and experts pore over such anecdotes for evidence of character flaws or influences that might somehow have shaped this man.

They listened as Fujimoto described a time when Kim Jong Un defied his mother's orders to remain seated at the table while everyone else finished their dinner. "Let's go, older brother," he said to Jong Chol, and they ran outside.

There was another time, when Kim Jong Un was about ten years old, that the young princeling became very angry at his aunt, Ko Yong Suk, for calling him "little brother."

"Don't treat me like a child!" the child yelled. So Fujimoto suggested calling him Comrade General, and the boy liked the name. "Everyone started calling him Comrade General after that," Fujimoto told me, chuckling, during one of our meetings in Japan. "So I'm like his godfather."

What he didn't mention was that Kim Jong Un wasn't the first Comrade General. Kim Jong Nam, the firstborn son of Kim Jong Il, had also been called Comrade General when he was the same age, about a decade before. But the winds had shifted, and it was now the third son who was favored as heir.

Certainly, the boy grew up thinking he was special. Fujimoto recalls Comrade General Jong Un's eighth birthday party, which he said took place in a party hall at the royal compound in Wonsan. It was attended by high-level officials rather than other kids.

Kim Jong Un was dressed in a black suit and a bow tie and was presented with bouquets of flowers. He looked quite uncomfortable. When the chef took his place at the table, he noticed another piece of paper next to the printed menu. It was the lyrics to a song called "Footsteps."

After toasts and congratulations to the young boy, the Pochonbo Electric Orchestra, North Korea's most prominent band at the time, famous for playing synthed-up versions of songs lauding the regime, played the song. It was easy to sing along after hearing the tune once, Fujimoto said, and soon everyone was joining in.

Tramp tramp tramp
The footsteps of our General Kim
Spreading the spirit of February
Tramp tramp tramping onwards . . .
Bringing us closer to a brilliant future
Tramp, tramp, tramp, ah, footsteps.

Kim Jong Il was born on February 16, and his birthday was celebrated with great fanfare every year. The message was unmistakable to everyone there: Kim Jong Il's successor, another General Kim, would lead them into the future.

From that moment on, even high-ranking officials bowed and deferred to Kim Jong Un whenever they saw him, his aunt and uncle told me. It was impossible for the boy to grow up as a normal child when the people around him were treating him like that, they said. And he quickly got used to giving commands.

As a boy, Kim Jong Un had been mad about all sorts of machinery, model planes and toy ships in particular. He wanted to know how they flew, how they floated. Even when he was eight or nine and still in Pyongyang, Kim Jong Un would stay up all night doing experiments with his machinery—and insisting on speaking to some expert or other even in the wee hours of the morning if he couldn't figure things out by himself. When he had questions or when something didn't function well, he would call for a nautical engineer to come and explain it to him, no matter how late it was, his aunt told me.

This, for her, revealed an aspect of his personality that had two sides: on the one hand, he had an incredible level of concentration, but on the other, he had a tendency to get hooked on an idea and take it too far. She didn't use the word "obsessive," but this was the trait she described. In fact, when later living with them in Bern, the boy always wanted his aunt and uncle to buy him model planes from the toy store or to take him to a park where enthusiasts used to fly their crafts, and the obsession would last long into his adult years.

Kim Jong Un himself seemed to confirm this years later, when he was heir apparent. "I have formed a close attachment with planes and warships since my childhood," he told a military official who asked his advice about a new model of gun one day in 2010.

He told the official how, as a child, he made a runway in the backyard of his house and played with his toy planes out there. The official took this as further proof of Kim Jong Un's unrivaled qualifications to lead, according to the North Korean version of events.[8]

It also explained his later becoming a pilot who would fly himself around North Korea, even building a brand-new airstrip at Wonsan so he could land near his summer residence. These days, when intelligence analysts comb through satellite images to figure out whether North Korea is going to launch a missile, one of the things they look for is Kim Jong Un's personal plane at a nearby airstrip.

Although Kim Jong Un's adolescent years coincided with the national famine, the Great Successor experienced none of its privations and probably never saw the suffering of his fellow North Koreans in person. Instead, he grew up in a world where everything revolved around him. Not only did he have specially appointed friends like Fujimoto, but he had teachers and coaches and cooks and bodyguards and drivers.

He grew up feeling like the most special little boy in the universe, a boy who would espouse self-reliance while, in fact, being reliant on this army of servants and supplicants and tutors.

Kim Jong Il's various children were shut into walled compounds with fifteen-foot-high iron gates or sequestered in the beachfront compound in Wonsan, where life was pure luxury. There were Sony televisions, computers, and video games so they could play Super Mario. There were pinball machines and grand pianos, Yamahas and Steinways, in every house.

The children had huge playrooms filled with more toys than any European toy store. There were mountains of Lego and Playmobil; boxes of jigsaws, more than they could ever get through; and plastic pistols with surprisingly realistic bullets. There was every kind of four-wheeled toy imaginable, but Kim Jong Un also had a real vehicle and a real gun: a car his father had had specially modified so the little boy could drive it at age seven and a Colt .45 pistol that he wore on his hip when he was eleven.

The houses had large, soundproofed cinemas with wood paneling to improve the acoustics and a black velvet curtain that would open when the lights went down. The children could sit in the soft armchairs and watch *Ben Hur*, *Dracula*, or James Bond movies.

In the kitchens, there were cakes and French pastries, smoked salmon and pâté, and tropical fruits like mangos and melons. They wore clothes made especially for them with British fabric that arrived by the Samsonite suitcase load. They brushed their teeth with imported Colgate.

There were gardens so large that they called them parks, with artificial waterfalls running into artificial lakes. They got around the compounds in golf carts or on mopeds. There were bears and monkeys in cages. Some of the compounds had large swimming pools; some had indoor and outdoor shooting ranges.[9]

Kim Jong Un passed his days listening to Fujimoto's Whitney Houston CD on the sushi chef's Walkman or playing basketball on courts at the official residences—often with kids brought in especially to play with the princes.

Kim Jong Un would obsessively analyze the basketball games, Fujimoto said. He would point out players' strengths and weaknesses, praising those who he deemed to have played well and scolding those who had not.

"He had the ability to make good judgments with solid reasoning; he knew when to praise and when to criticize," the chef recalled. When Kim Jong Un would talk about how harshly he'd criticized a player, he'd smile. He seemed to be practicing the art of command, and he was enjoying the terror that his absolute authority could inspire.

CHAPTER 3

ANONYMOUS IN SWITZERLAND

"I have formed a close attachment with planes and warships since my childhood."

—Kim Jong Un, from "Anecdotes of Kim Jong Un's Life"

KIM JONG UN WAS STILL VERY MUCH A CHILD WHEN HE DEPARTED for Bern, the capital of Switzerland, in the summer of 1996 to join his older brother Kim Jong Chol at school. The twelve-year-old had a pudding-bowl haircut and the start of what would one day become a very pronounced double chin.

He found himself in a chocolate-box picturesque city that felt more like a quaint town than an international capital. Bern was famous for its clock tower, known as the Zytglogge, which had led a young patent clerk called Albert Einstein to discover the theory of relativity some ninety years earlier. Einstein, riding home from work on a tram one evening in 1905, looked back at the clock, getting farther away from him, and wondered what would happen if he were traveling at the speed of light. The thought led him to solve the mystery of "space-time" that had been bothering him for years.

Kim Jong Un went on his own enlightening journey, traveling from famine-struck North Korea to one of the richest countries in Europe.

That August, *Mission Impossible* was on at the movies, and *Trainspotting* was about to open. Top-of-the-line personal computers used floppy disks and ran on MS-DOS.

The Summer Olympics were wrapping up in Atlanta. Bill Clinton was campaigning to be reelected president of the United States. The author George R. R. Martin that month published a fantasy novel called *A Game of Thrones.*

The North Korean princeling emerged from his compound cosmos into this new terrestrial world. It wasn't his first time abroad—he had traveled to Europe and Japan before—but it was the first time he had lived outside the confines of the North Korean royal court.

He joined his older brother, who had been living in Liebefeld, a decidedly suburban neighborhood on the outskirts of Bern, for two years with their maternal aunt, Ko Yong Suk, and her husband, Ri Gang.

"We lived in a normal home and acted like a normal family. I acted like their mother," Kim's aunt told me when I tracked her down in the United States almost twenty years later. "Their friends would come over, and I would make them snacks. It was a very normal childhood with birthday parties and gifts and Swiss kids coming over to play."

They spoke Korean at home and ate Korean food, and the boys' friends didn't know that Imo—as Jong Chol and Jong Un called her—was Korean for "Aunt," not for "Mom."

They enjoyed living in Europe and having money. Their family photo albums contain pictures of the future leader of North Korea swimming in the Mediterranean on the French Riviera, dining al fresco in Italy, going to Euro Disney in Paris—it wasn't Kim Jong Un's first trip there; his mother had already taken him a few years before—and skiing in the Swiss Alps.

They relaxed at a luxury hotel in Interlaken, the swanky resort town outside Bern that is the gateway to the Jungfrau mountains and home to a famous amusement park. He went twice to the Olympic museum in Lausanne, the Swiss city on the edge of Lake Geneva and the home of the International Olympic Committee. One exhibition at the museum really stuck with this machine obsessive: it was a feature where a visitor could request a video about an athlete or sporting event, and a robot in the basement would collect the video.

This was in the era before digital storage, and the robot machine made an impression on the boy who spent hours playing with planes and ships in his bedroom. Two decades later, when hosting the head of the

International Olympic Committee in Pyongyang, he would ask if the exhibition still existed. It did not.[1]

In Switzerland, all the members of the Kim family had carefully constructed identities to conceal who they really were. Ri was registered as a driver at the North Korean embassy and went by the name Pak Nam Chol. Pak is one of the most common Korean surnames after Kim. Ko, in keeping with Korean practice whereby women keep their surnames after marriage, had paperwork naming her as Chong Yong Hye.

Kim Jong Chol was officially Pak Chol, and Kim Jong Un was Pak Un. But the aliases were not new. All of them had been accredited to the North Korean mission to the United Nations in Geneva since 1991, and these diplomatic documents would have allowed them to travel freely in Europe.

The photo that was submitted to the Swiss authorities shows a young Kim Jong Un with chubby cheeks and puffy hair that appears to have been permed, just as Kim Jong Nam did when he went to Switzerland. It was apparently so they wouldn't stand out so much. He's wearing a navy-blue velour jacket zipped up over a white turtleneck—the finest '70s fashion but in the 1990s.

"Pak Un" also had another passport he could use to travel around Europe. A new Brazilian passport issued in 1996, perhaps specifically to allow him to move without being detected as North Korean, identified him as Josef Pwag—apparently the Portuguese rendering of Pak.

North Koreans on diplomatic passports can travel across borders but not without standing out. North Korea, then as now, was a pariah state with nuclear ambitions. Plus, North Koreans were a rarity, a novelty even. But an ordinary family of Asian Brazilians—Brazil has the largest Korean population in South America—on vacation in Europe rang no alarm bells.

The passport said that the teenager, shown in an unflattering photo with puffy hair and clearly identifiable as the young Kim Jong Un, was born in Sao Paolo on February 1, 1983. It listed his parents as Ricardo and Marcela Pwag.[2]

Ricardo Pwag was a North Korean who traveled frequently and extravagantly around Europe, flying first class on Swiss Air and staying in luxury hotels in Bern, Geneva, and Zurich. He appears to have been charged with buying buildings for the North Korean ruling class. Ricardo Pwag was probably Kim Jong Un's uncle, Jang Song Thaek.

With his new alias, Kim Jong Un settled in Liebefeld, where the architecture is more '70s concrete block than Alpine village. It is not dissimilar to the brutalist style of Pyongyang. Behind the main street in an "industrial alley," as the sign puts it, next door to a large wine trading company that looks like a monastery, is Number 10 Kirchstrasse. This was Kim Jong Un's home while he was in Switzerland. It's in a three-story, light-orange sandstone building surrounded by hydrangeas.

The North Korean regime had bought six apartments in the building shortly after their construction in 1989 for a price of four million francs—a little over $4 million at the time—for the family and some of the other North Korean dignitaries living in the Swiss capital. The family had three cars, with diplomatic plates and darkened windows, which they kept in the underground carpark.

Kim Jong Un joined his older brother at the International School of Berne, a private, English-language school attended by the children of diplomats and other expats in the Swiss capital. Tuition cost more than $20,000 a year.

The school was just a five-minute drive from the North Korean embassy, which was, and still is, located in a big house on a normal residential street, Pourtalèsstrasse, across the river from the city center. It's a well-to-do neighborhood lined with ambassadors' residences.

No one batted an eyelid when Kim Jong Un, sometimes wearing the school T-shirt, complete with Swiss flag and a bear, the symbol of the capital, was delivered to school in a chauffeur-driven car. Many other diplomats' kids arrived at school the same way.

The school, whose student population contains about forty nationalities, touts itself as being "perfectly situated in a neutral country." Indeed, Switzerland, famous for its discretion about everything from bank accounts to the schooling of dictators' children, was the ideal location for the secretive North Koreans.

When the news first emerged that Kim Jong Un would be the successor to Kim Jong Il, there was so much confusion that many reported tidbits of information that were in fact about his brother. Classmates recounted how the North Korean was introverted but was relatively fluent in English, but it turned out they were remembering the wrong North Korean, "Pak Chol" instead of "Pak Un."

One snippet—a penchant for the action star Jean-Claude Van Damme—did, however, appear to apply to the two boys, both of whom apparently loved to watch movies featuring him. In a coincidence that would play out later, Van Damme costarred in a Hollywood movie called *Double Team* with a certain basketballer called Dennis Rodman. The film came out in 1997, while Kim Jong Un was in Switzerland.

Kim Jong Chol even found a way to work the Belgian movie star into his schoolwork. "If I had my ideal world I would not allow weapons and atom bombs any more," he wrote in a school project while in Bern. "I would destroy all terrorists with the Hollywood star Jean-Claude Van Damme. Everybody would be happy: no more war, no more dying, no more crying."

Like a good North Korean socialist, or maybe just as an idealistic teenager, the poet says that everyone should have the same amount of money. "Only in my ideal world can the people have freedom and live very happily," it concluded.[3]

The apartment on Kirchstrasse was more modest than what he was used to back home, but Kim Jong Un could live a relatively normal existence there. And he could devote himself to his favorite pastime: basketball. It was his mother who first sparked his interest in the sport. There's an old tale that Korean mothers, North and South, like to tell their children: if you play basketball, you'll grow taller.

Kim Jong Un was short as a child, and his father was not a tall man—he was only five foot three, and famously wore platform shoes to try to compensate—so Ko Yong Hui encouraged her son to play basketball in the hope the tale was true. He grew to be five foot seven, so maybe it worked a bit.

She was thrilled to see her son taking to basketball, a sport that she believed would help him clear his mind and loosen his childhood obsession with planes and engines. Instead, Kim Jong Un's mother and aunt soon saw that basketball had become an addiction too—the boy was sleeping with his basketball in his bed—and one that came at the expense of his studies. His mother would visit Bern regularly to scold her son for playing too much and studying too little.

She arrived on a passport that declared her to be Chong Il Son, assigned to the North Korean mission at the United Nations in Geneva since 1987, but the Swiss knew exactly who she was. After all, she arrived in the country in a Russian-made Ilyushin 62 jet bearing the insignia of Air Koryo, the North Korean state airline. The plane, which bore the tail number P882, was for VIPs only. It even had a full bedroom onboard.

All sorts of bags and merchandise would be loaded on and off the plane, watched carefully by Swiss intelligence. They monitored Ko Yong Hui closely, keeping records of everything from her shopping expeditions on Zurich's Bahnhofstrasse, one of the world's most exclusive shopping avenues, to her hospital bills at fancy private clinics on Lake Geneva.

They also knew who her children were. They called Kim Jong Chol "the tall, skinny one" and Kim Jong Un "the short, fat one." But the new Swiss attorney general, Carla Del Ponte (who would later become chief prosecutor in the international criminal tribunals on Yugoslavia and Rwanda), had forbidden the Swiss authorities to monitor the children. In famously discreet Switzerland, they were allowed to just be children—even if they were the children of one of the world's most notorious tyrants.

When Kim's mother arrived in Bern, she would bring handwritten notebooks containing one thousand Chinese characters, which form the basis of most Korean words, that she had made and photocopied so the children could keep up with their language skills. She told her sons that they had to memorize five or six pages a day, the kind of homework that torments Korean children the world over.

She was what we today would call a tiger mother, pouring a lot of energy into her children's education and going through their journals and homework no matter how late she returned to the apartment at night.

But Kim Jong Un had other priorities.

Although he had come to think of himself as above everybody else since being anointed his father's successor at the age of eight, he knew he still had to obey his parents. He wouldn't talk back to his mother but would storm off in a huff and often refuse to eat his dinner as a way of showing his anger. Even then, he was short-tempered and intolerant. "He is stubborn," his aunt told me. "He wants to do what he wants to do."

Unsurprisingly, Kim Jong Un was also delighted when the summer approached and the school year finished so that he could go back home, where there was no studying, just basketball and beach.

Kim Jong Un's world was turned upside down in 1998. His mother had been diagnosed with advanced breast cancer and was starting intensive medical treatment in France. Her prognosis wasn't good.

The illness could also prove terminal for Kim Jong Un's guardians. Their link to the regime, the relationship that had vaulted them into this privileged position, was becoming weaker by the day.

They decided to abandon their charges and make a dash for freedom.

So after nightfall on Sunday, May 17, Kim Jong Un's aunt and uncle packed their three children into a taxi and went to the US embassy. Only their oldest, who was then fourteen, the same age as Kim Jong Un, knew what was going to happen next.

When they arrived at the embassy, they explained that they were North Koreans, that Ko was the leader's sister-in-law, and that they were seeking asylum in the United States. The US government didn't know at that stage who Kim Jong Un was, so they didn't initially mention that part.

The first thing the next morning, the Americans informed Swiss intelligence of the incredible defection, and together they worked out a plan: if the North Korean embassy came to their Swiss hosts and asked about the family, the government would plead ignorance.

The family spent all day Monday in the embassy answering questions. The following day, they were loaded into a minivan to make the four-hour journey over the border into Germany and north to the US Air Force base at Ramstein. They stayed in Germany for about two months while they were being debriefed and intelligence officials were checking out their story.

The interrogators wanted to know all their "secrets," but Ri Gang, Kim Jong Un's uncle, said they didn't know anything about North Korea's military operations, only about the ruling family's life. "We were just looking after the children and helping them study," he told me. They were granted asylum in the United States and settled down in Middle America, starting a dry-cleaning store like so many other Korean immigrants and watching their children flourish in their new environment.

I had tracked down the couple and spent a weekend with them, talking about the nephew who once passed as their son. I went to their dry-cleaning store and then back to their house, nearly identical to the others that lined their suburban street, with a neatly cut lawn and two cars parked in the driveway.

As we sat on their overstuffed black couches, the South Korean news broadcast on their television showed their former charge smiling with his cronies as they celebrated a missile launch. The newsreader uttered ominous warnings about the young North Korean leader. "They never say anything good about him," Ri muttered.

I asked the couple about the reason for their defection. They said it was because they wanted to get medical treatment for Kim Jong Un's mother. They had heard that the medical care in the United States was the best in the world, and they were prepared to take any steps to procure it for her, Ko told me.

Ri added that they believed that if they could convince the US government to allow Ko Yong Hui into the country, it could have helped to foster a better relationship between Washington and Pyongyang. Ri likened the idea to President Nixon's "ping-pong diplomacy" with China, which opened a new era of relations between the previously hostile countries.

This period was something of a high point in relations between the United States and North Korea. The Clinton administration had struck a nuclear deal with North Korea, and Bill Clinton had sent former defense secretary William Perry to Pyongyang to deliver a letter to Kim Jong Il.

This put in motion a series of meetings that led to the extraordinary sight of Kim Jong Il's second-in-command traveling to Washington as a special envoy. Wearing his North Korean military uniform, rows of ribbons across his chest, and his distinctive moon-shaped military hat with a red Communist star on the front, the vice marshal went into the Oval Office and posed for photos with President Clinton.

So it wasn't preposterous to imagine that a member of an "enemy" regime might come to the United States for medical treatment. But when Ko Yong Hui applied for a visa, her application was rejected. The thaw could happen only so quickly, it seemed.

But I could not believe that this was the full story of their reason for defecting. Ri and Ko's place at the heart of the North Korean regime depended entirely on their relationship with Kim Jong Un's mother. And now that she was dying—and her sons were getting older and outgrowing the need for a guardian—their position also appeared to be in danger.

After years of traveling and living in Europe, the couple—like tens of thousands of other North Koreans who have gotten a glimpse of the outside world over the past few decades—must have realized that North Korea was not the socialist paradise it was cracked up to be. Stories about the couple in the South Korean press—which admittedly does not have a stellar relationship with the truth—suggested that they sought asylum in the United States because they were concerned about what could happen to them after Ko's sister died or after Kim Jong Il died.

In fact, Kim Jong Un's mother lived for another six years, dying in a hospital in Paris in 2004, while his father defied strokes and other illnesses to make it to the end of 2011.

When he returned to Bern after the summer of 1998, Kim Jong Un did not go back to the private international school across the river. Instead, he made a new start at the public school in his neighborhood, Schule Liebefeld Steinhölzli. Starting a new school meant he wouldn't have to explain why his "parents" had changed.

The school was less than four hundred yards from the apartment block where the North Koreans lived, a five-minute walk down the concrete staircase, past the supermarket and other shops, and around the traffic circle.

When Kim Jong Un attended the school in the late 1990s, it had only two hundred students and nine classes. The education department liked to have many small schools so that no student would have to travel too far each day.

School started at seven thirty each morning but stopped at noon for a two-hour lunch break so the children could go home to eat. Even in the 1990s, there was an expectation that mothers would be waiting at home for their children.

At 2:00 p.m., the children would return for three more hours of lessons, except on Wednesdays, when there was no school in the afternoon. Wednesday afternoons is the time that Swiss kids go to the doctor or the dentist or—probably in Kim Jong Un's case—the basket-ball court.

The school is a cluster of two- and three-story functionally designed buildings. There's a garden out front where students grow corn, run-ner beans, and strawberries. In the school library, there are books about Picasso and Peter the Great in German and also books in English on display. Tools and vises are lined up neatly in the woodworking room, and artworks by students decorate the main foyer and the noticeboards. It is essentially an ordinary school.

Next to the school buildings is a large Astroturf field. On the day I visited, a group of kids from various immigrant backgrounds were play-ing soccer together. On the side, two boys speaking Arabic were racing a remote-control car, one chasing after it while the other tried to make a getaway.

When the news that Kim Jong Un would succeed his father broke in 2009, journalists flocked to the school for insights into the dictator-in-waiting. They inundated the school and tried to interview his former teachers.

A Japanese journalist took a photo of Kim Jong Un's class picture in a gallery in a hallway and then published it in his newspaper in July 2009. Thereafter, it was removed from the wall and stored somewhere private, and journalists were banned from the campus.

The photo still exists on the internet. The class, decked out in an array of 1990s fashion, with chambray shirts and oversized sweatshirts, is assembled under a tree in the schoolyard. Kim Jong Un stands in the center of the back row wearing a tracksuit, gray and black with red piping and big red letters reading "NIKE" down the sleeve. He's staring unsmiling at the camera.

Another photo taken around this time shows Kim with a smile, wearing a silver necklace over his black T-shirt and looking like a typical teenager. Another reveals some fuzz on his top lip and a smattering of pimples on his cheek.

Despite the school's efforts to get rid of the journalists, interest was so huge that the authorities organized a press conference in a classroom. Ueli Studer, the education administrator in the municipality of Köniz, which incorporates Liebefeld, confirmed that a boy from North Korea attended school from August 1998 to the fall of 2000. He was enrolled as the son of an employee of the embassy, Studer said, adding that this was not unusual given that some other foreign diplomats also sent their children to the school.

"The pupil was considered to be well integrated, diligent and ambitious," Studer continued. "His hobby was basketball." Along the bottom of the statement were boldfaced words saying that this was their final comment. To this day, these are the only details that the school has given.

Teachers there never met the boy's parents. Instead, various North Koreans would attend parents' nights in their place, apologizing and explaining that this was because the boy's parents couldn't speak German, recalled the school's principal at the time, Peter Burri.[4]

When he first enrolled at the school in Liebefeld, Kim Jong Un started in a "reception" class for children who did not speak German, spending several months learning his lessons in German but at a slower pace with simpler instruction.

At the time the boy enrolled, about a quarter of the students were not Swiss, so the authorities were used to dealing with children who arrived without being able to speak the local language. Kim Jong Un also had private German language tuition outside of school.

To find out more about what the young North Korean learned in school, I took the bus to Köniz one day and visited the municipality office. Marisa Vifian, head of the Köniz education department, pulled out a big white binder containing the school curriculum from the 1990s.

There was the usual lineup of classes—German, math, science, health, foreign languages, music, art, and sports—as well as units like "The World Around Us," which taught world religions and cultures. The school authorities assess the children based on ability rather than age. They'd rather play it safe and hold a child back a year and have him or her do well in a lower grade, Vifian told me.

Once he finished in the preparatory reception class, Kim Jong Un joined the regular sixth-grade class.

João Micaelo, then the fourteen-year-old son of Portuguese immigrants, clearly remembers the Asian boy in a tracksuit and Nike shoes walking into 6A, a class of twenty-two students. The kids were already seated at their desks when the new boy was brought in and introduced as Pak Un, the son of North Korean diplomats. There was a spare seat next to Micaelo, so the new boy, who simply went by the name of Un, sat in it.

The pair soon became close, bonding because of their seat placement but also because neither was particularly academic. In sixth grade, classes were split into two streams, and both Kim Jong Un and Micaelo were sent to the group of academically weaker students.[5] Kim Jong Un was embarrassed when he was called to answer questions in front of the class—not because he didn't know the answers necessarily but because he couldn't express himself. So Micaelo helped him with his German homework, while the newcomer helped his new friend with math.

Micaelo remembers Kim as quiet but said that he was very decisive and capable of making his point. "He was ambitious but not aggressive," he said.[6]

But other students remember the new kid being forceful because he had trouble communicating. While lessons were in High German, the more formal variety of the language spoken in official situations in Switzerland, families and friends spoke to each other in Swiss German, former classmates recalled. This is technically a dialect, but to an outsider, it sounds so different that it may as well be Dutch. It was frustrating to Kim Jong Un, who resented his inability to understand. "He kicked us in the shins and even spat at us," said one former classmate.[7]

In addition to the communication problems, the other students tended to think of Kim Jong Un as a weird outsider, his school friends recall, not least because the North Korean always wore tracksuits, never jeans, the standard uniform of teenagers the world over. In North Korea, jeans are a symbol of the despised capitalists.

One classmate remembered him wearing Adidas tracksuits with three stripes down the side and the newest pair of Nike Air Jordans. The other kids in the school could only dream of having such shoes, said Nikola Kovacevic, another former classmate who often played basketball with Kim after school, estimating a pair cost more than $200 in Switzerland at the time.[8]

As he moved into the upper years at school, Kim Jong Un improved his German enough that he was able to get by in class. Even the girl who got kicked and spat at conceded that he "thawed" over time as he became more sociable.

Still, he remained introverted. More complicated thoughts were beyond his German, so he tended to keep them to himself, Micaelo said.[9]

Kim Jong Un went on to pass the seventh and eighth grades and was there for a part of the ninth grade at the high school, the Köniz education authorities confirmed. His grades were never great. It surely didn't help that he was absent so often: 75 times in the first year, 105 in the second.[10]

Parts of the curriculum focused on social matters and would have presented a very different worldview to the one that Kim experienced in North Korea.

"Generally, people here are taught to respect each other," Godi Huber, who also works for the Köniz municipality, told me as I thumbed through the curriculum folders. "They learn about solving conflicts peacefully and how to live together harmoniously. These are our values."

In the days he attended school, Kim Jong Un's lessons included human rights, women's rights, and the development of democracy. One unit was even called "Happiness, Suffering, Life and Death."

Students learned about Martin Luther King Jr., Nelson Mandela, and Mahatma Gandhi. There was a strong emphasis on "intercultural education," Huber said, learning about cultural diversity; religious, ethnic, and social groups; the rights of human beings; and standing in solidarity with the disadvantaged.

It's hard to know what Kim Jong Un thought during these lessons. No such rights existed in North Korea. But this may not have been as jarring to Kim as it sounds because he had encountered very few North Koreans and almost none in situations outside of those that were carefully choreographed to show smiling citizens who beamed contentment at him. Kim could have told himself that his people didn't need all those fine ideals because they were evidently very happy under his father's leadership.

The teenaged Kim would also have learned about how the French populace rose up and stormed the Bastille, leading to the eventual execution of the king and queen. All students in Switzerland learned about the French Revolution as an example of how a society can change.

Kim Jong Un's class learned that the French Revolution began in no small part because of the population's unhappiness that living standards, having started to improve, did not continue to rise. Political scientists still talk today about the potentially destabilizing effect of rising expectations going unmet.

Does the Great Successor remember these lessons? Life has been improving for many North Koreans since Kim Jong Un came to power in 2011. They have more freedom to make money through their own enterprise, and those who make enough can buy cappuccinos, Rollerblades, and smartphones.

As a result, there are now obvious disparities between the way people live in the supposed socialist paradise. There's a 1 percent. Are the 99 percent, the North Korean equivalent of the bourgeoisie and peasantry, going to start resenting the gap between them and the elite and, more importantly, do something about it? Are they going to vent their anger if the small improvements in their standard of living do not continue?

The lessons on the French Revolution and the fate of Louis XVI don't augur well for Kim and his circle.

But back then, the student wasn't worrying about historical omens. He was busy playing basketball.

Every day at 5:00 p.m., when the school bell rang, Kim Jong Un would head to the basketball courts at his school or at the Lerbermatt high school, less than a ten-minute walk away. He was often with his older brother Kim Jong Chol and with an older North Korean boy who acted as their bodyguard.

Simon Lutstorf, a student at the Lerbermatt high school at the time, played basketball with the group several times a week between 1998 and 2001, often until eight o'clock at night. He just assumed that the Asian kid was associated with the Thai embassy, which was a short walk from the high school.

Kim Jong Un always wore the same outfit for basketball: an authentic Chicago Bulls top with Michael Jordan's number—23—and Bulls shorts, and his Air Jordan shoes. His ball was also top of the line: a Spalding with the official mark of the NBA.

Kim's competitive side came out on the basketball court. He could be aggressive and often indulged in trash talk.[11] He was serious on the court, hardly ever laughing or even talking, just focused on the game. When things went badly for him, he would curse or even pound his head against the wall.

Sometimes, in addition to the other Asian teenagers Kim Jong Un arrived with, a couple of adults came along and set up small camping chairs beside the court, keeping score on a little board and clapping when Kim landed a basket. Lutstorf described the scene as "really bizarre." "It was obvious that this guy, who we now know was Kim, was something special," he said.

Off the court, Kim Jong Un played basketball on his PlayStation. "The whole world for him was just basketball all the time," Micaelo said.[12] He had even been to Paris to see an NBA exhibition game and had photos of himself standing with Toni Kukoc of the Chicago Bulls and Kobe Bryant of the Los Angeles Lakers.[13]

A few of Kim Jong Un's closest friends in Bern went back to his home, which they described as spare, with no pictures on the walls. It did have a basketball hoop outside, however, and the teenagers would play out there often, sometimes making more noise than the neighbors would have preferred.

At the apartment, Micaelo met Kim Jong Un's "parents," his older brother, and his younger sister, Kim Yo Jong, who was known in

Switzerland as Pak Mi Hyang. They didn't have much to say to each other since the Koreans couldn't speak German and Micaelo couldn't speak English or Korean.

Still, Micaelo often went around for lunch, where a cook made "boiled chicken with strange sweet and sour sauces" that were not to the Portuguese student's liking.

Sometimes they would go to a local swimming pool in the North Koreans' darkened minivan, laughing the whole way. Another classmate, Marco Imhof, also went to Kim's apartment from time to time and noticed how the boy's personality changed to reveal flashes of temper. Once the boys were given spaghetti, but it was cold. He spoke "sharply" to the cook at the apartment, Imhof said, in a way that surprised him.[14]

Kim Jong Un had gadgets his friends could only dream of: a mini-disc player, which was the cutting-edge way to store music in the years before iPods; a Sony PlayStation; and lots of movies that hadn't yet been released in theaters. They loved watching action films, especially those featuring Jackie Chan or the latest James Bond.

But at a time when teenagers are usually pushing boundaries, Kim Jong Un was no party animal or playboy in training. He didn't go to school camp, parties, or discos, and he didn't touch a drop of alcohol.

Kim Jong Un "absolutely avoided contact with girls," a former classmate said, adding that she never had a substantial conversation with him. "He was a loner and didn't share anything about his private life. . . . When he was with somebody, it was Marco Imhof and Joao Micaelo."[15]

With these friends, he would talk about North Korea and what he'd done there during his summer break. He showed them photos of the beach at Wonsan and pictures of him jet-skiing. One day, while Kim and Micaelo were hanging out in the living room, the North Korean went off to his bedroom and came back with a photo of him and an older man. The man in the apartment was not his dad, Kim revealed. Instead, he introduced the man in the photo as his real father: Kim Jong Il, the leader of North Korea.

Micaelo thought his friend was talking nonsense and responded sarcastically, "Sure, your father is the president." Kim Jong Un just laughed but insisted that he really was the son of the North Korean leader. They dropped it.

But then one day, around Easter 2001, with only a couple of months to go until he completed ninth grade, Kim told Micaelo that his father had ordered him back to North Korea and that he would leave soon.[16] He offered no explanation for his sudden recall.

Kim's other friends received no such notice. The boy just stopped coming to school one day. Their teachers said they had no idea what happened to him either.

Just like that, Pak Un was gone.

CHAPTER 4

DICTATORSHIP 101

"I express my firm resolve to study harder and become a faithful man who relieve burden from the General who is so much concerned about the army's combat readiness."

—Kim Jong Un in 2006, from *Anecdotes of Kim Jong Un's Life*

BACK HOME, KIM JONG UN PREPARED TO JOIN HIS OLDER brother at Kim Il Sung Military University, North Korea's equivalent of West Point. It was their mother's idea to send them to the military academy, a way to bolster her sons' claims to succession.

His mother's ambitions were evident. One of the few photos of them together shows her leaning over the boy she called the Morning Star King as he colored. He is about six years old and dressed in a general's uniform with four stars on his shoulders.

Kim Jong Un had entered the university named after his grandfather in 2002 and began studying juche-oriented military leadership, the idea that North Korea could act alone to defend itself. It was an important ideological lesson even if it had no basis in reality. North Korea was entirely dependent on China for its stability.

That year was pivotal both for the heir apparent and for the regime.

First, it marked a new chapter for relations between North Korea and the United States—for the worse. At the start of 2002, President George W. Bush labeled North Korea part of an "axis of evil." Bush declared that, together with Iran and Iraq, North Korea was "arming to threaten the peace of the world. . . . All nations should know: America will do what is necessary to ensure our nation's security."

Just a couple of weeks after that speech, Kim Jong Il officially turned sixty. His birthday was always celebrated with great fanfare in North Korea, but this one was even more important than usual. In Korean culture, a man's sixtieth is a major milestone. It marks the completion of one sixty-year cycle of the lunar calendar and the beginning of the next.

In the meantime, Kim Jong Il's one-time consort, and the mother of Kim Jong Nam, died in Moscow that year. Between that and his milestone birthday, Kim Jong Il's mortality was clearly on his mind. There were signs of nascent preparation for succession.

For starters, there was a new "mother of the nation," a name previously reserved for Kim Jong Il's mother, in the propaganda. The Korean People's Army issued a sixteen-page pamphlet that year called "Our Respected Mother Who Is Loyal to Our Beloved Supreme Commander Is the Most Loyal among Loyalists." Songs about "Our Respected Mother" soon began to echo across the North Korean airwaves.[1]

These did not explicitly name Ko Yong Hui, but the cadres could read between the lines and see it was her. She elevated to become the next mother of the nation, an early indication that one of her sons was next in line for the leadership.

So efforts to crown one of her sons were well underway even before Kim Jong Nam's ill-fated trip to Tokyo Disney, although Ko took advantage of his embarrassing gaffe to push her sons' case.

Ko Yong Hui knew that she did not have long to lobby for her sons. She was losing her fight against breast cancer.

Kim Jong Un, meanwhile, was throwing himself into his studies at the academy, according to official North Korean accounts. The young man was such a natural at military strategy that he was instructing the instructors rather than learning from them, the state media reported.

Late one night in 2004, when Kim Jong Un was just twenty and partway through his course, he was "giving advice" to senior officials at 2:00 a.m., rebuffing their suggestions that he should go to sleep. The time is important—his grandfather was also renowned for working into the wee hours—so the detail was included to send a strong signal that Kim Jong Un was his grandfather's natural heir.

Instead of sleeping, Kim picked up a pencil, drew a picture of Mount Paektu, and wrote under it, "The Sacred Mountain of the Revolution. Kim Jong Il," the official history has it. He ordered this to be the cover of a book of military art about the "anti-Japanese revolutionary war," according to this version of events recounted by Kim Jong Un's image makers.

There may have been a granule of truth in the story, but most likely it was one of those events that takes on outsized significance in the hands of the state scribes. The officials with Kim Jong Un "were filled with deep emotion as they realized he would carry forward the bloodline of Mount Paektu in its purest form," the official account said.[2]

It's hard to exaggerate the importance of a pure bloodline in Korean culture. By claiming to be descended from the "Paektu bloodline," the Kim family was tapping into this long-held cultural belief in a purity that was distilled into these three Kims. It's the North Korean equivalent of tracing your ancestors to the *Mayflower* but in totalitarian overdrive.

Kim Jong Un's mother succumbed to cancer in May 2004, dying at a hospital in Paris. Her body was brought back to Pyongyang for a secret funeral and burial.

In public, the glorification of her as the mother of the nation continued. This could have worked as succession preparation for either of her sons, Kim Jong Chol or Kim Jong Un. Indeed, despite the fact that Kim Jong Un had been anointed when he was eight years old, it seemed that Kim Jong Il was keeping his options open by grooming both of them.

While Kim Jong Un was still at university, Kim Jong Chol was put into the Organizational and Guidance Department, arguably the most powerful agency inside North Korea. It oversees the Workers' Party of Korea, the cabinet, and the National Defense Commission. Kim Jong Il had begun his own political education there in 1964.

But as 2005 turned into 2006, there was speculation in the South Korean press that Kim Jong Chol had failed to prove himself as leadership material.

Perhaps as proof that he was no longer in contention—if he ever had been—Kim Jong Chol was spotted following his guitar idol, Eric Clapton, on a four-city tour in Germany. He had played the guitar from an early age and had an electric guitar and amplifier at home in Pyongyang.

Japanese television outlets filmed him in Frankfurt, Berlin, Leipzig, and Stuttgart, surrounded by a posse of bodyguards and in the company of a woman about his age. He was wearing a T-shirt, sometimes a leather jacket, and had floppy bangs hanging down over his round face. He did not seem thrilled with the media attention.

None of this was known in North Korea, though. The vast majority of North Koreans didn't even know that the Dear Leader had a son, let alone that he knew the chords to "Wonderful Tonight."

Meanwhile, the twenty-two-year-old Kim Jong Un went on to graduate—with honors, of course.

His graduation ceremony was held on December 24, 2006, an important day in North Korea. It was the fifteenth anniversary of Kim Jong Il's appointment as Supreme Commander of the Korean People's Army. It was also the eighty-ninth anniversary of his mother's birth. No date is too minor for the North Korean regime to justify a celebration that helps it reinforce its personality cult.

Kim's final dissertation was called "A Simulation for the Improvement of Accuracy in the Operational Map by the Global Positioning System (GPS)." Kim Jong Il apparently approved of this technical treatise, saying that it reflected the "great military strategy theories" developed by him and his father, Kim Il Sung.

Whether or not there was really a dissertation, Kim Jong Un was presented with a badge and a certificate declaring him to be a top student at this elite academy. He took the opportunity of his graduation to hold forth about his father's brilliance.

"While learning the Supreme Commander's juche-based military ideas and the art of warfare during my university days, I keenly realized that our General is a military genius, indeed," Kim Jong Un told a meeting of the of commanding officers of the Korean People's Army that day.

Kim Jong Un credited his father with formulating unparalleled military ideas and vowed, even though he'd not yet been announced as successor, to "become a faithful man who relieves burden from the General who is so much concerned about the army's combat readiness."

This was all according to the North Korean account of the meeting, in a thin 2017 booklet called *Anecdotes of Kim Jong Un's Life*, published, according to the foreword, to address the supposedly huge international interest in the third Kim.

The book claimed that there had been 67.4 million stories published in English about Kim Jong Un in one ten-day period—that's 230,000 an hour. "No other politician captured such keen attention of the world" in the history of media.

The numbers seem to be typical North Korean exaggeration, and the book failed to mention that the attention was due to Kim Jong Un's reckless threats and general brutality rather than being driven by admiration for the young leader.

The succession preparations took on a new sense of urgency in the summer of 2008, with Kim Jong Il's stroke. He was in a coma, "in a bad way," when a French brain specialist, François-Xavier Roux, arrived in Pyongyang to treat him.

North Korean officials had phoned Roux, the chief of neurosurgery at Sainte Anne Hospital in Paris, for advice in 1993 after the Dear Leader fell while horse riding and suffered a head injury. He never knew why they'd chosen him. When they called for him again in 2008, he was flown to Pyongyang with a team of doctors in great secrecy to treat a mystery patient. It turned out to be Kim Jong Il himself, and he was in a "life-threatening" condition.[3]

It became clear why the North Koreans had sought out a foreign doctor—none of them had wanted to make decisions for their Dear Leader, and certainly not ones where his life was at stake. They needed someone who was "not emotionally involved." At his father's bedside in that hospital room was his youngest son, Kim Jong Un. But it was "very difficult" to get a sense of the son's personality because "he didn't speak to anyone" in the medical team, according to Roux.[4]

The French doctor visited again in September and October to check on his patient's recovery. There was a significant risk that he would have further strokes, the doctor said.

Clearly time was not on Kim Jong Il's side.

Less than five months later, Kim Jong Il officially notified the top military and civilian authorities that he was naming Kim Jong Un as his successor. Kim Jong Il didn't even bother to go through with the charade that his own father had arranged for him in 1980: calling a Workers' Party Congress and making it look like the top apparatchiks had a say in the matter. He simply anointed his son.

First, Kim Jong Il informed the top officials in the Workers' Party on January 8, 2009—Kim Jong Un's twenty-fifth birthday—that he had chosen his youngest son as his successor.

Then the news was announced down the hierarchy. Apparatchiks like Thae Yong Ho were informed. Thae was at work in the European division of foreign ministry in Pyongyang, a large building on Kim Il Sung Square in the center of the capital, having returned from a posting to the embassy in London the previous year.

His "cell" in the Workers' Party of Korea—the Communist organ through which the Kims have kept a grip on North Korea for more than seven decades—was called to a meeting. They assembled as instructed and were informed that Kim Jong Il had chosen his son, the Comrade General, to succeed him. They were told that this was about continuity, a message that was repeatedly reinforced throughout what Thae remembers as a very quiet meeting.

"No one ever doubted this decision," Thae told me some years later in Seoul. "In North Korea, we are taught from a very young age that the revolution will be continued from generation to generation."

Before that time, even relatively high-ranking officials like Thae knew almost nothing about North Korea's royal family. From his time abroad in Europe, he knew that Kim Jong Il's children had been educated in Switzerland, but he did not know how many children or what their names were.

The roll-out was slow and indirect, disseminated almost subliminally, to the general populace, especially those in the "hostile" northern regions, where life was toughest and loyalty to the regime was flimsiest.

It began in 2009 with "Footsteps," the song that the Japanese sushi chef had heard in the privacy of the royal compounds more than a decade before. Now, ordinary North Koreans began hearing the bouncy Soviet-martial-style tune and its "aaaah, footsteps" refrain.

"It was actually fun singing together," Min-ah, a young North Korean mother from the northern border city of Hoeryong, told me near her new home on the outskirts of Seoul as she reminisced about the time her neighborhood watch group—the grassroots level of surveillance in the police state—began learning the song and about the third generation.

"Footsteps" began playing on television and radio and was sung in neighborhood watch groups and Workers' Party cells. It was printed in the notebooks that soldiers carried. North Koreans sent abroad to earn money for the regime also started hearing the song at their weekly ideology sessions.

"We were told to memorize the song and were told that the 'Comrade Leader' was so great," Mr. Kang, who was also from Hoeryong, told me. Before he escaped from Kim Jong Un's clutches, he'd been a drug dealer.

"We knew that he was going to be the leader after Kim Jong Il, but we knew nothing about him. We had no idea what he looked like; we had no idea how old he was. We knew only how great he was."

This song's significance was also noted in the South. A South Korean intelligence analyst sitting in his office outside Seoul was monitoring the North's state broadcaster, Korean Central Television. It was showing Kim Jong Il at a concert in the countryside somewhere, surrounded as usual by his closest aides, including his sister and her influential husband, as well as the propaganda chief.

Then the letters appeared at the front of the stage: "Footsteps." The choir began to sing. A light went on in the intelligence analyst's head: North Korea's succession question had been answered.[5]

South Korea's intelligence services knew next to nothing about Kim Jong Un. During the course of 2009, they knew so little about him that they even misspelled his name and could only guess at his correct age. "Everything about Kim Jong Un is cloaked in mystery, be it his photo, birth date or job title," a South Korean newspaper wrote at the time.

In the United States, the Central Intelligence Agency got wind of Kim Jong Un's anointment and started thinking about ways to influence him. American spies approached Eric Clapton about playing a concert in North Korea, knowing that the Kim boys were big fans of the British guitarist. Clapton was amenable to the idea, but it went nowhere. The spies also talked about trying to get a former Chicago Bull to play intermediary. They settled on Dennis Rodman. That idea went nowhere either—at least, not under the CIA's direction.

Inside North Korea, Kim Jong Un's age was going to be an issue. Political and social relationships in both Koreas are still bound by Confucianism, which involves a strict hierarchy that equates age with importance. Kim Jong Un was only twenty-five years old, a mere child in a political environment where his grandfather's octogenarian comrades were still in positions of power.

What's more, there was no preexisting myth that had been crafted about Kim Jong Un. The North Korean regime had exaggerated Kim Il Sung's exploits to turn him into a legendary anti-imperialist guerrilla who had triumphed over the Japanese. Then there was the story of the bright star and a double rainbow above Mount Paektu for Kim Jong Il.

Kim Il Sung spent a quarter century consolidating his power, not making his total authority official until 1972, when a constitution with a position of "Supreme Leader" was adopted. He spent the next twenty years paving the way for his son to succeed him.

Kim Jong Il was promoted up the party during the 1970s and was heir apparent from 1974. At the Sixth Congress of the Workers' Party in 1980, he was officially unveiled to the world as his father's successor. So when Kim Il Sung died in 1994, the regime had had plenty of time to get used to the idea that his son, who was then the respectable age of fifty-two, would take over and the "Paektu bloodline" would be continued.

Kim Jong Il, however, had not begun to prepare the system for his son—who was so young he would still have been doing his compulsory military service if he was any other twenty-five-year-old North Korean man—to carry on the family business. Kim's stroke changed his calculation about the future, and he spurred his inner circle into action.

Starting in 2009, Kim Jong Un was rapidly elevated through a series of increasingly powerful civilian and military positions, and the influential propaganda and agitation department began creating a personality cult around him.

North Koreans began hearing about the "Leader Comrade," and the state outlets began to talk about "a historic time of transition." It was only after this that the name Kim Jong Un began to appear. Posters went up everywhere heralding Comrade Kim Jong Un, the successor of the Paektu bloodline, as "our people's glory."[6]

The official narrative described him as a "Brilliant Comrade" and a "Young General," a "morning star shining over the whole nation." The North Korean regime sent a booklet to every unit of the Korean People's Army called *The Material in Teaching the Greatness of Respected Comrade General Kim Jong Un.*

Among the supposed great feats it listed was that at age three, Kim Jong Un would fire a gun and hit a light bulb a hundred yards away. Another version of this story had him hitting a target ten times in ten seconds. By the time he was eight, he could not only drive a truck, but he could drive it at eighty miles an hour. Plus, he knew everything there was to know about the military, whether it be the army, the navy, or the air force. It was hard to swallow even in North Korea.

During the course of 2009, the North Korean constitution was revised to strengthen the power of the country's supreme leader even further and to make clear that the armed forces should be looking after the "core of revolution"—the core being, of course, the Kim family. Kim Jong Un was reportedly given a place on the National Defense Commission. The Korean People's Army was no longer known as the "Kim Jong Il armed forces" but as the "Kim Jong Un armed forces."[7] The kid who paid little attention at school was soon being heralded as a "genius among geniuses."

Kim Jong Un's pledge to the generals that he would carry on the revolution was printed in the pamphlets and distributed to every unit of the Korean People's Army.

The adulation for his mother continued. An eighty-five-minute documentary called *The Mother of the Great, Military-First Korea* appeared on state television.

It showed photos and footage of Ko Yong Hui being a devoted follower of the regime during the mourning period for Kim Il Sung in 1994. And it showed her accompanying Kim Jong Il during his guidance visits to military, industrial, and cultural sites during the 1990s—footage that was certainly never broadcast at the time, when the "first ladies" were entirely invisible.[8]

One scene showed Ko speaking at a party marking her fiftieth birthday party. "The General said to me once, 'You must tell the people how hard these past seven years have been for me,'" Ko said, talking about the years since Kim Il Sung died and during which famine ravaged the country. "I have personally seen how difficult these seven years have been for the Peerlessly Great General," she simpered.

They weren't that difficult. Kim Jong Il was eating caviar and lobster while his compatriots starved. For two years during the height of the famine, he was the world's largest buyer of Hennessy Paradis cognac, importing almost a million dollars' worth of the liquor a year.

But the propagandists had an alternative history to write. And that required bestowing legitimacy on the princeling.

Hence the documentary. The goal was clear: Ko Yong Hui was the newest "Great Mother" of the nation, following in the footsteps of Kim Il Sung's and Kim Jong Il's venerated mothers. It was inevitable that her son, with that pure Paektu blood coursing through his veins, would be the next leader of North Korea.[9]

At their compulsory weekly education sessions, people around the country were having messages drilled into them about the incredible feats of this young genius. They heard the one about firing a gun when he was three years old and the ones about riding horses and driving cars at an age when most kids are learning their ABCs.

"It was hard for people to believe these things—we just laughed at them. It may have worked for kids but not for adults," Mr. Kang, the drug dealer, told me. "But if you questioned it, you'd be killed."

Some of its efforts to sell the new leader pushed the boundaries of credulity, even in this totalitarian state. One officially sanctioned biography called *The Childhood of Beloved and Respected Leader, Kim Jong Un* claimed that he had perfect pitch, that he could ride the wildest horses at age six, and that, when he was just nine, he had twice beaten a visiting European powerboat-racing champion. The youngster had driven at speeds of 125 miles per hour, it said. It was so unbelievable that the textbook was recalled after whispered criticisms began circulating that it "distorted and exaggerated" the leader's early years. It was revised to make it more credible.[10]

Worse still, the regime was about to commit its biggest error ever, one that was entirely self-inflicted and that would shake the system to its very core.

On November 30, 2009, a Sunday, the regime abruptly announced that it was devaluing the currency, the North Korean won. The news came down through the Workers' Party hierarchy, with high-ranking officials in Pyongyang the first to know and ordinary people in the boondocks the last.

The North Korean cash squirreled away in wardrobes around the country became almost instantly worthless. Citizens had one week in which they could convert 100,000 won, worth about thirty dollars or a one-hundred-pound sack of rice at the time, into the new currency, which would have two zeros knocked off the end. One hundred old won would, from then on, be worth one new won.[11]

Chaos and panic enveloped the country. The elites in Pyongyang who had heard the news first rushed to change their won into foreign currency or to spend as much as they could—on food, clothing, anything—before the change took place.

But for everyone else, the news arrived too late. Families who had been toiling to drag themselves into the emerging middle class had their life savings obliterated overnight.

Mr. Hong was one of those who'd turned his miserable state-mandated job into one that actually earned him a living. He'd been working as a border guard near the North Korean city of Hyesan and had branched out into the money transfer business: he used his connections on both sides of the border to secretly get money from the outside world to North Koreans inside.

This highly subversive business is nevertheless commonplace on the border now, as North Koreans who've escaped to South Korea and China want to send money home to relatives. Through his industrial zeal, Mr. Hong had built up a nice little nest egg for his family. He'd managed to save 30,000 North Korean won, a huge amount in an area where 10,000 won could buy a reasonable house.

He could buy meat and fish for his wife and their elementary school–aged daughter to eat every day, sometimes more than once a day. They had all the trappings of wealth that Kim Il Sung had long ago talked about—although the Great Leader had said these benefits would come by creating a socialist paradise, not by smuggling cash across the river.

But with the currency reforms, Mr. Hong's savings were wiped out, and his family's lifestyle was gone almost overnight. Untold numbers of other North Koreans who'd turned into secret capitalists suffered the same debilitating fate. That marked a turning point in the way Mr. Hong and his neighbors thought about the country's leaders. For the first time, he realized he was being cheated by the system.

He recounted the turmoil that the currency reforms caused in his hometown and how it proved to be the final straw for him. "I thought that Kim Jong Il really cared for the people, but when the currency reforms happened and all my savings were wiped out, I knew that wasn't the case," Mr. Hong told me in the rundown commuter town outside Seoul where he had been living since escaping at the end of 2015.

As the value of the North Korean won plummeted on the black market, the regime banned the use of foreign currency and imposed strict new rules about when markets could be open and what products they could sell.

It was not enough. Inflation spiked. Food shortages worsened. Around the country, people were dying. Some were having heart attacks from the shock of losing everything; others were killing themselves.[12] The regime, realizing the potential for disruption and perhaps unrest, raised the amount that could be changed into the new currency to 300,000 won and then to 500,000. Some workplaces raised salaries or offered to pay workers their wages at the old rate.[13]

The whole idea of devaluing the currency seemed designed to crack down on the private markets that had taken root after the famine and the growing economic influence of the traders. The move wiped out their savings, except for the biggest fish, who could save their money in foreign currency.

Some reports from inside North Korea suggested that the effort was undertaken in Kim Jong Un's name, part of an effort to signal his emergence on the political scene.

If this was true, Kim Jong Un never shouldered any of the blame for the fiasco, at least not publicly. That went to Pak Nam Gi, a seventy-seven-year-old technocrat who had been chief of the planning and finance department in the Workers' Party.

In January of 2010, Pak was sacked from his position. By March, he had been charged with "deliberately ruining the national economy." He was executed at a firing range in Pyongyang.[14] Someone had to take the fall for this debacle.

Not only did the system try to divert any blame from Kim Jong Un, but it tried to make him look like the good guy. The Central Committee of the Workers' Party of Korea gave out 500 won of the new currency to every household at the end of 2009. It was "consideration money from General Kim," the committee reportedly told the citizenry.

Despite this attempt to buy favor, the environment was not exactly conducive for a tricky transfer of power. But with Kim Jong Il's health continuing to deteriorate, what choice did the regime have?

With the country in economic turmoil and dissatisfaction simmering just below the surface, Kim Jong Un's next audition was designed to prove his military chops. Tyrants the world over know that there's nothing like a brazen military victory to distract from troubles at home.

The princeling is thought to have been the mastermind behind the sinking of a South Korean naval corvette, the *Cheonan*, at the end of March 2010. The 1,200-ton *Cheonan* was struck by a torpedo during a routine patrol in the West Sea near the North-South maritime border, the scene of previous naval skirmishes. Forty-six South Korean sailors were killed. It was one of the bloodiest incidents since the end of the Korean War in 1953.

An international investigation into the attack found evidence that pointed overwhelmingly in the direction of North Korea, saying the only plausible explanation for the sinking was a torpedo fired by a North Korean submarine.

There were suspicions among analysts in South Korea that Kim Jong Un was behind the attack, trying to burnish his credentials with North Korea's top brass.[15] He had his bespoke degree from Kim Il Sung Military University, but he didn't have any on-the-ground experience. So he urgently needed some if he was going to lead a country that had, under his father, espoused a military-first policy prioritizing the Korean People's Army.

Another crucial rite of passage was completed in August, when Kim Jong Un accompanied his father on a trip to China, apparently so Kim Jong Il could make a formal introduction to the regime's historical patrons in Beijing. There are rumors that during this trip, they toured parts of northeast China, where Kim Il Sung had cut his teeth as an anti-Japanese fighter.

With the formal introductions to their Chinese comrades completed, the *Cheonan* sunk, and the myth of the Paektu bloodline aggressively propagated, Kim Jong Un apparently had all the qualifications he needed for a promotion. On September 27, 2010, Kim Jong Un was made a four-star general in the Korean People's Army, which, his father said in the announcement of his son's elevation, "is demonstrating its might before the world as a powerful revolutionary army of Mt. Paektu."[16]

That was on a Monday. The following day, the regime called a Workers' Party representatives' conference for the first time in forty-four years. Posters up in Pyongyang urged cadres to "greet the conference of the Workers' Party of Korea as an auspicious event which will shine forever in the history of our party and country!" The *Rodong Sinmun*, the official mouthpiece of the Workers' Party, reported that the conference would "shine as a notable event in the history of the sacred Workers' Party."

At the conference, Kim Jong Un was named vice chairman of the Central Military Commission and appointed to the Central Committee of the Workers' Party, moving him up the ranks of the two branches that keep the regime in power—not a bad start to the week for a twenty-six-year-old.

By Friday, the regime had released the first official photo of Kim Jong Un, running it in full color on the front page of the *Rodong Sinmun*. In the front row sat Kim Jong Il, in his trademark olive-green jumpsuit, surrounded by the top brass, many of them festooned with military decorations. And there was the young Kim Jong Un, the only one dressed in a black Mao suit, his hair in a peculiar pompadour. The echoes were clear: he looked like a young Kim Il Sung.

For the outside world, what had been suspected was suddenly patently clear: the rumored successor had come fully into view.

Further confirmation, as if any were needed, came less than two weeks later, when Kim Jong Un appeared next to his father at the celebrations for the sixty-fifth anniversary of the communist Workers' Party of Korea.

They stood on the balcony of the Grand People's Study House, a huge library overlooking Kim Il Sung Square in the center of Pyongyang. Kim Jong Un was expressionless as he clapped at the appropriate times during the parade, standing closer to his father than the men in military uniforms and high-ranking party officials but still keeping a respectful distance. His father was the star of the show.

Several of the men on that balcony would not be around much longer.

Kim Jong Il seemed frailer than ever, walking with a limp and having trouble using his left hand, even for applauding. He would be dead in just over a year.

Vice Marshal Ri Yong Ho, the chief of general staff in the Korean People's Army, who gave a speech that day lauding the North Korean system, would be purged from this system within two years. After that would be the man in the black suit and darkened glasses—Kim Jong Un's uncle, Jang Song Thaek, who'd be brutally thrown out too.

As the regime focused on cementing the idea of hereditary succession into the third generation, anyone who might question or rival the new young leader would be cast aside.

Even Marx and Lenin, whose portraits had hung over the square for decades, would soon be removed.

But the sixty-fifth anniversary tableau offered a vision of communist unity as thousands of troops marched through the square, shouting for the long life of their system.

From that point on, Kim Jong Il was rarely seen without Kim Jong Un at his side.

There he was, following his father on a tour of new apartments built in the capital, all smiles, clapping at the residents' accordion performances and pouring celebratory rice wine for them. He was with Kim Jong Il as he gave on-the-spot guidance about the construction of the power station. And he was present alongside his father during a performance of the Electronic Band of the Song and Dance Ensemble of the Air Force Command early in 2011. They played snappy numbers, including "Where Are You, Dear General?" and "We Will Become a Shield in the Sky."

All the while, half a world away, events were taking place that must have shaken the Kims to their core. In the final days of 2010, autocracies with dynastic designs began falling in the Middle East.

In Tunisia, resentment over economic inequalities brought protesters into the street. In January 2011, the government was overthrown. The protests became contagious. Thousands upon thousands gathered in Tahrir Square in Cairo, demanding the resignation of President Hosni Mubarak, the authoritarian ruler who seemed to be preparing to pass power on to his son, Gamal.

The following month, Mubarak resigned. By then, the Arab Spring movement had spread to Libya, where Colonel Muammar Gaddafi, who had ruled through fear for more than four decades, was positioning his second son, Saif al-Islam, as heir apparent.

Another month, another authoritarian leader was threatened. In March, it was Syria's turn. Protestors demanded that Bashar al-Assad, who inherited the leadership from his father, release political prisoners, sparking a brutal, years-long civil war.

One can only imagine the horror with which these events were watched from Pyongyang. The general populace would have had little idea what was going on. Although many people did manage to break through the ban on foreign media, few of them chose to watch international news, preferring the escapism of illegal action movies or soap operas.

But for the North Korean regime, the sight of autocrats falling would have been deeply disquieting.

The regime stepped up its succession preparations. State media began mentioning Kim Jong Un much more often, usually preceded by a new honorific "Beloved and Respected Comrade General." The authorities reportedly ordered that no babies from then on could be called Jong Un, and any North Koreans who already had that name—a relatively common one based on two Chinese characters that mean "proper" and "kindness"—had to change it.

In schools around the country, Kim Jong Un was gradually being introduced into the curriculum. During ideological education sessions, students were taught that Kim Jong Un was Kim Il Sung's grandson.

Hyon, who at the time was a sixteen-year-old high school student in Hyesan, on the North Korean border with China, remembered being told that Kim Jong Un had an extraordinary childhood. He got the laughable spiel about Kim Jong Un being able to drive when he was three years old. He had to take down revolutionary memos in his special notebook. He had to learn the song "Footsteps," of course.

Government officials would hold events in their school halls or convene the students in the playgrounds and then would proceed to read out lectures about Kim Jong Un. They were supposed to cheer "long life" throughout, the phrase chanted about the earlier Kims at every opportunity.

A rumor went around Hyesan that once Kim Il Sung had asked Kim Jong Un to get him an apple. Kim Jong Un didn't just get him a single apple; he asked for a shovel because he wanted to bring the whole tree to his grandfather. This was a not-very-subtle parable about the need to go the extra mile for the Great Leader.

The teenage Hyon wondered at the time if the powerful secret police had planted the rumor, hoping that it would then be spread around through word of mouth. This kind of message could be much more effective than putting it on the front page of the papers—again. It was the North Korean version of going viral.

By the time Kim Jong Un took over leadership, his succession seemed natural and inevitable.

PART TWO

THE CONSOLIDATION

CHAPTER 5

A THIRD KIM AT THE HELM

"The entire army should place absolute trust in and follow Kim Jong Un and become human rifles and bombs to defend him unto death."

—*Rodong Sinmun*, January 1, 2012

THE YOUNG MAN HAD GOOD REASON TO BE SOLEMN. HIS FATHER had died. Kim Jong Un found himself the leader of the totalitarian state that his family had more or less invented. He was now entering the most important year of his life, the year that would show whether he was capable of keeping his family's grip on the country or whether the brutal, anachronistic system would finally tear itself apart.

He had to assert his authority over men who'd been working for the state for longer than he'd been alive and keep a lid on a population that had been cut off from the outside world for decades. And he had to repel an international community that was expecting—and, in many cases, hoping—that he would fail.

The first order of business was to turn the personality cult up to full blast.

On December 17, 2011, Kim Jong Il had suffered a massive heart attack, the result of "great mental and physical strain," while traveling by train to give on-the-spot guidance in the north of the country, the veteran newsreader Ri Chun Hee announced in a quivering voice during a special midday bulletin on state television two days later.

She had tearfully announced Kim Il Sung's death in 1994. Then, as now, she assured her audience that North Koreans had no need for concern. They had Kim Jong Un, the "Great Successor to the revolutionary cause," to lead them.

The twenty-seven-year-old was now "leader of the party, military, and the people," and the young scion would "brilliantly succeed and complete" the revolutionary creed established by his grandfather almost seven decades before, the broadcast continued.

The announcement ricocheted around the world. North Korea was now entering a highly unpredictable new phase. The regime was attempting the unprecedented: a transition to a third generation of supposedly socialist, highly totalitarian, and definitely untested power.

South Korea put its military on high alert. Japan activated an emergency response team. The White House was on tenterhooks and was "in close touch" with both of its allies on North Korea's doorstep.

In North Korea, the propaganda had been written. The senior officials had been put in their places. All the steps necessary to ensure Kim Jong Un could succeed his father had been taken, even if they'd been taken hurriedly.

Now Kim Jong Un had to step up and play his role.

The first, and most important, part was that of Bereft Inheritor. Kim Jong Un made sure the North Korean people saw him as the natural continuation of a line that had ruled the nation for the previous six decades. Like his father seventeen years earlier, he was now modeling the kind of ashen-faced sorrow he expected to see throughout the population.

Kim Jong Un went to the Kumsusan Memorial Palace, a thirty-five-thousand-square-meter, five-story mausoleum in the northeast of Pyongyang, where his grandfather had lain in state for the past seventeen years.

It was originally built as Kim Il Sung's official residence but was converted into a permanent memorial at a cost rumored to have hit $900 million, money spent when the famine was at its peak. Still, the regime's priority was not feeding its starving people but creating a behemothic tribute to the man who'd presided over the mismanagement that contributed to the deaths.

Kim Il Sung's embalmed body had lain in a glass case there, a menacing presence even in death. Every day, untold numbers of North Koreans in their Sunday best rolled into the massive building on long travellators more usually associated with airports. A steady stream of foreign visitors went in too, for taking outsiders to pay homage to the dead despot was important to maintain the lie that the Great Leader was internationally revered.

On my trips along the travellators into the mausoleum, I always found it fascinating to look at the North Koreans moving in the opposite direction. As they rolled along past me, I wondered what they made of this whole place. Maybe they were disgusted at the resources devoted to a corpse, or maybe they were genuinely moved by the sight of a man they'd been told was a demigod. Many were crying. For others, it was at least an opportunity to put on their best clothes and have a day away from the drudgery of ordinary life.

Now, Kim Jong Il was lying in state there too.

When they went into the mausoleum, Kim Jong Un and his sister, Kim Yo Jong, led the black-clad senior officials who went to pay their respects before their father's body. Both were wiping away tears.

Their father was lying on a platform, dressed in his zip-up jacket, his head resting on a round pillow and his body covered with a red sheet. Around the bier were the red begonias grown to bloom on his birthday, a flower named Kimjongilia. In North Korea, even Mother Nature was forced to bend to serve the myth of the glory of the Kims.

Then, eleven days after Kim Jong Il's death, came the public farewell.

Kim Jong Un sent his father on his last journey, the long black funeral cortege rolling through the white streets to complete a twenty-five-mile circuit through Pyongyang. The snow was falling thick and fast in a show of "heaven's grief," as a North Korean newsreader later described it.

The procession contained two American-made Lincoln Continentals: one carrying Kim Jong Il's portrait, wider and longer than the car itself, and another bearing his casket, wrapped in the flag of the Workers' Party, the traditional Communist hammer and sickle joined by a calligraphy brush to represent scholarship.

As the hearse rolled slowly through Kim Il Sung Square, eight men walked alongside. At the front right of the car was Kim Jong Un, clutching the side mirror as if to steady himself in his grief or perhaps as if to hold on to his beloved father as long as he could. His expression was as dark as his coat. But none of Kim Jong Il's other sons were visible. There was no sign of Kim Jong Un's older half brother, Kim Jong Nam, or his full brother, Kim Jong Chol.

Instead, the group of eight included Jang Song Thaek, Kim Jong Un's uncle, a gregarious character who had an important role managing the North's economic relationship with China. Jang was part of the inner circle thanks to his marriage to Kim Jong Il's sister, Kim Kyong Hui. Both of them had been promoted to the politburo the previous year, at the same conference where Kim Jong Un was named heir apparent.

The streets were lined with mourners who were wailing and beating their chests, convulsing in tears and falling to the ground in a way that could look extremely melodramatic to outsiders. The theatrics were Korean soap opera crossed with Latin American telenovela with a heavy dollop of bizarre.

North Koreans don't need to be told to mourn their leaders in this way. They know what is expected. Certainly, you would not want to be the North Korean caught on camera crying less passionately than the people around you. But some of it was no doubt genuine. Almost all North Koreans have grown up knowing nothing else, worshipping the Kims like gods. Some are true believers.

In the days after Kim Jong Il's death, the state media held up the intense public mourning as a sign of how deeply the people loved their leader. "The wailing of people greeting and sending off the hearse in tears seemed to shake the land," the official news agency reported.

This outpouring of grief was repeated across the country. Soldiers, schoolchildren, government officials, everyone gathered at monuments around the country to pay their respects—complete with unrestrained sobs, rending of black clothes, and full prostrations on the snow-covered ground—to Kim Jong Il. Kim Jong Un ordered warm drinks and extra medical care for the mourners out on the snowy streets, the state media said.

After the funeral, Kim Jong Un watched over a military parade in front of the Kumsusan Memorial Palace, where the Korean People's Army pledged its allegiance to the young new leader. They vowed to act as rifles and bombs to protect him and to wipe out North Korea's enemies if they dared "intrude into the inviolable sky, land and seas of the country even by 0.001 mm."

Kim Jong Il had declared a three-year mourning period after the death of his father, during which time he consolidated his grip on the regime and tried to hang on through the famine.

But the Great Successor didn't have any downtime. The man now known as the "Beloved and Respected" Comrade Kim Jong Un got busy "turning sorrow into strength," as newsreader Ri put it. From that moment on, he devoted all his time and energy to staying in power. For that, he needed to establish his own power base, one that owed its loyalty directly to him, not to his father.[1]

It was easy to make fun of the new young leader, and he would soon become the butt of many a joke.

For starters, there was his cartoonish appearance, with his idiosyncratic fade haircut, his rapidly expanding girth, and his penchant for attire that is fashionable only in Communist holdover states.

The photos of the Busy Dictator published in the state media looked like something out of the *Onion*. He popped up from a tank, his round, smiling face encased in a soft black helmet. The jolly dictator was shown supervising the production of a giant vat of lubricant. It was the kind of lubricant used for greasing engines, but North Korea could hardly have chosen a more joke-inducing factory for that photo shoot.

Kim Jong Un gave himself a vast array of elongated titles—he had soon collected hundreds of appellations of varying degrees of obsequiousness. Some were standard Communist fare like First Secretary of the Workers' Party. (He posthumously made his father General Secretary for eternity.) Others were standard but even more obviously undeserved, like chairman of the party's central military commission and first chairman of the National Defense Commission.

But some were pure hyperbole, like Invincible and Triumphant General. He was the Guardian of Justice, the Best Incarnation of Love, the Decisive and Magnanimous Leader. And there were many with the suns: the Guiding Ray of Sun, the Sun of the Revolution, the Sun of Socialism, the Bright Sun of the Twenty-First Century, and the Sun of Mankind. There was no honorific too superlative for the new leader.

Even the stories in the North Korean media became ever more fabulous, like the one by the Korean Central News Agency that announced that some of its scientists had discovered a "unicorn lair." Naturally, the story went viral immediately as people around the world tittered at this tale that was fanciful even by North Korean standards.

It turned out to be a translation issue. The report was in fact about a mythical creature linked to an ancient Korean kingdom—not so different from the Loch Ness monster. But that didn't stop the most laughable version gaining traction.

On two occasions, the state media reported that the Great Successor had climbed "through thick snow" to the top of Mount Paektu, the mythical peak from which he claims his divine right to lead. As proof, the papers showed the overweight man on top of the nine-thousand-foot mountain—wearing a long woolen coat better suited for Pyongyang parades and black leather dress shoes. So great was the leader that he didn't even require hiking gear to climb mountains.

Kim Jong Un was naturally moved by the power of the snowcapped volcano. With its unique prose style, the *Rodong Sinmun* newspaper reported that the "majestic spirit of Mount Paektu" was reflected in the eyes of the "gifted great person" and that, in that mountain, he saw "a powerful socialist nation which dynamically advances full of vigor without vacillation at any raving dirty wind on the planet."

Stories about him soon took hold in the popular imagination outside North Korea.

In China, he was quickly nicknamed "Kim Fatty the Third," despite the belated efforts of the Chinese censors to scrub the moniker from the internet.

There were the completely unfounded reports that he'd had a girlfriend, the leader of North Korea's most prominent girl band, executed because she and her bandmates had been making and selling lesbian porn films. She turned out to be not just alive; she became Kim Jong Un's key envoy during a period of cultural engagement. There were rumors that he'd spent $3.5 million on sexy lingerie for his Pleasure Squad, although there was never any evidence that he'd created a harem like his father had.

And when Kim Jong Un disappeared from sight for six weeks in 2014, and then reappeared with a walking stick, it was said that he had so great a predilection for Emmental cheese, a legacy from his days in Switzerland, that his ankles had given way. It seemed more likely that he was suffering from gout, a form of inflammatory arthritis that has been known as "the disease of kings" because it is caused by an overindulgent lifestyle. The true reason for Kim's disappearance remains unknown.

Even usually sober publications such as the *New Yorker* and the *Economist* couldn't resist the urge to mock: the former depicted Kim Jong Un on the cover as a baby playing with toy missiles, while the latter had his idiosyncratic hair blowing up into a nuclear cloud.

Kim Jong Un did indeed have a wobbly start. His first attempt at showing his military muscle ended in humiliating failure—apparently giving sustenance to all those snide suggestions that his leadership would not succeed.

He'd been running North Korea for only four months. The regime was gearing up to celebrate the centenary of "Eternal President" Kim Il Sung's birth on April 15, 2012. Even eighteen years after his death, Kim Il Sung's birthday was still being celebrated as the Day of the Sun, the holiest day of the year in North Korea. It is a day of military parades and fireworks and bowing before statues and other reminders of the Great Leader's general ongoing magnificence.

More than a simple anniversary, the centenary was an opportunity for the young dictator to reinforce the myth of the Paektu bloodline and affirm his divine right to lead North Korea. He planned two weeks of extravagant celebrations to mark the occasion.

He intended to start with a bang.

On April 13, the Korean Committee of Space Technology launched what it said was a new earth observation satellite. It was called Lode

Star-3, an auspicious name as every North Korean knew that a lode star had appeared in the sky over Mount Paektu on the day that Kim Jong Il was born.

The North Korean space committee had announced plans for the launch the month before. The ink was barely dry on the Leap Day agreement that Washington and Pyongyang had signed on February 29. In it, North Korea agreed to stop launching missiles and conducting nuclear tests in return for food aid.

The United States and other countries warned the Kim regime not to go ahead with the launch, viewing the rocket as a weak disguise for a long-range missile.

But the state media insisted that Pyongyang was simply exercising its sovereign right to the peaceful use of space. It took journalists from around the world to the launch site. Soon after dawn, the rocket lifted off. It flew for only ninety seconds before crashing into the sea between the Korean Peninsula and Japan.

The regime could hardly ignore it, given all the fanfare it had created and the fact that international media had recorded it. Kim's scribes simply said that the satellite "failed to enter its preset orbit" and that scientists were investigating the problem.

Even that modest and undeniable announcement was a break with the past. Kim Jong Il never conceded any kind of shortcoming. But Kim Jong Un publicly admitted a failure. It was an early sign that, while he was following in his father's footsteps in some ways, he would also do some things differently. He would prove to be much more forthcoming about North Korea's weaknesses and what needed to be done to fix them.

Anyway, Kim soon had reason to cheer. It wasn't long before the North Korean scientists fixed the problem. By the end of the year, they had put a satellite into orbit—a rickety one but in orbit all the same.

Kim Jong Un wasn't going to allow an early stumble to define him. Two days after the humiliation of the failed launch, the Great Successor returned to the balcony in Pyongyang, looking out over the square named for his grandfather. It was the same balcony where he had walked with his father barely eighteen months before, watching over a huge military parade and making his official debut to the world.

There, he delivered a speech. Much of what he said was standard North Korean bluster about how its "mighty military" would achieve "final victory" against the imperialists. But the speech was an event in itself. Kim Jong Il spoke in public only once, and then only a single phrase, during his entire seventeen years in power. "Glory to the heroic soldiers of the Korean People's Army!" he said during a military parade in 1992.

Yet here was a young man holding forth for twenty minutes in front of a bank of seven microphones, speaking to the people just a few months into his tenure. Far from being nervous on his first public appearance as leader, he looked relaxed as he joked and smiled with his top aides on the balcony.

This young leader was already so different from his father. Yet so much was familiar. North Koreans watching couldn't help but be reminded of Kim Il Sung, their Eternal President. Kim Jong Un had adopted a gravelly voice just like his grandfather, and he was again wearing his grandfather's trademark Mao suit, a red Kim Il Sung pin over his heart.

Flanked by generals in military uniform and other top officials, Kim Jong Un watched as tens of thousands of soldiers marched through the square below, holding aloft giant portraits of his grandfather and father. He saluted his predecessors as the soldiers chanted his name in sharp unison. All this was now his.

He may have been a gift for comedians and cartoonists, but it was not through luck, chance, or accident that Kim Jong Un has defied the odds to remain in control of his regime.

Everything that he has done since his first days in power has been carefully calculated to help him achieve his only goal: to remain, as his image makers put it, the Ever-Victorious, Iron-Willed Commander of North Korea.

In the outside world, there was a tendency to diminish Kim Jong Un's power, to say that he was just a figurehead and that the old guard was really running the show.

It did seem to be true that the Great Successor got some guidance in his early months and years. His aunt, Kim Kyong Hui, was his most important advisor. She had been very close to her brother, Kim Jong Il, and was a crucial pillar in his regime. She took the lead in ensuring her nephew got the education and support he needed as he took over the leadership. She also made sure the Kim family coffers were safe.

Her husband, pallbearer Jang Song Thaek, became the "Control Tower," looking after day-to-day operations of the regime. It was Jang who decided what messages got to Kim Jong Un and with what priority, putting his own spin on them as he delivered them.[2]

A third official made up the triumvirate of close advisors: Choe Ryong Hae, who at that time was the director of the General Political Bureau, the agency within the Korean People's Army that administers political education within the military. This was a crucial role that gave him authority in both the military and the Workers' Party.

These three supported and guided the young leader as he started his new role, but North Korea's regime operates on a system based on a Supreme Leader. Kim Jong Un wielded absolute power. This would be illustrated very soon through the fates of these three closest advisors.[3]

As he cemented his hold on the leadership and the regime, Kim Jong Un very deliberately retreated inward, forgoing the kinds of pilgrimages to Moscow and Beijing that his father and grandfather had made. He tried to make sure that no one else left the country either. He immediately set about sealing the borders to make sure that there was no exodus of people or sense that his grip on the state was anything less than iron clad. He clamped down on the flow of information, employing advanced technology to catch those who dared watch a South Korean drama or listen to a Chinese pop song.

He injected a new dose of terror into society, ensuring everyone lived in constant fear. The general populace came under new levels of repression, and elites in the regime who accumulated too much power risked being exiled to the far corners of the state—or worse.

Kim needed a cohort of supporters around him who also had a vested interest in his success, so he went about figuring out who to keep and who to eliminate. He got rid of potential rivals to the leadership, dispatching his uncle and eventually his half brother in brutal fashion to make it clear that his ambition knew no boundaries.

He allowed more economic freedom—distinctly capitalist markets became central to most people's lives—as a way to give the population a sense that their standard of living was improving.

That freed him up to pour all the regime's resources into developing the missile and nuclear weapons programs, pressing ahead with breathtaking speed and accomplishment to demonstrate a credible threat to the Kim regime's mortal enemy, the United States of America.

Even the ridiculous appearance was by design.

While other dictators have tried to hide the fact that they're aging and might therefore be mortal—just look at the way Saddam Hussein and Muammar Gaddafi dyed their hair—Kim Jong Un did the opposite. The young autocrat made himself the reincarnation of his grandfather. His hairstyle was straight out of the 1940s Soviet Union, and he walked with a limp. He had turned his voice into a low rumble reminiscent of his grandfather's, overlaid with a two-packs-a-day rasp. And most noticeable of all, he gained more and more weight between every public appearance.

In the summer, he wore the white, short-sleeved, comrade-style shirts that his grandfather sported. In the winter, he had the same huge fur hats. He even wore old-fashioned, square glasses. The whole look was vintage Kim Il Sung to remind North Koreans of the good old days.

The mimicry worked.

The first time he saw Kim Jong Un, with his substantial girth enveloped in a Mao suit and his unusual short-back-and-sides hairstyle, the high schooler from Hyesan immediately thought of his history lessons and the family reminiscences about the good times the country enjoyed under Kim Il Sung. "I thought about Kim Il Sung's time and time when North Koreans' lives were better, and I think a lot of other North Koreans thought that way too," Hyon told me.

"Just like South Koreans have fond memories for Park Chung-hee, North Koreans have fond memories of Kim Il Sung because during his reign, North Koreans lived better than South Koreans," he explained.

But Kim Jong Un didn't stop at appearances. Kim Il Sung had been a huge personality, and he had parlayed that into a charismatic regime that revolved around him alone. Kim Jong Il did not have this kind of demeanor. He was notoriously reclusive and standoffish and quite obviously disliked human contact.

Kim Jong Un seemed to be very much his grandfather's grandson, someone who seemed to enjoy North Korea's version of retail politics, of getting out and meeting his constituents. He didn't need their votes—the leader of North Korea is always elected to the Supreme People's Assembly, with 100 percent turnout and 100 percent in favor—but he did want enthusiasm, and so photographs of him being adored and being adoring were shared to perpetuate the myth.

In newspapers and on television screens, Kim Jong Un made sure to show himself as a man of the people. Everywhere he went—schools, orphanages, hospitals—he was tactile, smiling broadly and hugging everyone, from children to the elderly. Giving on-the-spot guidance at a farm, he petted a baby goat on the head.

The state media exploded with reports of people around the country supposedly randomly interviewed about their thoughts about their new leader. Everywhere from foodstuff factories to medicine manufacturing plants, North Koreans were quoted pledging their allegiance to the new leader, described as the "eternally immovable mental mainstay of the Korean people."

One woman couldn't contain her admiration: "I'm convinced he is the master of our destiny," she said on state television. "As long as he is with us, we will not fear anything."

The state media was glowing in its appraisal of Kim's debut, and many people were initially encouraged. Families around the country were given unfathomably decadent rations—like fish and meat, a rarity—to mark the change in leadership. They were gifts from the Great Successor to the people. Optimism grew.

Min-ah was only a couple of years younger than the new leader, and her life was relatively good back then in 2012. She was relatively well-off by provincial North Korean standards. She lived in Hoeryong, a bustling trading post on the North Korean border with China, and her husband was a truck driver, a good job because it allowed him to run a lucrative smuggling business on the side. They had a house with a small yard and, soon, a young baby. Once their daughter started kindergarten, they had enough money to bribe the teachers to treat her well. They were part of the new North Korean middle class.

Still, she hoped that the ascent of Kim Jong Un, a millennial like her, would herald a new era for North Korea—an era of better relations with China, which tolerated but didn't exactly embrace North Korea, and with the outside world. An era of economic prosperity, where North Koreans might begin to enjoy some of the riches and freedoms they saw in the South Korean dramas they secretly watched late at night.

But nothing improved. In fact, in some ways, life got worse. The border was fortified, making it more difficult for people to smuggle goods across the river. As a result, prices went up. The cost of laundry powder doubled and then tripled.

Disappointment began to set in. Min-ah's husband and closest friends began joking about their new demigod. If Kim Jong Un can be leader, then I can be the leader too, they laughed. In the police state of North Korea, such talk was seditious, and if someone betrayed their words to the authorities, the consequences would be severe: almost certain detention in a political prison camp.

"Everybody knew that Kim Jong Il and Kim Jong Un were both liars. We knew that everything we heard on the news was lies, but it's impossible to say anything because you're under such tight surveillance," Min-ah told me a few years after she and her husband and their two young daughters escaped to South Korea. "If someone is drunk and says Kim Jong Un is a son of a bitch, you'll never see them again."

Kim Jong Un had successfully taken over, but he had not yet proven that he knew how to make a success of the decrepit kleptocracy that was his inheritance.

CHAPTER 6

NO MORE BELT TIGHTENING

*"We must grow the valuable seeds, which the great Comrade Kim Jong Il
sowed, to build an economically powerful state and improve the people's
livelihood, and lead them to bloom as a glorious reality."*

—Kim Jong Un, April 15, 2012

KIM JONG IL WAS FIFTY-TWO YEARS OLD WHEN HE TOOK OVER
the running of North Korea, and the country was very vulnerable. The
Soviet Union had collapsed, and famine was about to explode. North
Korea's economy, already in a state of extreme disrepair, was about to get
even worse.

The second-generation leader couldn't risk adding any more uncer-
tainty into this volatile equation. He just had to hold on and hope that the
propaganda and the all-encompassing surveillance would see him through.
Against the odds, Kim held on and kept the family business intact for seventeen years. His principal accomplishment was to have endured that long.

Kim Jong Un did not have the option of just holding on. He was
only twenty-seven when he inherited this state. He could theoretically
rule for decades. So, to prove his right to rule, he needed to do much
more than his father. He actually needed to show that life was getting
better in North Korea if he wanted people to continue supporting his
regime and the grossly unfair society it had created. He needed to give
people a sense of a better life.

But to achieve tangible economic growth, he didn't embark on a grand or coherent plan such as the Chinese-style "reform and opening" or Soviet-style perestroika. Instead, he loosened the very restrictive rules a little. He simply stopped stifling enterprise.

Small acts of private enterprise were tolerated, if not endorsed. There would be no more clamping down on people who were trying to make ends meet by selling rice cakes or cutting hair or selling DVD players brought in from China, which handled almost all—about 90 percent— of North Korea's trade. Farmers could keep a little of their harvest to sell privately. Big changes to the monetary system were abandoned in favor of some gentle market forces that might provide enough growth to satisfy the people.

North Koreans "will never have to tighten their belts again," the Great Successor declared when he delivered his first public speech, marking the occasion of his grandfather's one hundredth birthday. Kim Jong Un told the bedraggled populace that they would be able to "enjoy the wealth and prosperity of socialism as much as they like."

It was a bold claim and a risky promise that challenged North Korea's miserable economic record.

While other countries in Asia had boomed during the '80s and '90s, North Korea's economy remained stuck somewhere between the Victorian era and the worst days of Stalin.

China joined the World Trade Organization. Communist Vietnam pressed ahead with its "doi moi" reforms that allowed more and more private enterprise. And South Korea was catapulting itself into the leagues of the world's richest countries.

Meanwhile, in North Korea, the fields were plowed by oxen. Trucks burned wood, not gasoline. Factories ground to a halt because of the lack of electricity and raw goods. In 2005, North Korea's GDP per capita was about $550—36 times smaller than the South's. North Korea was wedged in the United Nations' economic tables between Mali and Uzbekistan, while South Korea was up with Portugal and Bahrain.

North Korea's economic handicaps date back to division of the Korean Peninsula in 1945, which created a fundamental economic imbalance between North and South. The mountainous North is rich in mineral resources like coal and had been developed during the Japanese colonial period as the industrial heartland. The southern half had been the "rice bowl" that had provided the food for the peninsula and for parts of Japan.

With the division, South Korea wanted for industry and North Korea for sustenance. While the South began an impressively fast industrialization process, fueled by government support for companies like Samsung and Hyundai, the North's deficiencies were exacerbated by Kim Il Sung's promotion of his juche policy even as the regime relied heavily on the Soviet Union and China for support.

While the South moved toward capitalism, the North had a Communist-style, centrally planned economy. The state theoretically provided food, housing, clothing, education, and healthcare in return for the people working on state farms, in state factories, or, for the educated, in state institutions.

The system worked, in a fashion, during the 1960s and 1970s, when North Korea could barter its coal and other commodities for food and goods from China and the Soviet Union. But then China began its metamorphosis into a capitalist behemoth, and the Soviet Union collapsed. North Korea's downward economic spiral accelerated. With the famine, the country came as close to the brink of collapse as it had ever been.

It was during this time that the centrally planned socialist economy began to unravel. The regime, unable to supply rations any longer, had no choice but to allow people to buy and sell food to survive.

Under Kim Jong Il, the government retroactively allowed the changes that had spontaneously taken place already. Experts have called this process "marketization from below."[1]

The ad hoc markets that had emerged during the famine became tolerated. Grasshopper traders—people who sold goods on the street and could pack up and hop away quickly—became commonplace. Corruption took off as people paid border guards and others in positions of authority to turn a blind eye to their trading and smuggling. While the state economy ground to a halt, the private economy did indeed begin to grow.

The famine had unleashed an unregulated, scattershot kind of capitalism that was hard to repress, and it has accelerated rapidly under Kim Jong Un.

The Great Successor understood that by simply allowing a constrained form of capitalism, he could give people the ability to earn their own money and let them work their way to a better life. And it cost his government nothing.

So, since that first speech in 2012, Kim Jong Un repeatedly talked about the paramount importance of raising living standards.

A year later, he would make an even bolder claim. Having already had the constitution amended to declare the North a nuclear state, Kim Jong Un revived the "byungjin" policy of his grandfather. During a Workers' Party meeting in 1962, Kim Il Sung had espoused a "simultaneous progress" policy that would pursue the development of the economy and national defense at the same time. "A gun in one hand and a hammer and sickle in the other!" was Kim Il Sung's revolutionary slogan at the time.

Fifty years later, Kim Jong Un again promoted the idea that this regime could pursue both nuclear weapons and economic development—that North Koreans could have both guns and butter.

Up on the border with China, Mr. Hong, the money transfer merchant who'd had his life savings wiped out in the 2009 currency reforms, found the new leader's promises far from convincing.

If Kim Jong Un cared so much about them, why were North Koreans in far-flung areas still eating corn instead of rice, and why didn't even the well-to-do have bathroom essentials? "When Kim Jong Un said he was going to make the country strong and prosperous, no one believed it," Mr. Hong told me. "How could we be strong and prosperous if we didn't even have toilet paper?"

But the Great Successor had to choose this course to have a chance at staying in power. He understood that North Koreans, having had a taste of capitalism and the relative riches it can bring in a dilapidated Communist economy, had rising expectations. Plus, almost everyone in North Korea knew China was much richer and that South Korea was much, much richer.

Did Kim Jong Un remember his lessons on the French Revolution from his time at school in Switzerland? If he was to keep a grip on this totalitarian state and head off possible dissent, he needed to maintain a sense that life was getting better. He had initially concentrated on the crony capitalists who kept him in power, and this had been effective in his first years as leader. That would suffice for only so long. With economic disparities widening, he would need to make sure the ordinary people also felt like their lives were improving.

But Chinese-style reform and opening—allowing information to flow in at the same time as loosening up on the economic controls—was not an option for Kim. Allowing the population to have access to the truth would mean they would also see that the Great Successor was, in fact, not so great. But small economic "improvements"—North Korea doesn't call them "reforms" because that implies there's something wrong with the system—pose relatively little risk.

Instead, he allowed the markets, called "jangmadang," to blossom.

From the smallest of towns to the biggest of cities, there's at least one bustling marketplace. Across the country, these markets have become the center of daily life. They are overwhelmingly run by women, who, once married, are no longer required to work in state jobs. So while their husbands go off to coal mines without electricity or hospitals without medicine, the women make proper money.

People with permission—or with enough money to buy permission— to travel to China cross the Tumen River and bring back rice cookers, high-heeled shoes, solar panels, deworming tablets, colorful shirts, cell phone cases, and screwdrivers. Sometimes they bring literal kitchen sinks. About 80 percent of the products in North Korea's markets are made in China.

Those who can't travel set up shop as hairdressers or bike repairers, open restaurants, or sell homemade sweets. Some entrepreneurial types make money by renting out their cell phones for calls to South Korea or their apartments to couples wanting some privacy.

These markets have become the biggest agent for change that North Korea has ever experienced. People across the country have seen their living standards improve—just as Kim Jong Un promised. Maybe things didn't improve as much as many citizens, such as Mr. Hong, wanted, but they're still heading in a positive direction. There is now a middle class in North Korea.

There are now more than four hundred government-approved markets in North Korea, double the number that existed when Kim Jong Un took over the country.[2] The city of Chongjin alone has about twenty. The markets in Sinuiju and the "smugglers' village" of Hyesan, both close to the border with China, as well as those in the port city of Haeju, have all grown rapidly and visibly in recent years.[3] Satellite images show new markets popping up all over North Korea and old markets moving into bigger, newer buildings.

With an average of fifteen hundred stalls in a market, there is stiff competition to secure a prime spot. A good stall in a prominent place in Hyesan was going for about $700 in 2015—an astronomical sum in North Korea. But there is so much demand for stalls that even these expensive slots are being snapped up as soon as they become available.[4]

At every turn, there is someone seeking to make money from the markets. The security services extract bribes from those seeking to cross the river into China. The supposedly communist authorities have embraced the decidedly capitalist concept of tax. People running stalls in the markets must now pay 10 percent of the value of their sales to the market management office. South Korean researchers estimate that the authorities rake in about $15 million a day in stall rental fees from merchants, while other estimates suggest the state can earn almost a quarter of a million dollars in a single day by levying taxes on stall owners.[5]

Each market is run by a manager, someone who is almost always a man and who is well connected with local bureaucrats. This is a powerful role that comes with the opportunity to make a lot of money—and, of course, an obligation to pay kickbacks to higher-ups who put them in the job.

As the state economy has failed, with industry grinding to a halt thanks to a lack of electricity or raw goods, the markets have become the lifeblood of North Korea.

South Korea's intelligence service estimates at least 40 percent of the population in North Korea is making money through their own endeavors. This, the intelligence service says, is similar to the levels of marketization seen in Communist Bloc countries like Hungary and Poland before the Soviet Union collapsed.

The southern spies love to report signs of imminent collapse in North Korea. But their numbers in this case might, in fact, be too low. Other surveys have found that more than 80 percent of the population now makes its living through market activity.[6] Once entirely reliant on the state, they are now part of North Korea's burgeoning entrepreneurial class.

An even higher percentage gets its food from the markets—about 85 percent, according to a survey by the South's Korea Development Institute. Malnutrition remains a big problem, with many North Koreans still struggling to get variety in their diets. The United Nations estimates 40 percent of the population is undernourished, and stunting and anemia are still major concerns. But the explosion of market activity means that people are not dying from hunger anymore.

North Korea's economy, far from being a defunct state teetering on the edge of Soviet bloc–style implosion, has become relatively stable. North Korea does not produce reliable statistics, but outside estimates suggest that it has been growing. South Korea's central bank, which is always conservative in its figures, suggests that North Korea's economy has grown by about 1 percent a year under Kim Jong Un. One South Korean think-tank, the Hyundai Economic Research Institute, predicts growth might hit 7 percent.

Even by the South Korean central bank's more cautious estimate, North Korea's annual output has more than doubled since Kim Jong Un became leader.

The millennials, who were born or grew up during the famine years—Kim Jong Un's generation and younger—did so with markets as part of their daily life. They are often called the native capitalists—or the Jangmadang Generation.

Hyon, the high school student in Hyesan, was a native capitalist and an ambitious member of the Jangmadang Generation. He was born near the border with China in 1994, when Kim Jong Un was ten years old.

He never thought about university. He didn't worry about mandatory military service either. He was from a family with good political standing, so he used his grandfather's connections in the police to fake some documents and avoid being conscripted. He wanted money, and he wanted freedom. He found both on the road.

All these goods coming in from China need to be transported, whether over the river into North Korea or to the hundreds of markets scattered around the country. As a result, a bustling logistics industry has grown up to support the markets.

Travel within the country had traditionally been tightly controlled, with people prevented from going outside their county or province without the necessary permits. It was a way of keeping the population under control and limiting the flow of information. But the rules have eased, and palms can be more easily greased under Kim Jong Un.

Thanks to his grandfather's political links, Hyon was also able to use his grandfather's networks to get travel permits to move freely around North Korea. And because his mother had escaped to China, he had access to outside funds.

So he used $1,500 that his mother had sent him—the fruits of her own entrepreneurial efforts over the river—to lease a truck and start a transportation business with two friends.

Never mind that private vehicle ownership is still not allowed in North Korea. When there's money to be made, rules can easily be bent. Vehicles technically belong to state institutions. But managers at state factories, at state companies, or in military units can often be convinced to allow employees to use their pool cars or trucks in return for fees and a share of the profits.

A taxi or a minibus that had been officially assigned to a factory suddenly becomes a "servi-cha"—a combination of "service" and the Korean word for "car"—that will take paying passengers places, whether across town or across the country.

A truck assigned to a farm can easily become a delivery vehicle for market wholesalers, trundling over potholed roads and laden with imported consumer goods or homegrown harvests. Trains were once the main method of transportation, but they are slow and unreliable because of the lack of electricity and an aging infrastructure. Trucks are now preferred.

Since the servi-cha and trucks are officially registered as state vehicles, they are not bound by the usual restrictions to stay within a certain geographical area. When the drivers approach checkpoints, the guards check if they've prepared their bribes by asking them if they've done their "homework." Those who don't "do their homework" are liable, in the code language of the checkpoints, to have to "stay and finish their homework" or have their cargo confiscated.[7] Everyone has an incentive to make this system work.

Vehicles registered to powerful entities like the Ministry for the Protection of the State are particularly lucrative when repurposed as they can travel long distances without the worry of being held up at checkpoints.

This new transport service has been helped along by another crucial tool of the global logistics industry—and another thing that was, until relatively recently, banned in North Korea: the cell phone.

Markets used to be the preserve of runner merchants, traders who would physically take their goods to the bricks-and-mortar market and try to find customers for them. Now, a merchant needs only a cell phone. She or he can talk to wholesale and retail merchants to agree on prices and quantities and then call truck or bus drivers to arrange for delivery. The runner merchant has been replaced by the sedentary merchant— someone who sits back and conducts all the business over the phone, selling goods and calling in people to move them around.[8]

Cell phones have also helped to stabilize prices. People know when a new shipment of rice is coming across the border, so they'll wait rather than pay high prices when stocks are low.

In this new environment, Hyon began driving around the country, delivering goods and staying with his aunts or other relatives in various cities, including the capital of Pyongyang. He also acted as a supply chain manager for his aunt, who was married to a military official and lived in Pyongyang. Being an officer in the military used to be a plum job in North Korea, but now it was his aunt who was the main earner in the house. "Because of his position, my uncle could provide protection for my aunt's business. It's the women who can really make money," Hyon said.

For his part in the chain, Hyon would use middlemen in rural areas to buy stock for his aunt in Pyongyang to sell in the markets there at a higher price. Through the middlemen, he would buy huge quantities of beans to be delivered in increments to avoid raising suspicions.

"I couldn't just go out and buy two tons of beans. Because there was a shortage of crops in North Korea, you can't be seen with that much food," Hyon, who is tall and athletic and doesn't look like he suffered from childhood malnutrition, told me over coffee in a trendy café in southern Seoul where reggae was blaring from the speakers. He was attending university in the South and looked the part in shiny white trainers and immaculately coifed hair.

Food was a relatively safe business to be involved in. Trading in, say, DVD players was more profitable but much more sensitive. DVD players with USB drives from China were very popular and would fetch about twenty dollars each in North Korea. And well-connected traders could bring in whole train cars of DVD players—sometimes four thousand at a time—and make a lot of money. "But you had to be really powerful to deal in the DVD players because they were illegal," Hyon told me.

Whether the trade was in beans or DVD players, every part of the process involved business-minded people.

Hyon would order the beans and send people to pack them into sacks. Then he'd hire porters to deliver the sacks to the train station. He would bribe the guards to turn a blind eye to the shipments—usually three or four kilograms of rice per ton of beans. And he would mete out the deliveries, sometimes over a month, so it wasn't obvious just how much he was shipping. There were teams in Pyongyang who could be hired to offload the beans once they reached the station there and deliver them to his aunt.

"Of course you have to smooth the way with money," he said, describing how he conducted business. "But you also need connections. I bribed powerful officials to allow things to be offloaded in Pyongyang."

Then his aunt would send him money and instructions for the next order, and he would do it all over again.

Hyon threw himself into the opportunities that marketization presented. Many others adapted out of pure necessity.

Jung-a, who also lived on the border, was just eleven years old when Kim Jong Un became the leader of North Korea, so she was born into an environment that was becoming increasingly market driven. She was twelve when her father deserted and escaped from North Korea, leaving her mother with no choice but to turn to the markets to try to make a living.

Still, her mother, Mrs. Cho, was hopeful when Kim Jong Un took over. "We thought that because he was a young leader, maybe things would get better, they would become easier," she told me after they'd escaped to South Korea. But the Great Successor gave them nothing. "I had to do everything myself," she said.

To make ends meet in Kim Jong Un's North Korea, Jung-a had to drop out of school. She finished elementary but never started middle school.

Instead, several times a week during planting and harvest seasons, and for regular weeding and tending in between, Jung-a and her mother would walk for about three hours from their house in the center of Hoeryong to their small plot of land in the foothills of the mountains, where they grew corn.

They would skip breakfast and leave their house at 4:00 a.m. to arrive at their plot, which covered about one-third of an acre, at 7:00 a.m. or so. The land technically belonged to the state pig farm, but the farm manager was renting it out in small sections to locals like Mrs. Cho—for a handsome sum. Mrs. Cho, a small woman with a pained expression engraved into her face, agreed to pay the manager 440 pounds of corn to rent the plot for the year. Of course, the manager wasn't paying these earnings to the state so that Kim Jong Un could fund his "Socialist Paradise." He was selling the corn at the market, like everyone else.

After their morning's work, Mrs. Cho and Jung-a would stop for lunch—of a sort. They usually ate corn noodles with a soup made from ground beans. They ate it cold to avoid the cost, in both time and money, of lighting a fire to heat it. In the summer, they might have a little seasonal spinach or cucumber on the side. Then they'd get back to work.

Sometimes they'd splash out and cook rice for dinner, but usually they just ate more cold noodles. Then, at around 8:00 p.m., they would start the trek back home.

At harvest time, they hired a man with a cart to deliver the corn payment to the farm manager on the make, and then he would haul the rest of it into town so Mrs. Cho could sell it in the market. Many people ate corn—corn noodles, corn "rice," corn husk soup—because it was so much cheaper than rice.

With the money Mrs. Cho made from selling corn in the markets, she would buy soybeans—she'd tried growing them on her plot, but they were too labor intensive—and with the beans, she'd make tofu at home.

With eight pounds of beans, which cost 18,000 North Korean won in the market, she could make tofu that she could sell for 30,000 won.

It was Jung-a's job to sell the tofu from their house. "I couldn't play with my friends; I missed going to school," she told me when I went to visit her and her mother in their tiny apartment outside Seoul. "It was so boring being home all the time, and I was very envious when I saw my friends coming home for lunch with their schoolbags."

But for Mrs. Cho, keeping Jung-a at home not only helped to bring in money but also saved on another expense: school. North Korea is nominally a socialist state, where housing, education, and healthcare are theoretically free. In practice, though, everything comes at a price.

Teachers ask students to pay them fees in return for instruction. The fees are not usually denominated in cash but in goods: soybeans, rabbit skins, things that the teacher can then sell for a profit in the market.

Technically, students could continue going to school if they didn't pay the fees, but they wouldn't get much of an education. They'd have to sit in the back of the class, if they were lucky, and would get no attention at all. The ostracism means that students whose parents can't afford these "fees" usually stop going to school.

Mrs. Cho felt bad that her daughter was lonely and at home, so she bought a simple television set that she could have on during the day. But it was a miserable existence for Jung-a.

After buying firewood and food for themselves—once they sold all the tofu, they bought cheaper food to eat—Mrs. Cho would make a 5,000-won profit on a good day, enough for two pounds of rice. On a bad day, because of bean price fluctuations or insufficient demand, they made no profit at all.

Their lives saw a lot of toil for very little gain. Mrs. Cho soon found herself with constant back pain and became increasingly reliant on her daughter to earn their tiny income. So, one day, despite everything she'd heard about South Korea being full of beggars and torture being widespread, Mrs. Cho and Jung-a decided to flee.

That's how we were able to talk in their new home. Mrs. Cho, who now had the obligatory perm of a middle-aged South Korean woman, was pounding her lower back with her fists and grimacing as we sat on the floor talking. Jung-a was asleep on a futon beside us. She was now eighteen and had been up studying all night. She was trying to catch up on her education, to get a high school diploma so she could compete in South Korea's schooling-obsessed society.

Even after she arrived in South Korea, Mrs. Cho continued to hope that life in North Korea would get better. "I learned that he was educated overseas, so I thought that he was going to open the door to the outside world," she said wistfully of Kim Jong Un.

But the news she heard from home suggested that, for people like her, life was just as tough as it had always been.

Selling homemade tofu and carting beans around the country were businesses that existed in a kind of gray zone in North Korea. It was always dicey because such transactions could easily be deemed illegal if Mrs. Cho or Hyon got the wrong checkpoint guard or couldn't muster the right bribe.

Yet there was nothing gray about what Mr. Kang was doing. His business was definitely illegal, no matter which way you looked at it.

He'd been a drug kingpin in Hoeryong, just across the river from China and the farthest part of the country from Pyongyang. For decades, this part of the nation was considered deprived even by the standards of North Korea. People considered politically unreliable were exiled there if they were lucky and to the nearby concentration camp if they were not.

Like many people on the border, Mr. Kang took advantage of his location at the edge of a booming China. He had a Chinese cell phone that could pick up a signal from Chinese cell towers, and he made money by connecting North Koreans with people in the outside world, including South Korea. He arranged for family members in North Korea to cross the border to be reunited, briefly, with relatives in South Korea. And he was one of many people involved in the money transfer business, arranging for remittances from family members in the outside world to get to designated recipients—all for a hefty fee, of course. The commission on money transfers generally works out to 30 percent.

But the riskiest, and most lucrative, of all Mr. Kang's enterprises was selling ice, a methamphetamine that was popular across the river in China and is widely used in North Korea, not least because of its appetite-suppressing abilities. Entrepreneurial scientists have turned the chemical factories of Hamhung, once a core part of the socialist state, into private meth labs. It is the North Korean equivalent of *Breaking Bad*.

Drug dealing was a risky business. The standard sentence for drug dealers and manufacturers is a couple of years in a prison camp, although there have also been reports of executions for those running large-scale drug rings.

But if things go right, it's a lot more profitable than clocking in at your job in a dormant factory while your wife sells homemade tofu or rice cakes in the market.

In the years leading up to Kim Jong Un's succession, Mr. Kang had built a thriving business. His wife stopped working as a teacher and started working in the drug-dealing business. They had a baby. Drugs and money were flowing, and they were living well. They had a Japanese fridge, a leather sofa from China, and two TVs, one of them from Japan. They had a maid who would cook and clean for them in return for two pounds of rice a day.

When their daughter started going to school, the teachers doted on her. They lavished her with special attention and took pains to make sure she understood the lessons properly. She was treated better than the children of high-ranking officials because Mr. Kang was giving the teacher one hundred Chinese yuan a month—about fifteen dollars—and treating her to expensive spreads in local restaurants.

When, in 2010, he first began hearing about Kim Jong Un, Mr. Kang was also hopeful, thinking that this young man would lead North Korea to open up to the outside world. The opposite happened. Security all along the border was tightened as the authorities tried to batten down the hatches ahead of the second transition of power.

Mr. Kang's export business got more difficult as China cracked down on drug usage and the North Korean state accelerated preparations for the Great Succession. So he rerouted it: the drugs that once flowed into China now stayed at home to be consumed entirely by North Koreans.

"Even though they tried to crack down on that too after Kim Jong Un came in, it's impossible to stop anyone from doing anything in North Korea," Mr. Kang told me in a restaurant near his new home outside Seoul. The hot plate between us sizzled with meat and kimchi. "You can always bribe your way out."

Mr. Kang escaped to South Korea in 2014, when he was forty-two. When I met him, he looked like any other ordinary, middle-aged man; he was wearing a red hiking parka and black hiking pants. He had not been hiking. A perm gave his hair some extra lift. To wash down his pork, he ordered a bottle of soju—not the ordinary soju but the one with the red cap: the strong one.

Kim Jong Un's efforts to clamp down on illegal drugs did not work. At the time he left North Korea, Mr. Kang estimated that about 80 percent of the adults in Hoeryong were using ice, consuming almost two pounds of the highly potent drug every single day.

"My customers were just ordinary people," he said. "Police officers, security agents, party members, teachers, doctors. Ice made a really good gift for birthday parties or for high school graduation presents," he said. Teenagers were using it. Even his seventy-six-year-old mother was using it—to boost her low blood pressure.

For many North Koreans, taking meth became an essential part of daily life, a way to ease the grinding boredom and deprivations of their existence. For that reason, drugs can never be eradicated, he said.

"Honestly, it makes you feel good. I used to feel that if I didn't do it, then I didn't really feel right; my day didn't get off to the right start. I felt like I was barely human," he said. "It helps you release stress, and it really helps relations between men and women," he added without even a snicker.

Although it was technically illegal, Mr. Kang was open about his drug selling. His neighbors knew, and the police knew, but he tried not to flaunt his wealth to avoid attracting wider attention.

The police themselves were also seizing new opportunities to become not just rich but also high. They provided protection in return for regular doses of ice. "They would come by my house during their lunch break, and of course I didn't charge them." Mr. Kang laughed. "The head of the secret police in my neighborhood was almost living at my house. He'd come by every day."

Despite the tighter border crossings, Mr. Kang, one of the pioneers in the ice business, was still managing to make between $3,000 and $5,000 a month from his illegal businesses—an enormous sum of money in China, let alone North Korea. And the more he earned, the more influential he became.

"In North Korea," he told me, "money begets power."

CHAPTER 7

BETTER TO BE FEARED
THAN LOVED

"Our service personnel and people will never pardon all those who dare disobey the unitary leadership of Kim Jong Un."
—KCNA, December 13, 2013

KIM JONG UN KNEW THAT IT WOULD NOT BE ENOUGH TO ALLOW people to toil in the market economy and work their way to a slightly better standard of living. He also had to make sure they knew they could lose everything—and he meant everything—if they dared cross him.

He had to embody the dictum laid out five centuries earlier by the Italian politician Niccolo Machiavelli in his book *The Prince*: that it is better to be feared than loved.

In the first years of his reign, Kim Jong Un put the country, already the world's most isolated, on lockdown. He had security along the river border with China further reinforced. He had patrols stepped up. His efforts to thwart attempts to escape were much more draconian than his father's. The Great Successor wasn't taking any chances with the flow of information and people across the river into China. He cracked down on anything and everything that could challenge his fledgling rule.

The Kim regime had endured for seven decades by trapping the entire population inside the country and repeatedly drilling into them, starting from kindergarten, the myth that they lived in a socialist paradise and were the happiest people in the world.

Kim Il Sung constructed this narrative, but he clearly knew that the farce was going to be a hard sell, because he also built a surveillance state that still, to this day, monitors and controls every aspect of every North Korean life. Officials check how deeply citizens bow before statues of the leaders, how ardently they listen during compulsory ideology sessions, how often they try to skip out of sweeping the road at dawn. In this police state, anyone can be an informant or be turned into one: a wife, a colonel, a vegetable seller, a teacher, a coal miner, a child.

Long after the Soviet Union's glasnost, and long after China creaked open its doors, the North Korean regime still tries to enforce a near-total information blockade. By denying the citizens access to the outside world, the Kim regime has been able to perpetuate its myths.

To punish anyone who dares question the leadership, the Great Leader also stole Stalin's notorious gulag system. Huge concentration camps in remote regions, often with bitter climates, housed anyone who dared to dissent—and often their whole family, for good measure.

It's hard to exaggerate the all-encompassing nature of the regime fictions. "It's like a religion," Dr. Yang, a physician from the border city of Hyesan, told me. "From your birth, you learn that the Kim family are gods, and you are taught to be absolutely obedient to them. It's a reign of terror. The Kim family uses terror to keep people scared."

Every home, every school, every hospital, every public building, and even every subway car must contain framed photos of Kim Il Sung and Kim Jong Il, which must be cleaned every day with a special cloth that is kept in a special box. Placards and billboards through towns and cities, and even messages carved into mountainsides, extol the greatness of the Kim regime.

Every television channel is devoted to regime propaganda. The movie theaters show only North Korean films, with catchy titles like the sixty-two-part *Nation and Destiny*. Every household has a radio attached to the wall that can never be turned off and can never be tuned to a different station.

Open a North Korean newspaper, and you will see story after story about the genius and beneficence of Kim Jong Un. There is nothing the Brilliant Comrade does not know, according to the universal fiction of North Korea. He dispenses advice on catfish farming and livestock breeding, at greenhouses and tree nurseries, at construction sites and shipyards. He inspects production lines for shoes, face cream, and bean paste and has wise instructions to impart at every turn. He has thoughts on music, architecture, and sport. He is a military genius who has guided the progress in the nuclear and missile programs as well as commanding conventional drills at sea and on land.

There is no alternative point of view. And, for all but a handful of the elites who get Kim Jong Un's explicit permission, there is no internet access. Cell phones are not connected to the outside world. There are no underground newspapers. There is no graffiti. In fact, there isn't a single known dissenter in the entire country.

The regime begins the process of indoctrination early.

During one trip to Pyongyang, I went to a nursery with a sign across the front saying "Thank you, Respected General Kim Jong Un." Inside, it was decorated with cartoon racoon soldiers holding rocket-propelled grenade launchers and sailor ducklings with machine guns. The toddlers posed with plastic Kalashinikovs while visiting reporters took photos.

Min-ah's daughter was in kindergarten when she first learned about Kim Jong Un. She was four. She and her classmates were given sweets, shown a photo of the new leader, and told what a special leader he was. She has one abiding memory of that time. "His face was fat like a pig," she recalled a couple of years later from the safety of Seoul.

As Kim Jong Un was settling into leadership, the education department ordered high schools across the country to teach a new course devoted to him. The curriculum amounted to eighty-one hours of lessons on Kim Jong Un, in addition to the ones focused on his father, grandfather, and grandmother.[1] Additional history classes told high schoolers about American soldiers cruelly thrusting bayonets through North Korean babies during the Korean War, and the economics lessons taught about how, thanks to the juche philosophy, North Korea could be self-reliant.

Outside of school, North Korean children between the ages of nine and fifteen had these messages further drilled into them at obligatory Young Pioneer Corps meetings. Being admitted to the Young Pioneers is often considered the most momentous day in a child's life, with membership conferred in a ceremony held at schools on a regime anniversary, like Kim Il Sung's birthday or Foundation Day. Parents attend, and the child often gets a gift-wrapped present like a pen or a schoolbag. North Koreans don't celebrate their own birthdays, just that of their leader, and for many children, this is the only time in their lives they ever get a present.[2]

Man-bok was in his second year at university when his class was told that Kim Jong Un would be the next leader of their country. Since kindergarten, through school, during military service, and then once he started studying science at college, Man-bok had grown up with Kim Il Sung and Kim Jong Il looming over his studies. Students at his university had to endure ideological education for ninety minutes every day. Over and over again, they were told about the glorious history of the North Korean revolution led by Kim Il Sung with the help of his wife Kim Jong Suk, carried on by their son Kim Jong Il.

Man-bok was sick of it; he wanted to learn about science, not about these supposed comrades. He was fed up with a life of doublethink.

Then, one day soon after that first announcement, he saw the heir apparent on TV, a chubby kid his age, surrounded by old generals who were addressing him using a very respectful Korean word for "offspring."

The student thought it was a joke. "Among my closest friends, we were calling him a piece of shit," he told me. "Everyone thinks this, but you can only say it to your closest friends or to your parents if you know that they agree."

But it was no joke. With the ascent of Kim Jong Un, Man-bok came to realize that this system had spawned its third-generation leader. Given his youth, this man might be around for a very long time.

Elsewhere around the country, during compulsory military service, in factories and mines and government ministries, and at Women's Federation and neighborhood watch meetings, other North Koreans were being taught about the Genius Among Geniuses.

To support his claim to the leadership, Kim Jong Un had North Korea's ten commandments revised in 2013. Kim Il Sung had developed these Ten Principles on the Establishing of the Monolithic Ideology of the Party almost forty years earlier in an attempt to provide some heft to the personality cult.

Every single principle contains the leader's name and makes reference to his absolute authority and the need to believe in it unconditionally. Principle Two demands "accepting the Great Leader Comrade Kim Il Sung's thought as one's own belief and taking his instructions as one's creed." And Principle Four is "highly revering the Great Leader Comrade Kim Il Sung is the noblest duty of the revolutionary warriors who are endlessly loyal to the great leader."

When he took over, Kim Jong Un apparently decided they needed updating. He had the principles revised to include venerations of his father, Kim Jong Il, and provide a closer link between the system and himself. "The Great Comrade Kim Il Sung and Comrade Kim Jong Il are extraordinary patriots, great revolutionaries and loving parents of the people. They dedicated their everything to their fatherland, revolution and people," the revised version states.

But Kim Jong Un stopped short of having his own name added or his portrait installed in every home. Careful not to overreach, he concentrated instead on elevating his father, hoping that would bolster his legitimacy as the scion of this glorious system.

North Koreans are required to memorize the principles and be able to recite them on demand.

They have the updated principles drilled into them at the ideological education sessions held twice a week in their neighborhood groups or in their workplaces. In these compulsory sessions, they must sit through the latest descriptions of the leader's greatness and the United States' iniquity. This is how many first heard about the astounding feats of the Comrade General Kim Jong Un in 2009.

Every Saturday, and sometimes more often, citizens must also attend self-criticism sessions, where they are required to detail their own shortcomings of the previous week and often offer up those of the people around them. These are often exercises in going through the ideological motions: citizens describe how they could have worked even harder, until their fingers bled or they fainted, in the service of the Great Successor. But they can also be forums for condemning rivals or retaliating against an annoying neighbor.

Even hairstyles are strictly controlled in North Korea. Women are not permitted to dye their hair, although perms are common among married women. A story went around in the outside world that shortly after Kim Jong Un took over, he had ordered all men to get his pompadour. That was not true, but it is true that North Korean men must have short hair. A range of recommended styles adorns the walls of barber shops, including, yes, several with very short sides and very high tops. It's not compulsory, but an astute North Korean would know that there's no better way to show his loyalty to the leader.

Even those sent abroad legally to earn money for the regime are not exempt from these education and self-criticism sessions. In fact, because these people are catching glimpses of the real world, the regime goes to great lengths to try to keep them ideologically uncontaminated.

"We would hear about how Kim Jong Un was working so hard for the party and for the nation and for the people," said Mr. Song, who was a construction worker in Russia, earning foreign currency for the North Korean regime and a little bit for himself, when Kim Jong Il died. "He had done this and this and that, and Kim Jong Un was working so hard for all of us. It just didn't make sense. Anybody who had served in the military knew that it was ridiculous to say a young child could shoot a rifle or even see over the dashboard of a car," he said. But he couldn't say anything about it at the time.

No one in North Korea can say that this young emperor has no clothes and expect to live.

But almost everyone knows it, for the state once called the Hermit Kingdom is hermetic no more. Despite the regime's extreme efforts, it has not been able to completely shut out the rest of the world.

In the wake of the famine, when food and clothes came in over the Chinese border, so, too, did information. People who had snuck across the river came back talking about what they had seen: a country where people have so much to eat they didn't finish everything on the table and where dogs ate better than North Koreans.

Gradually, more sophisticated forms of information began to arrive.

Traders now smuggle flash drives and micro-storage SD cards into North Korea, often buried in sacks of rice or bags of batteries, to sell secretly in the markets. These small storage devices are easy to hide from the authorities and to share among friends.

Activists in South Korea try to help with this by putting USB drives in huge balloons that they float across the border when the winds are right or in bottles that they float up the river when the currents are favorable. Most are loaded with action movies and soppy soap operas. Some contain books and encyclopedias. Others hold peppy South Korean K-pop. Some contain porn.

All of it is gobbled up by North Koreans hungry for information.

"When you go into the market, you say to the vendors, 'Do you have anything delicious today?' or, 'Do you have any good beer?'" Mrs. Kwon told me of her former life in the northern city of Hoeyrong. "Then you say, 'OK, fill it up to the max.' That means that you want one with lots of movies on it."

DVD players with USB drives have become hot-ticket items in the markets. Small portable DVD players called "notels"—a combination of "notebook" and "television"—are particularly popular. They have a DVD drive as well as USB and SD card ports and a built-in TV and radio tuner and can be charged with a car battery. They sell for about fifty dollars, and maybe half of urban households have one.[3]

When she went to the market, Mrs. Kwon would sometimes take old USB sticks to swap, or she would just buy new ones. A sixteen-gigabyte flash drive cost less than two dollars and would contain a wealth of outside information.

"I loved looking at their houses; I love looking at how they were living, everything," she recalled, telling me how she particularly loved *My Name Is Kim Sam-soon*, an old rom-com centered around a chubby, forthright woman who finds and then loses a heartthrob doctor. "It was like a fantasy," Mrs. Kwon said. "Of course I wanted to live like them, so I dreamed about that kind of life and about coming to South Korea."

Although she does not live a fairytale existence in the South—she has a small apartment in a satellite city outside Seoul—the spark came from those glimpses of the real world.

The glimpses of fridges, sofas, TV sets, cars, and the rest of daily life in the South undermine one of the core myths of Pyongyang's propaganda—that South Korea is a destitute and desperate place and that North Koreans have a happier life.

The smallest details in these movies and dramas could be hugely influential on people who have never watched anything other than regime media. The smallest detail could expose the biggest lies.

Watching social interactions in the South can also be illuminating. Young North Koreans, particularly women, noticed how people in the South would often use polite language to each other, using levels of Korean that denoted respect. It was a stark difference from the talking down to younger people and women that was commonplace in the North.

Jung-a, who should have been at high school but was instead selling homemade tofu, remembered her surprise when she watched a film called *Ninja Assassin* that was on one of the flash drives she got in the market. The high-action, often bloody martial arts film was American, but it starred a muscled South Korean pop star called Rain. It was eye-opening for her.

"At school in North Korea, we were taught that South Koreans look different from us," she told me. "But when I saw this movie, I saw that they looked just the same as us and spoke the same as us."

She particularly loved K-pop songs. "North Korean songs all sound the same, and the words are all strong and tough. I was used to songs that were about Kim Il Sung and the generals and patriotism," Jung-a said. "Then all of a sudden I heard these songs that were in Korean but sounded totally different."

This kind of information had percolated throughout North Korea and had undermined the faith that people might have had in the third-generation leader, Dr. Yang, a gruff man in his forties, told me during a break from seeing patients at the hospital in Seoul where he now works.

"People don't expect anything from this young leader," he said. "I think more than seventy percent of people are dissatisfied with the Kim Jong Un regime. They know that Kim Jong Un is not a capable person."

In North Korea, he was technically a doctor, working in a big provincial hospital. But the hospital had no medicine, and the doctor earned practically nothing—3,500 won a month, not even enough to buy two pounds of rice—so his real job was smuggling. He would pick medicinal herbs from the mountains—something North Korean doctors are good at since they don't have actual pharmaceuticals and are instead forced to take "herbal vacations"—and sell them in China. With the proceeds, he would buy home appliances like rice cookers, portable DVD players, and LCD monitors and bring them back into North Korea.

Because of this work, he knew the regime propaganda for what it was.

"They told us that the reason we were poor was because of sanctions," he said. "But I lived near the border, so I knew that the reason that North Korea didn't develop was because there was no reward for anybody to work harder. They were going to have to work for free either way."

Why, then, if so many North Koreans know about the outside world, and know that the regime is lying to them, has the system survived? The answer lies in the unparalleled brutality of the regime, which has no compunction in meting out severe punishments for the smallest hint of disaffection.

To enforce the lie that he's the best man for the job, Kim Jong Un has perpetuated North Korea's political caste system with zeal, rewarding those deemed most loyal to him and ruthlessly punishing those who dare question him.

This caste system is another legacy of his grandfather. When he was creating his ideal state, Kim Il Sung borrowed some of the feudal practices of the Chosun Dynasty, which had ruled Korea for five centuries until almost 1900. He adopted the Chosun-era system of guilt by association. It is this system that, even now, can lead to three generations of an entire family being imprisoned, sometimes for life, for one person's wrongdoing.[4]

He also stole the discriminatory class system called *songbun* from the Chosun era, dividing North Korea into fifty-one different categories that fall into three broad classes: loyal, wavering, and hostile.

To this day, in Kim Jong Un's North Korea, the loyal are given every advantage. They are the 10 to 15 percent of the population who are considered the most politically committed to the system and have the most interest in it continuing. They get to live in Pyongyang and receive better schooling, including the possibility of attending Kim Il Sung University. They are set up for plum jobs and have a head start on Workers' Party membership. The loyal caste live in better apartments, wear better clothes, eat better and more food, and are more likely to be able to visit a doctor who actually has medicine.

At the bottom are the hostiles: the Japanese collaborators, the Christians, the skeptics. They comprise about 40 percent of the population and are generally banished to the inhospitable mountains of the north, where winters are unbearable and food is scarce even by North Korean standards.

These "undesirables" have no social mobility and no hope of advancement. Their lives revolve around a collective farm or factory— an assignment that, for the last few decades, has meant fending for themselves.

In between the loyal and the hostile is the wavering class, the ordinary people who make up about half the North Korean population. They exist in a kind of limbo. They have no chance of going to college or having a professional job, but if they're lucky, they might secure a good assignment during their military service that will help them work their way to a slightly better standard of living.[5]

Someone born with bad *songbun* has no hope of moving up the social hierarchy. The upper levels, however, can plummet all the way to the bottom if they put a foot wrong.

Through this system, and the constant threat of being demoted down the classes, Kim Jong Un has been able to maintain power. If you're a member of the loyal class—living in Pyongyang and able to earn some money on the side of your ministry job to send your children to university—you would think twice before openly questioning whether the leader could really drive a car at age five or criticizing the decision to spend millions on nuclear weapons instead of on hospitals and schools. There is always someone to keep an eye on you and report if you're not sufficiently devoted to the regime. At the grassroots level, it starts with the *inminban*, literally "people's group," a kind of neighborhood watch system. Each neighborhood is broken down into groups of thirty or forty households, with a leader who is always an interfering middle-aged woman. It is her job to keep an eye on what people in her assigned households are up to. North Koreans like to say that the leader of their neighborhood group is supposed to know how many chopsticks and how many spoons each house has.[6]

She is responsible for registering overnight visitors—in North Korea, a person can't stay at a friend or relative's house without notifying the authorities—and often, together with the local police, conducts dead-of-night raids to ensure there are no forbidden guests or that residents like Man-bok or Jung-a are not watching South Korean movies. She inspects everyone's state-issued radio to make sure they haven't tuned it to anything other than the state station. She checks cell phones to make sure they don't contain unauthorized music or photos from the outside world.

She also encourages neighbors to report on one another. If a family is thought to be eating white rice and meat suspiciously often, people might wonder how they're making their money. If the blue light of a television set is flickering against the curtains late at night, long after the state television channels have stopped broadcasting, people will wonder what the occupants are watching.

If someone's having an affair, the neighborhood leader will find out about it. This is no small matter in North Korea, which takes a dim view of women, in particular, who have premarital or extramarital sex. The couple's transgression will be reported to their employers, and both will be put through a humiliating public criticism session.[7]

North Koreans live in a system where every aspect of their lives is monitored, where every infraction is recorded, where the smallest deviation from the system will result in punishment. It is ubiquitous, and it keeps many people from even raising an eyebrow at the regime.

The neighborhood leader needs to report transgressions in order to stay in good stead with the higher authorities, especially the two main security agencies.

The Ministry of People's Security performs standard policing duties and runs labor camps for those deemed to have committed "normal" crimes like assault, theft, drug dealing, and murder. The name of these prison camps in Korean translates as "a place to make a good person through education." Prisoners are generally sent to them for fixed terms and can hope to be released one day.

The Ministry for the Protection of the State deals with political and ideological crimes. This agency is responsible for maintaining the total blackout of all information other than state media and ensuring that everyone is strictly adhering to the propaganda.

It investigates political crimes—committed by people who question the regime or try to escape its clutches—and runs the network of unimaginably brutal prison camps for those accused of political wrong thinking and wrongdoing.

Aware that outside media has crossed his country's borders, Kim Jong Un has given new powers to the special unit of the security services charged with enforcing the ban on illegal foreign media: Group 109. Its mission is to find media produced in foreign countries, especially that stored on cell phones and USB drives, and confiscate it. The unit looks at a device's history particularly closely, searching for evidence of file sharing.

People caught with such illicit content are liable to be detained and questioned. Some are able to bribe their way out of trouble with money or even cigarettes, plus the confiscation of the device in question. In fact, many North Koreans think that officials deliberately look for foreign media on citizens' phones or during late-night raids on homes as a way to make some money on the side of the low-paying state jobs.

When he had the North Korean Criminal Code revised in 2012, the year after he took power, Kim Jong Un had a special section added to address foreign media. This is considered tantamount to subversion and is much harder, or, rather, much more expensive, to wriggle out of. People caught running industrial information smuggling operations are at risk of being referred for prosecution, where conviction is guaranteed, and sent to a labor camp for their crimes.[8]

Not that the other components included after Kim Jong Un took power were any less draconian. Drawing up a plan for the economy in a haphazard manner and not properly selecting winning athletes for important competitions are listed as political offenses. Any gathering not authorized by Workers' Party and state authorities is banned, as is criticizing or expressing dissatisfaction with the state, even privately. Anyone who takes part in a riot or demonstration "with anti-state purposes" faces a life sentence of "reform through labor" or the death penalty. Anti-state "propaganda and agitation" carries the threat of death.[9]

Even with this enhanced effort to guard against "ideological corruption," the regime has not wholly prevented people from getting snatches of the outside the world.

Man-bok, the science student, watched war movies, gangster movies, and R-rated movies. He listened to the news. He grew more and more disaffected. "The regime tried to brainwash us," he said, "but we in the younger generation know the truth."

To mention the criminal code is to suggest there's an orthodox rule of law in Kim Jong Un's North Korea. There is not. Sometimes the authorities will bother themselves with a quasi-judicial process but certainly nothing that the outside world would recognize as a fair trial. There's no defense attorney, no jury of one's peers.

Often, the authorities don't even bother going through these limited motions. Some people who are thrown into the most brutal political prison camps don't know why. There are four such camps, each covering hundreds of square miles of rugged terrain in the northern reaches of the country. They are surrounded by high barbed-wire perimeter fences, as well as pit traps and minefields, and reinforced with watchtowers manned by armed guards with automatic rifles.

Once in these penal labor colonies, prisoners are held incommunicado and are considered to be outside the protection of the law because they are deemed to be counter-revolutionaries not worthy of legal protection.[10]

The prisons operated by the secret police are by far the most brutal, with inhumane conditions that large numbers of prisoners do not survive.

Once imprisoned, people are starved. Food is so scarce that inmates hunt for frogs or rats to eat. It's the only protein they'll get. They search for edible weeds, anything to supplement the "soup" they're given, the chief ingredients of which are water and salt.

Still, they must perform arduous work and often dangerous manual labor, sometimes for as long as eighteen hours a day. They dig mines by hand using only picks and shovels. They log trees with axes and handsaws. Farmwork is done with only the most basic tools. Women make wigs and false eyelashes or sew garments, all of which are sent to China and onward to the outside world. Prisoners who do not meet their production quotas can expect to have their food rations cut further and to be beaten.[11]

Severe beatings and torture are commonplace, including pigeon torture, whereby prisoners' hands are tied behind their back, and they're hung from a wall, forcing out their chest. They're made to stay that way for hours, often until they pass out or vomit blood.

Plane torture and motorbike torture are also customary; prisoners are forced to hold out their arms either to the side or in front for hours on end. They usually collapse before being allowed to let their arms fall to their sides.

Worse still are the sweatboxes. Prisoners are locked into wooden boxes so small that a person can't fully stand up or lie down. Instead, they are forced to kneel in a crouched position, their buttocks pressed into their heels. This cuts off the circulation and leaves their rear ends solid black with bruising. If left long enough in there, the person will die.[12] The guards are trained to be merciless, and if they show even the most trivial form of kindness, they are liable to be punished themselves.

Rape and violent sexual assault are also part of the punishment cycle. Women who wind up in prison after being repatriated from China have reported being forced to have abortions—often induced through beatings—or having their newborn baby killed in front of them. Some have even reported being forced to kill their babies or be killed themselves.

This is especially likely when the baby is considered to be "impure"—to have a Chinese father.[13]

The United Nations' special commission of inquiry into North Korea's human rights abuses found that these violations were not "mere excesses of the state" but "essential components" of its totalitarian system.

"The gravity, scale and nature of these violations reveal a state that does not have any parallel in the contemporary world," the commission concluded in a landmark 2014 report. It recommended the Kim Jong Un be referred to the International Criminal Court to face charges of crimes against humanity.

The testimony presented to the commission came from numerous prisoners who had endured the prison camps and lived to tell the story. All of them were incarcerated in the camps during the Kim Il Sung and Kim Jong Il eras and later managed to escape from North Korea and describe how they had been treated.

There is no doubt that Kim Jong Un has taken full advantage of the repressive system set up by his grandfather and perpetuated by his father. Satellite images show that the extensive network of prison camps, located both on the outskirts of cities and in huge compounds in the mountains, continues in his era.

Those images also show new or expanded prison camps, including one near the political-prisoner Camp 14, in the center of the country. Inside a 5.6-square-mile enclosed area with clearly visible security perimeters are guard barracks and checkpoints. The reeducation camp, Prison No. 4 on the outskirts of Pyongyang, has a clearly visible limestone quarry just outside the penitentiary walls and a conveyor belt to transport the limestone rocks into the camp for prisoners to crush.[14]

But the outside world has heard very little of what conditions are like inside these reeducation camps and concentration camps in the Kim Jong Un era.

During my years covering North Korea under the third-generation leader, I searched for people who had been inside the prisons after 2011. Even after talking to activists who help North Korean escapees, including former prisoners, and experts on North Korea's prisons, I couldn't find a single person who'd emerged from the camps after Kim Jong Un rose to power. No one I asked even knew of such a person.

Maybe the inmates have remained inside the prison camps. Maybe they haven't been able to escape the prison of North Korea. We just don't know. But we are sure that this penal system endures.

When the International Bar Association asked three renowned human rights judges to hold a hearing on North Korea's prison camps in 2017, one of them said they were just as bad as—and perhaps even worse than—the Nazi concentration camps of the Holocaust. He should know. Thomas Buergenthal was held in Auschwitz and Sachsenhausen as a child, as well as the ghetto of Kielce, Poland. He went on to serve on the International Court of Justice.

"I believe that the conditions in the [North] Korean prison camps are as terrible, or even worse, than those I saw and experienced in my youth in these Nazi camps and in my long professional career in the human rights field," he said after hearing from former North Korean prisoners and guards.[15]

Like the UN commission, these jurists concluded that Kim Jong Un should be tried for crimes against humanity because of the way his regime uses political prisons to control the population.

Many people wonder why North Korea hasn't collapsed, like the Soviet Union, or changed, like China.

There are several reasons.

It's partly because life is in fact getting better for many North Koreans, thanks to their ability to earn their livings through the markets. A person who ate meat twice a year might now be able to eat it twice a month. A farmer who can sell his crops can bribe his daughter's way to the front row of the classroom. Money has enabled some small freedoms, which may feel like outsized changes in repressive North Korea. One of the most often overlooked factors is the fact that the Kim family has created a strong national identity and given people some reasons to be proud, sometimes based on misinformation but sometimes not. Even after escaping, North Koreans have told me they are proud of their plucky defiance of international bullies and especially of their nuclear prowess.

But the biggest reason is fear.

The punishments are so harsh that North Koreans who object to the system would rather escape than try to argue for change from the inside.

"Even if you know things, you are not supposed to say them," Mrs. Kwon told me. "If you speak up, you don't know what kind of punishment you might face. So instead of trying to do something to change the system, it's better just to leave."

Yet only those with a very strong will to escape actually try to leave, she said. Even if they make it out, they know there's a likelihood that their family members will be punished.

And so it continues.

CHAPTER 8

GOODBYE, UNCLE

"Despicable human scum Jang, who was worse than a dog, perpetrated thrice-cursed acts of treachery in betrayal of such profound trust and warmest paternal love shown by the party and the leader for him."

—KCNA, December 13, 2013

THE MOST DANGEROUS TIME FOR A NOVICE AUTOCRAT IS THE first two years in power. It's then that he has to figure out who's loyal and who's expendable. It's during those first two years that someone else who wanted the job is most likely to make a play for it. This is especially the case when the leader inherits his supporters from his predecessor.

So when Kim Jong Un took over, he followed the model used by his father and grandfather and set about making sure the handful of elites who could keep him in power were rich and happy—and getting richer and happier.

Like his patriarchs, he has managed to survive as a dictator by controlling an entire nation through a relatively tiny group of people. It was another rule espoused by Machiavelli: don't worry about the general population; just be sure to enrich a small, elite group.

He is what academics call a "small coalition leader," someone who keeps his regime stable through the support of relatively few well-rewarded people while letting the rest of the population languish.

Within the small coalition category, Kim Jong Un belongs to a subset that Bruce Bueno de Mesquita, a political scientist who has studied successful tyrants, calls the "greedy kleptocrats." Other members of this subset include Ferdinand Marcos of the Philippines and Mobutu Sese Seko of Zaire, now the Democratic Republic of the Congo.

They want to live well, so they steal a lot of money from state coffers, and they make sure that the people who keep them in power also live well. As for those privileged elites, they know that they're much more likely to retain their positions when power passes from king to prince than when it passes to someone outside the family. So they have an interest in the son succeeding.

Kim Jong Un's first order of business was to determine who would stay in his small coalition of elites.

Even a novice knows that getting rid of potential rivals or critics at the beginning is crucial. Mao Zedong did it in China, Kim Jong Il did it when he took over, and Kim Jong Un followed in this tradition.

Generally, the risk in this early period is killing too many people, not too few, Bueno de Mesquita told me when I went to see him in his office at New York University. If you get rid of too many, those who remain think their leader is indiscriminate and have a reason to live in fear. But if you kill too few? Well, that's easy enough to fix.

There's a good reason for terrifying the people at the top. Contrary to popular perception, most dictators are not overthrown by an angry populace marching in the streets. The vast majority are removed by insiders from the regime. The biggest risk to dictators is not the struggle between the privileged and the masses but a struggle among the elites.

"As far as authoritarian leadership dynamics are concerned, an overwhelming majority of dictators lose power to those inside the gates of the presidential palace rather than to the masses outside," said Yale scholar Milan Svolik, who studied 316 dictators and found more than two-thirds were overthrown by their rivals.[1]

This is how leaders from Nikita Khrushchev in the Soviet Union in 1964 to Robert Mugabe in Zimbabwe in 2017 lost their power. Their one-time allies seized it from them.

Often the trigger for a leadership challenge is money. Greedy kleptocrats frequently lose power when their supporters realize they won't be able to protect them for much longer, Bueno de Mesquita said. Once Reza Pahlavi, the shah of Iran, fell ill, his henchmen sat on their hands. Marcos's military realized, too, that the aging Filipino president wouldn't be able to deliver anymore.

But if they navigate the early challenges and survive their first two years, most dictators die in their sleep.

So, from the moment he took control of the regime, Kim Jong Un got to work becoming the most Machiavellian figure of our time. No one was safe, not even the men who had supported him through the transition period—*especially* not the men who'd supported him through the transition period.

One of the first to disappear was Vice Marshal Ri Yong Ho, one of the pallbearers during Kim Jong Il's funeral. He was chief of the Korean People's Army's general staff and had kept the military loyal to the Kims during the handover from second to third generation.

But that didn't protect him. In the middle of 2012, Ri was publicly relieved of his positions—for health reasons, according to the official account. South Korea's intelligence service said he'd been banished to the northern part of the country. Others speculated that he'd been executed. Either way, he was never seen again. His face was even edited out of photos and his name deleted from all documents. He simply ceased to appear anywhere.

The same happened with General Hyon Yong Chol, who was promoted after Ri was purged to become North Korea's equivalent of a defense minister. He vanished at the start of 2016 and was reported to have been executed for insubordination and treason. Among his many alleged transgressions, according to South Korea's intelligence agency, was falling asleep while Kim Jong Un was speaking.

But he was not quietly eradicated: he was publicly executed by antiaircraft guns, a method that would have blown him to a pulp.[2] Other officials would certainly have made a mental note to stay wide awake in meetings from then on.

Other times, the disappeared would return months or years later with their tails between their legs. Whatever had happened during their absences had made them devoted disciples of the young chieftain.

Choe Ryong Hae—a man often referred to as "North Korea's number two"—was removed from his positions in the inner sanctum of the Workers' Party. He was reportedly sent for reeducation for several months on a cooperative farm. But he was apparently declared trustworthy again and, in 2016, was elevated to even higher positions.

The most shocking purge came at the end of 2013. Another pallbearer was dispatched, this time in an even more dramatic fashion.

Jang Song Thaek was Kim Jong Un's uncle by marriage. He and Kim Jong Il's sister, Kim Kyong Hui, had fallen in love while studying at Kim Il Sung University together.[3] The Great Leader was apparently unimpressed by the upstart young man, but his daughter was insistent on marrying the gregarious Jang.

They had become a power couple in the regime, both becoming close advisors to Kim Jong Il. Jang was put in charge of economic projects, leading everything from coal mine development to construction. He traveled so often for the regime—buying resources needed for his building projects or products that Kim Jong Il wanted—that he became known as "the Kim Jong Il Who Goes Abroad."[4]

He also played a crucial role in the preparations for Kim Jong Un's succession. When Kim Jong Il died, Uncle Jang's place at the very top of the regime was evident when he had walked directly behind Kim Jong Un when they were pallbearers. If he hadn't been dyeing his hair pitch black for years, he might have been called the éminence grise of the regime.

Several people who'd met him told me he was charismatic. He was considered good looking, and he liked to drink, play cards, and sing karaoke. He was known as a dealmaker and a good one at that. He drew people into his orbit.

Uncle Jang was no angel. He was what might euphemistically be called a ladies' man or, less euphemistically, a predator. One of the apocryphal stories about him is that he personally held "auditions" for the women who became part of Kim Jong Il's notorious Pleasure Brigade, his own personal harem.

His outgoing personality and ideas about opening up had landed him in trouble before. Once, during a dinner party in the 1990s, Jang had the temerity to suggest that the regime's policies might be misguided, given that people were starving. Kim Jong Il was incensed, throwing a silver napkin ring at him. His wife tried to calm the situation, and Jang not only apologized but sang a song to the leader.[5]

Then he landed in a reeducation camp in the countryside in 2004 after Kim Jong Il found out he was throwing wild parties for government officials. Such raucous, reward-laden parties were the preserve of the leader alone.

There were other problems. Kim Jong Il's sister was rumored to be a raging alcoholic, and their daughter, Kum Song, committed suicide in Paris in 2006. She'd been studying there but had reportedly overdosed on sleeping pills after her parents opposed her plan to marry a boyfriend they considered unsuitable. She was found dead in her villa by her maid and chauffeur.[6] The irony of this tragedy was that Kim Il Sung had opposed Jang Song Thaek as his daughter's husband for the same reasons.

But Jang was a political striver. As Kim Jong Il's health worsened, he was given a number of increasingly important positions. In 2010, he was promoted to vice chairman of the National Defense Commission, making him one of the most important officials after Kim Jong Il.

He was widely seen as a man who could act as a kind of regent or caretaker during the transition from Kim Jong Il to the young and inexperienced Kim Jong Un. He might not have had Paektu blood running through his veins, but his marriage to Kim Jong Il's sister made him the next best thing.

Crucially, Jang was in charge of all-important economic relations with China, North Korea's neighbor and benefactor. The two countries' relationship had once been described as being "as close as lips and teeth," but as China had embraced capitalism with zeal, they were more like relatives awkwardly trying to find common interests to chat about at a family wedding. Still, after the collapse of the Soviet Union, China was North Korea's only economic benefactor and major political ally. Plus, with their 880-mile-long land border, it was North Korea's main gateway to the outside world.

Under Jang's direction, North Korea had been trying to develop special economic zones within the country—the exact kinds of zones that reformist leader Deng Xiaoping had championed in China several decades before. The zones were a safe way for a Communist regime to open a window to capitalism, allowing investment and trade but in strictly controlled circumstances. If the zones went well, the contagion of capitalism could be allowed to spread. If they didn't please the regime, they could be sealed off.

China had for some years been trying to nudge North Korea along this path. Kim Jong Il pretended to be interested as he was taken on a tour of high-tech companies in the southern Chinese city of Shenzhen in 2006.

After Kim Jong Un took over, however, the regime announced the creation of more than a dozen special economic zones, many of them along the border with China, in an experiment designed to attract foreign investment and loosen some red tape to see whether this kind of economic opening could work within North Korea's political strictures.[7]

Jang was in charge of these efforts. He used it to make a significant fortune of his own along the way, siphoning money from coal exports to line his own pockets. He was in this for himself. But in the North Korean scheme of things, it was easy for Jang to look like a relatively enlightened official.

"Jang was a reformer. He wanted to reform the political environment as well as the economy," said Ro Hui Chang, who was a senior official in charge of the construction workers that North Korea sends abroad to earn money for the regime.

Ro had been part of the money-making elite in North Korea under both Kim Jong Il and Kim Jong Un. He'd been posted to the Middle East and had overseen the regime's army of construction workers who were building soccer stadiums and apartment towers in Kuwait and Qatar. Then he went back to Pyongyang for a while before he started managing laborers in Russia when Kim Jong Un took over.

He'd landed this plum position because of his good family background. Ro's uncle was a police chief. Ro would go over to his apartment and listen while his uncle and Jang sang and played the accordion. Jang thought the boy was "adorable" and told the young Ro to call him "Uncle."

Ro grew up wanting to be like these two "uncles." "Jang was my role model since childhood," he told me, recalling how spirited they both were when they were singing or playing table tennis. When Ro started going to business meetings, he tried to be the same kind of jovial character as Jang, inspiring people with his gregariousness.

Jang believed that the North Korean economy had ground to a halt in the 1990s and that bold change was needed, Ro said. He wanted North Korea to follow China's example. All it would take was a new mind-set. Ro and the other Jang devotees supported any idea that would allow North Korea's anemic economy to flourish.

The uncle wanted to replicate the fast-paced development next door, with Beijing's cooperation—and money. He wanted to offer greater legal protection for foreign investors as a way to attract outside money from business operators who insisted on making profits and being able to repatriate them. When talking to potential Chinese partners, he was embarrassed that he couldn't offer even minimum protections for their investments, such as a legal system in case of disputes.

But with this kind of talk, Jang ran afoul of more conservative factions in the Workers' Party, who told Kim Jong Un that Jang's ideas were threatening the party's survival. He had amassed too much power and was promoting too different a vision for North Korea's future. Rivals within the regime began to whisper in Kim Jong Un's ear about their concerns. Wasn't Jang getting a bit too close to China?[8]

These suggestions burst into the open during a trip to China in August 2012, when Jang received red-carpet treatment on a par with that lavished upon Kim Jong Il. An advance party had paved the way, and China's ambassador to Pyongyang was waiting in Beijing to greet Jang.

Jang then went to see Chinese president Hu Jintao, and photos of the meeting disseminated by the Chinese government showed the two men in dark suits sitting in the Great Hall of the People discussing special economic zones on their shared border like a couple of heads of state. But Jang wasn't the head of his state.

South Korea's government, meanwhile, kept suggesting that it was Jang, not Kim, who was really in power in North Korea. This might have been a form of psychological warfare. If it was, it appeared to work. There was room for only one charismatic leader in Kim Jong Un's North Korea.

For all the outward signs of closeness—sitting together at military parades, walking together at Kim Jong Il's funeral—Kim Jong Un harbored a deep resentment toward his uncle and aunt. He blamed them for preventing him from ever once meeting his exalted grandfather, Kim Il Sung.

It would have been so much easier for the young despot to claim the right to rule if there was a photograph of him as a little boy sitting on his grandfather's knee or perhaps out at a shooting range with him. Such a photo would have helped bolster his legitimacy to lead.[9]

But Kim Jong Un didn't have this photo. And he'd always resented Jang for favoring his older half brother, Kim Jong Nam, to inherit the leadership of the country. Jang and Kim Jong Nam had shared similar ideas about China and economic reform, and that made Kim Jong Un suspicious.

By the end of Kim Jong Un's first year in power, Jang's star was waning. He was made chairman of the commission to turn North Korea into a sports power—a move that might look like a promotion but was, in fact, a demotion. Sports are a second-tier issue compared to weighty matters like national security. Then, at the start of 2013, Jang, who was still technically vice chairman of the National Defense Commission, was excluded from North Korea's equivalent of a National Security Council meeting.[10]

It was around this time that Kim Jong Un hosted the American basketballer Dennis Rodman for the first time. At a game in Pyongyang, a waiter brought what appeared to be a pitcher of cola out to the Great Successor, who was sitting in a red armchair and having the time of his life, the Worm beside him and the Harlem Globetrotters on the court in front of him. Uncle Jang saw the impure drink and had it sent back, ordering a pitcher of water to be brought out instead, according to one person who witnessed the incident. Uncle Jang was treating Kim Jong Un like a child—and in public.

But his relegation to the sidelines became more apparent when Kim sent another aide, not Jang, as a special envoy to China in May.

By the end of 2013, Jang had served his purpose. He had been useful for the inexperienced leader as he was cementing his position. He had been a valuable mentor and advisor. And he had been instrumental in securing the materials and contracts that were needed to build the huge showcase developments like the apartment towers and amusement parks that Kim Jong Un wanted constructed as a tangible sign of progress being made under his leadership.

But it was time for Jang to go.

Kim Jong Un's father had also been wary of his own uncle. When Kim Jong Il was rising up the ranks in the 1970s, he removed a potential rival for the leadership by sidelining Kim Il Sung's younger brother. But in that case, the uncle was simply demoted to peripheral roles.

Demotion was not sufficient for Kim Jong Un; he decided to make a lesson out of Jang's departure. The young leader had quietly dispatched a number of senior officials, but in getting rid of Jang, he decided to send a message to the apparatchiks who kept him in power: watch your step; no one is safe in my North Korea, not even my own family members.

Just a few days shy of his second anniversary as leader, the Great Successor was presiding over an extended meeting of the politburo of the Workers' Party, sitting in the center of a stage with a huge portrait of his father behind him.

Jang, in a black Mao suit and purple-tinted glasses, was facing Kim in the center aisle of the second row. Partway through the meeting, an official began reading out a long diatribe against Jang, accusing him of trying to accumulate his own power. He was suspected of selling the country's mineral resources to Chinese companies too cheaply and of trying to undermine the Kim regime, or, as a North Korean newsreader put it, of "vicious efforts to create a faction in the party, creating illusions about himself," and trying to "emasculate the monolithic leadership of the party."

Kim Jong Un was not going to be emasculated.

The politburo accused Jang, a notorious philanderer, of leading a "dissolute and depraved life," including "improper relations with several women" and a habit of wining and dining at "deluxe restaurants." It went on, charging him with using drugs and gambling.

Jang was stripped of all his titles and expelled from the party. For maximum dramatic effect, two uniformed soldiers hauled him from his seat and marched him out of the hall.

In fact, this spectacle appeared to have been staged by the regime. Jang had been arrested and thrown into a special detention facility several months earlier, and his two closest aides were arrested and executed. Two weeks after that, a grim-faced Jang was hauled out of his cell and installed in the front row of the politburo meeting so that Kim Jong Un's henchmen could arrest him again, this time in public and in front of all his peers.[11]

The footage of Jang being humiliated and carted away was broadcast on Korean Central Television, the first time since the 1970s that North Korea had released the footage of the arrest of a senior official. The following day, the *Rodong Sinmun*, the mouthpiece of the Workers' Party, devoted its entire front page to Jang's crimes and punishment. The state news agency released an extraordinarily long prosecutorial attack against the uncle.

It was a stunning display for this most reticent of regimes, which had long preferred to dispatch fallen cadres behind its tightly closed doors.

To ram the message home, Kim ordered his uncle to be executed four days later. A special military tribunal found Jang had been plotting to overthrow Kim Jong Un and declared him a "traitor for all ages."

When the tribunal handed down its decision at the trial, or at what the North Korean regime at least called a trial, Jang's wrongs were described as a betrayal of Kim Jong Un himself.

Jang had shown "dirty political ambition." He was "despicable human scum." He was "an anti-party, counter-revolutionary factional element and despicable political careerist and trickster." He was "worse than a dog."[12]

The state propagandists poured all their energies into their condemnation of Jang, lapsing into language that sounded almost Shakespearean. He had "perpetrated thrice-cursed acts of treachery," they said.

As evidence of his treachery, the tribunal cited the fact that Jang didn't clap much when Kim Jong Un was "elected" to a new post in the Central Military Commission. While everyone else was breaking out into cheers so enthusiastic that they "shook the conference hall," Jang was a picture of arrogance and insolence, the tribunal said. He took his time standing up, and when he did, his clapping was halfhearted.

The North Korean scribes accused Jang of "dreaming different dreams while in the same bed." Those dreams centered on a reformed economy with himself, not Kim Jong Un, at the head of it. Jang may have been inside the regime, but he wanted to take it in a different direction.

Some analysts viewed Jang's execution as a sign of Kim Jong Un's weakness, of just how threatened he was by his mercurial uncle. They saw it as proof of the lack of cohesion in the young leader's regime, a signal that he was having trouble rallying the old guard around him. In fact, it was a sign of strength. Kim Jong Un was fully in control, so in control that he could dispose of his uncle and his uncle's clique just by giving the order.

He had deliberately staged an unequivocal display of how savage he could be and sent a clear message to anyone else in the regime who might think about promoting his own ideas or creating his own coterie.

It had been nearly two years to the day since Kim Jong Un had taken over the state. And almost as if he'd been reading a textbook, he had figured out who was loyal and who was expendable. He was going to make it past the two-year mark in eye-popping style.

Jang was gone, and his wife, Kim Kyong Hui, was never seen in public again. Rumors swirled about her. Maybe Kim Jong Un had his aunt put under house arrest. Maybe she was ill. Maybe she was spending her days drinking. Maybe she was dead.

Jang's execution was exceptional even by North Korean standards, not least because it involved unprecedented transparency from within the regime itself.

North Korea's experiment with news management over the death of Jang didn't entirely have the effect the regime intended. The world had come to expect ever more outlandish tales from the depraved North Korean regime, and this apparent disclosure of truth would also be exaggerated.

Instead of sending a message of coherence and power, it allowed the international media to have a speculative field day about what other depravities might be happening in the weird world of Kim Jong Un. The world's imagining quickly reached fever pitch.

The most ludicrous rumor was that Kim Jong Un watched while a pack of 120 ravenous Manchurian hunting dogs tore a naked Jang to pieces. That story first appeared on a satirical Chinese-language website and was then printed almost word for word in a Hong Kong tabloid called *Wen Wei Po*, known for its colorful stories and for not always bothering itself with facts.

Then a relatively serious newspaper, the *Singapore Straits Times*, picked it up and retold it in English. A commentator opined that if an outlet based in Hong Kong, a territory that is part of greater China, could run such a story, it must mean that Beijing was extremely unhappy with Kim's decision to get rid of the two countries' middleman. It didn't seem to occur to the commentator that a sensationalist tabloid might not bother itself too much with actual facts.

There's long been a tendency, concentrated in but not limited to the scurrilous tabloids, to print anything about North Korea. This is partly a response to the regime's knack for the bizarre—Kim Jong Un beaming over a barrel of lubricant—and the public's willingness to believe almost anything about a regime that is both cartoonish and exceptionally bloodthirsty at the same time.

The hungry dogs story started to gain traction. It was repeated by more reputable news organizations, even as they conceded they could not verify the tale. From then on, it became difficult for the truth—that he was probably shot by a regular firing squad—to compete. The truth could not get in the way of a good story and a pack of ravenous hounds. Besides, Kim Jong Un's press department was hardly likely to call the newspapers to insist on a correction.

Even if it was less spectacular than the Hong Kong tabloids would have the world believe, Jang's sudden and spectacular demise did send a chill through China's relations with North Korea—and through what might be generously called North Korea's business community.

Dozens, perhaps even hundreds, of Jang's associates disappeared around the same time. Some of them were not just purged from the system but more likely executed. Those outside North Korea at the time fled.

Ro was one of them. He was on a business trip in Russia when he heard the news that Uncle Jang had been executed. He was told to report to a North Korean security service official, which made him nervous. So he decided to flee.

He made his way to South Korea, where he started a business selling medicinal herbs from a Seoul basement squeezed between an acupuncture clinic and some kind of karaoke hall where K-pop was blaring into an empty room. It was a strange afterlife for a once-powerful apparatchik, but Ro was simply grateful to be alive.

CHAPTER 9

THE ELITES OF PYONGHATTAN

"A large number of monumental edifices of eternal value have been built across the country and streets and villages have turned into a socialist land of bliss."

—Kim Jong Un, April 27, 2012

RI JONG HO WAS ANOTHER NORTH KOREAN FAT CAT. HE WINED and dined. He traveled. He had a car with a chauffeur. He made money, lots of it. Some for the Kim regime and some for himself.

He enjoyed an "upper-class existence" in North Korea. "People might not like me saying this, but my life wasn't that tiring," he told me a year after he'd moved to the United States with his family. "I was rich."

The family was part of the privileged capitalist class at the center of the regime, people enjoying a new standard of living under Kim 3.0. They're the North Korean version of the Masters of the Universe, married to the Real Housewives of Pyongyang. They're the nouveaux riches in a country of the ancient poor. Under Kim Jong Un, they are prospering like never before.

"When it comes to getting rich, there are few rules anymore," Ri told me when I met him near Tyson's Corner, an upmarket commuter suburb outside Washington, DC. "Every North Korean breaks the law. Kim Jong Un breaks the law as well. Because everyone does it, the authorities just close their eyes."

This is the price of Kim's "small coalition."

The young leader could squash his rivals, just as he had done to Uncle Jang. But he had to keep some supporters, and he had to keep them happy by keeping them rich.

Enter the "donju," the North Korean "masters of money." This catch-all phrase refers to the class of entrepreneurs who supported Kim Jong Un's regime and became wealthy beyond their wildest dreams in the process. They are the Russian oligarchs of North Korea.

Uncle Jang was the ultimate master of money, but Ri, who knew Jang, wasn't doing too badly for himself either.

The masters of money are officials in the Workers' Party or the military. They're people running state businesses at home or abroad. They're the ones trying to attract investment into North Korea. They are officers in the security services, married women who are exempt from state jobs because they're supposed to be home cooking and raising children, and border traders with good political networks or the money to buy good political networks.

With some creative accounting, these people can make amounts of cash that, not too long ago, would have been unfathomable—thousands, sometimes tens of thousands, of dollars. Those at the top with access to lucrative industries like mining can easily become millionaires. And this money flows through North Korea under the watchful eye of—but existing almost entirely independently of—the state.

The capitalist class that emerged after the famine of the 1990s started with ordinary people who were trying to fend off starvation. But it soon included officials in the Workers' Party and the military who could use their positions to start up money-making ventures.

Since Kim Jong Un came to power at the end of 2011, their ranks have exploded. There are now untold thousands of North Koreans who have a financial interest in his leadership. They are the aspirational middle class as well as the entrenched elites.

They have a role model in the form of the Great Successor, who enjoys all the trappings of his position.

Kim Jong Un has at least thirty-three homes throughout North Korea, South Korea's intelligence agency estimates, of which twenty-eight are linked to private railway stations. The residences have layers of fencing around them that are clearly visible from satellites. The buildings on the compounds are connected by underground tunnels and house huge subterranean bunkers for the leader and his family to hide in if they come under attack.

The Great Successor lives in the lap of luxury. His main compound in northeast Pyongyang covers almost five square miles and is known as No. 15 Official Residence or the Central Luxury Mansion. It was remodeled soon after Kim Jong Un took control of the country. The Olympic-sized swimming pool with a large, twirling waterslide—where Kim Jong Un probably played as a child—was filled in, and a new swimming pool with a pool house was constructed.

The renovations were estimated to have cost tens of millions of dollars; indeed, some reports suggest Kim Jong Un spent $175 million on it, an impossible figure to verify. Kim had an entire office of moneymakers, like Ri Jong Ho, out there generating the funds to maintain such a lifestyle.

At another compound on the outskirts of Pyongyang, in the Kangdong district, Kim has a bowling alley and shooting range, horse stables, a soccer field, and a race track. And then there's the huge waterfront compound in Wonsan, which Dennis Rodman described as a cross between Disneyland and Kim Jong Un's own private Hawaii.

Kim travels often in his own private jet, a Soviet-era Ilyushin IL-62 with a cream and wood-paneled interior, not dissimilar to the American president's plane, Air Force One. It's officially called Chammae-1, or Goshawk-1, after the North Korea's national bird, but in the outside world, wits have nicknamed it Air Force Un. He'd sit onboard in his big leather chair at his desk with a MacBook on it, talking into one of his several phones and tapping his cigarette into a crystal ashtray as he was flown around his kingdom.

For fun, the man who played with model planes as a teenager now flies himself around in the light aircraft at his royal disposal. His regime even claims to be building planes that are very similar to the American-made Cessna 172 Skyhawk. In 2015, North Korean television showed Kim inspecting and then appearing to fly one of the small planes, cheered on by a crowd of air force pilots. "The plane built by our working class had the top-notch performance; it was easy to maneuver, and the engine sounded just right! Well built!" he told the engineers.

The masters of money don't enjoy the same lifestyle, but they have certainly experienced an increase in their standard of living under the new leader. And Kim Jong Un uses the success of the new entrepreneurs to support his claim that life in North Korea is getting better for everyone.

It's a neat symbiotic relationship. This system has earned Kim Jong Un a nickname in North Korea: Nanugi. It means "the person who shares," because the leader is sharing the burden of the infrastructure projects, and the profits, with those below him.

These masters of money are now "sharing" every sector of the North Korean economy, from canned food and shoe production to domestic tourism and coal mining.

But the bargain is most evident in the skyline of Pyongyang, now called Pyonghattan by outside visitors. In a Potemkin village, it's the façade that matters. The entrepreneurs are funding the ambitious projects—the architecturally impressive apartment towers, fancy new museums, and recreation centers—that Kim Jong Un takes the credit for.

The new buildings may embrace 1990s Chinese-style architecture and 1980s building quality, but they are a sharp improvement on the Soviet brutalism of before. The marquee Ryomyong Street complex, launched in 2016, houses more than three thousand apartments in no fewer than forty-four high-rise buildings, one of which is seventy stories high. The mostly green-and-white buildings—for the complex is supposedly eco-friendly—are built in a style considered modern by North Korean standards.

Kim Jong Un celebrates these developments, which mirror the kinds of projects underway in second- and third-tier cities across China, as a sign of North Korea's progress.

Ryomyong Street—Kim Jong Un named it based on the words meaning "place where the dawn breaks on the Korean revolution"—was opened with extraordinary fanfare in 2017. Tens of thousands of North

Koreans, including many in military uniform, were gathered around the complex, chanting in unison and waving colorful pompoms as Kim drew up in his stretch Mercedes limousine. The flags of both the North Korean state and the Workers' Party fluttered in the April sunshine. A brass band trumpeted. Brightly colored balloons were released into a sky so blue it seemed to also have been organized by the regime. Everything was perfect in the Socialist Paradise.

The Great Successor walked along the red carpet and up onto the dais and watched while his top economic aide lauded the regime for building the complex.

"The construction of Ryomyong Street is truly a significant, great event," the official, Premier Pak Pong Ju, said. "It shows the potential of socialist Korea, and that is scarier than the explosion of hundreds of nuclear bombs above the enemies' heads."

Then the Great Successor cut the red ribbon.

The complexes had ostensibly been built as a reward for the scientists and engineers who were working in North Korea's nuclear and missile programs. Rising above the Taedong River, they look impressive from a distance. "Just like Dubai," a government minder told me one glorious sunny day as we stood on the southern side of the river, looking across at the towers. I asked him if he'd been to Dubai. He'd never even been to China.

But up close, there were literal cracks in the façade. On Changjon Street, the Pyongyang equivalent of Park Avenue, the tiles were falling off the new apartment buildings within a couple of years. When I went to the Mirae Scientists' Street to visit an apartment—highly choreographed by the regime's propagandists—a woman with a key had to come turn on the elevator for us.

In most cities, the most sought-after apartments are those on the high floors, the ones with commanding views, but not in Pyongyang. There, the best apartments are fourth floor and below. No one wants to live in a twentieth-floor walk-up.

The new entrepreneur class was central to this effort. The state could provide the labor—what else is a million-man army good for?—but the masters of money were called upon to use their networks and capital to provide the raw materials for construction. In return, they made money by flipping the apartments allotted to them when construction was completed. Sometimes they were given as many as ten, on which they could make as much as $30,000 in profit on each.[1]

Private property ownership is still technically illegal in North Korea, but that hasn't stopped the emergence of a vibrant housing market. Sometimes people lease out the right to live in the apartments assigned to them by the state; at other times, masters of money sell the apartments they've been allocated in these new developments for substantial profits.

As a result, real estate prices have soared, with prices in Pyongyang increasing as much as tenfold. A decent two- or three-bedroom apartment in the capital costs up to $80,000, but a luxury three-bedroom apartment in a sought-after complex in central Pyongyang can fetch $180,000. It is an unimaginable sum in a country where the official government salary remains at about $4 a month.

Another reason for the real estate boom is the almost complete lack of a banking system. The masters of money can't stash their cash in an interest-bearing account or investment fund, so they channel it into bricks and mortar.

Ri Jong Ho's entrepreneurial good fortune began in the mid-'80s, when he began working for Office 39. By earning money for Kim Jong Il's slush fund, he was enabling the Dear Leader to buy all that cognac and sushi. That made Ri an important person to the regime, and he lived a good life as a result.

His last job was in the Chinese port city of Dalian, not far from the border with North Korea, where he was the head of a branch of Taehung, a North Korean trading company involved in shipping, coal and seafood exports, and oil imports. He had previously been president of a ship-trading company and chairman of Korea Kumgang Group, a company that formed a venture with Sam Pa, a Chinese businessman, to start a taxi company in Pyongyang. Ri showed me a photo of him and Pa onboard a private jet to Pyongyang.

As head of the Dalian branch of the Taehung export business, Ri would send millions of dollars in profits—denominated in American dollars or Chinese yuan—to Pyongyang. In the first nine months of 2014, until his defection in October that year, Ri said he sent the equivalent of about $10 million to the regime. Despite all the sanctions, the US dollar is still the preferred currency for North Korean businessmen since it is easiest to convert and spend.

It didn't matter that there were supposedly stringent international sanctions in place. Ri's underlings simply handed a bag of cash to the captain of a ship leaving from Dalian to the North Korean port of Nampho or gave it to someone to take on the train across the border.

But Uncle Jang's downfall at the end of 2013 spooked many masters of money, including Ri. He and his family escaped from Dalian to South Korea and then eventually to the United States.

He clearly made a tidy sum of money for himself on the sidelines of his official job. The family lived a comfortable life in the Virginia suburbs. But even in the United States, Ri was cagey about meeting me and careful about what he said. "There are so many other stories, but I can't tell you all them. Do you understand?"

He gives occasional public speeches about the North Korean regime—and much more private advice to the American government—while his children work on their English and study to go to an American university. They want Ivy League or, failing that, Georgetown.

During my years of reporting on North Korea, the rise of the masters of money was plain to see. No one illustrated the trend better to me than the manager of the March 26 Electric Cable Factory in the center of Pyongyang.

When I first visited his factory in 2005, he was a skinny guy in the summer version of a Mao suit. Dark trousers hung off a gangly frame. He showed me around the pristine factory and told me about a new decentralization pilot program that had given a handful of factory managers, including him, more authority over hiring and business decisions. This was part of a regime effort to convince outsiders that the North Korean economy was on the up and up. The manager even had an "employee of the month" board on the wall to incentivize harder work, but I didn't find his pitch very convincing.

When I went back to the factory in 2016, the manager was still there, running it. But he was almost twice as wide. By then he sported a double-breasted suit, and he had the ruddy flush of someone who was eating and drinking well. I could see large cartons of Canadian-made chemicals in his factory—despite the sanctions that should have stopped them—and wondered what other business ventures he was involved in, in addition to his official job. He was a good example of the conundrum that is North Korea: it was plain to see that he was flourishing inside the system, but how he was doing it remained a mystery.

I met another master of money in Dandong, the Chinese border city that acts as the commercial gateway to North Korea. Pak was the manager of several factories inside China that employed hundreds of North Korean workers to make manufactured goods, he told me. He was vague, fearing that being identified in any way could get him in serious trouble with the regime in Pyongyang. But he told me the goods his workers produced went into South Korean and Chinese products—all which found their way into the global trading system without anyone knowing they'd been made by North Korean hands.

Since taking over the running of the factory, Pak had instituted a number of changes aimed at making the workers more productive and the factory more profitable. The workers used to get a two-hour lunch break, during which time they'd eat simple food like dumplings. That meant output plummeted in the afternoon because they were too hungry to work.

"So I opened a cafeteria for them and said they could eat as much as they wanted for free, but they had only twenty minutes for lunch," he told me as we tucked into plate after plate of Chinese food in a restaurant, with frequent exhortations of "pleased to meet you" in Korean as he raised his glass. "They loved it, and I got an extra hour and forty minutes of work time at much greater efficiency."

After a few months in China, new arrivals from North Korea have a noticeably rosier skin tone because they're eating properly. While starvation is no longer a threat in North Korea, malnutrition is. People there often struggle to get enough variety in their diet. "Now I feed them three meals a day, and the cost is nothing compared to the increased productivity and profits," Pak said.

All the profits went back to Pyongyang, Pak told me, his Tissot watch glinting as he gesticulated. That seemed unlikely, but he wouldn't confess to taking a cut for himself. Later, he showed me photos on his Samsung Galaxy smartphone—one of the best-selling products from South Korea.

Although we both knew he was telling me only part of the story of his dealings in China, the manager was emblematic of the economic freedoms that have developed since Kim Jong Un became leader.

Even state-run companies are increasingly operated according to market principles. Once charged with following orders from the top, managers can now hire and fire workers—previously unimaginable in the Communist nation—and run their operations in the way they think most profitable.

Pak flatly denied being a capitalist or making any money for himself, almost spitting out those words. But still, he was happy to talk about his corporate role models, like Microsoft founder Bill Gates and the leaders of South Korean conglomerates such as Samsung and Hyundai, the engines of the country's rapid industrialization in the 1960s and '70s. He'd learned a lot by studying how they ran their companies, he said.

"Perseverance, the need to diversify," he cited as some of the lessons. "We're living in a world where new things keep appearing. Who would have thought Nokia would have collapsed? Their mistake was sticking with the same product."

But the only guidance we really needed came from the Great Successor. "Two years ago, Kim Jong Un promised prosperity, that we North Koreans would also live a very good life," Pak said, being careful to loyally stay on message. "Now it's been three years, and the harvest is getting better; economic growth is improving."

While much of this is wishful thinking, it's not entirely wrong, as the South Korean central bank figures attest. The single-digit growth rates are not much compared to other developing economies—China was well into the double digits during its heyday—but it's enough to add a ring of truth to the regime's insistence that life is getting better.

There is much more diversification and autonomy in this increasingly capitalist economy. Groups that are technically state-run are in fact controlled by masters of money and are in some ways turning into diversified conglomerates reminiscent of those in South Korea. Samsung started as a fruit and dried fish exporter but, in the space of a few decades, turned into one of the world's biggest manufacturers of smartphones, televisions, and computer chips.

Air Koryo, North Korea's national airline, now runs a taxi company, petrol stations, and a travel agency, as well as making Airline brand cigarettes and tinned food like mackerel and pheasant. The Masikryong group operates Kim Jong Un's landmark ski resort near Wonsan as well as running bus lines and selling bottled water.

The North Korean company My Hometown began by making premium 7.27 cigarettes—named after the date when the armistice ending the Korean War was signed. This date is celebrated in North Korea as Victory Day and is associated with the regime (high-ranking officials travel in black Mercedes sedans with license plates bearing the number 7.27). These cigarettes sell for more than imported brands like Marlboro and Rothmans and are Kim Jong Un's smoke of choice.

My Hometown also makes soju liquor as well as sporting goods including basketballs and soccer balls, soccer shoes, and sports clothing modeled on Adidas and Puma. The all-female North Korean cheering squads who went to the Winter Olympics in South Korea in 2018 were carrying My Hometown bags.

Grocery store shelves across the country are stocked with cans of North Korean–produced fish and peaches. This is partly because of Kim Jong Un's promotion of domestic industry for its own sake, but it's also because of his desire to fight against what he has called "import disease." He likes to claim that North Korean products are better, but he is also trying to combat the impact of international sanctions, which have made it harder to get everything from missile parts to teapots. He may also be trying to regain some control over the economy by undercutting private traders. Having state enterprises make products that are cheaper than imports and then selling them in state outlets is a good way to put the competition in the markets out of business.

On a visit to a cosmetics factory in Sinuiju, on the border with China, Kim Jong Un even said that North Korean products should be as good as French brands and help bring about "the dream of the women who want to be more beautiful."

The masters of money are also running the mines, selling coal and other minerals like iron ore to China for the regime—and taking a healthy cut for themselves along the way. Some who have escaped suggest the cut could be as much as one-third.

There's now a booming transport industry in a country where, just a few years ago, people needed a travel permit to cross county lines. Now there are taxis and tour buses, courier services and private trucking companies, like the one Hyon started on the border.

There are even domestic tourism companies in a nation where people never had the money or opportunity to take a vacation before. From Sinuiju on the western border to Wonsan and Mount Kumgang in the east, North Koreans with fancy cameras can be seen going sightseeing and stopping for lunch in hotel restaurants.

These businesses operate as a kind of public-private partnership where masters of money are given license to expand state entities and cream off the profits, provided they pay a certain proportion back to the state.

For example, an entrepreneur might rent space in a state factory producing shoes. The factory manager and the Workers' Party chairman affiliated with the factory pocket that rent and often additional payments that are called allowances for expenses but are in fact another form of bribery. The entrepreneur uses the space to operate his own business—hiring his own labor and buying his own raw goods to make much better shoes and keeping the profits. If he's especially cozy with the cadres running the factory, and the profits are especially good, they might allow him to use state vehicles or other perks.[2]

Or a master of money might buy mining and mineral rights from the central government authorities and then take over mines that have been abandoned because of a lack of electricity and the equipment needed to bring out the minerals. They invest in the mine to get it up and running again. They hire workers who, unlike when working for the state, will receive a decent wage. They pay off ministry officials and buy protection from local party cadres and officials in the prosecutor's office. Then they rake in the cash and pay a share of their profits—about 30 percent—to the regime as "loyalty funds."[3]

The prospects for earning serious money this way has made going into business much more attractive than going into the Workers' Party.

While I was in Dandong one time, I visited a factory where thirty North Korean women were making clothes for a Chinese company. This has been one of the main ways that Kim Jong Un has earned money for his regime. Experts estimate Kim Jong Un has sent about one hundred thousand people abroad, bringing in about $500 million for the regime each year.

The manager of the factory, a North Korean who gave his name as just Kim, showed me around the workshop, where the women were lined up in rows, sewing black men's work trousers for a Japanese brand while North Korean radio blared through the factory.

Over a two-hour lunch washed down with a Chinese firewater that tasted slightly better than its name in English—Black Soil—Manager Kim talked about doing business in China and his plans for expansion.

But he became most animated when talking about his daughter back in Pyongyang, who was a teacher. He complained that she studied too much and always had her nose in a book. He wants her to become a Workers' Party member so that she could become a trader like him and go out to make money. "That's where the future is," he told me.

Although party members have an advantage, the overlap between those with economic and political power is strong but not complete. Some have political connections and good social standing and parlay that into huge amounts of money. Others with political power use it to extract a share of the profits—in bribes or in kind—in return for protecting the entrepreneurs. Entrepreneurs without political influence simply buy it.

But it is a risky and fluid environment. Everyone is constantly jockeying to show his or her loyalty to the regime and amass more economic power. If a cadre member becomes jealous of the money a rival is making, he or she could report the rival and the entrepreneur to the authorities for corruption and other economic crimes.

That's when money and networks really come into play—and why these players need connections in the security services. Many entrepreneurs make sure to bribe their local security officials as insurance against a business relationship gone bad. But there are times when even paying off officials and building a network can't save a cadre fallen from grace. Just ask Uncle Jang.

While people like Ri flourished at the top of the regime, there were plenty of more independent agents at the grassroots level who were allowed to get rich and help stabilize the system by spreading that wealth around.

"I was selling crabs, shrimp, and mushrooms to China and Russia," one of these self-made masters of money, Oh Yuna, told me one day after she'd escaped to South Korea. She sent out one-ton containers full of sought-after seafood, sometimes five containers at a time. "So I was rich," she said.

North Korean crabs can fetch twenty dollars a pound in China, and one container can carry tens of thousands of pounds.

Oh was based in Rason, an area near the borders with China and Russia, where the warm-water ports of Rajin and Sonbong had been combined into a special economic zone. It was one of the most free-wheeling parts of North Korea.

The SEZ was started by Kim Jong Un's father in the 1990s but never took off. It has developed quickly, however, under the Great Successor. This cloistered zone gives local entrepreneurs more creative license and the proximity of the country's two major trading partners supplying the demand, while its relative isolation within North Korea has enabled the regime to cordon it off and control the spread of capitalism.

Oh became a master of money by bribing the right cadres to let her trade goods in the markets. This way, she became rich the old-fashioned way—by having a good nose for it.

"I was very good at business," she told me over lunch in an Italian restaurant near her home outside Seoul. "I made sure I put very good quality crabs and shrimp and fish in my boxes. Some people filled their boxes with inferior seafood then put a layer of top-quality seafood on the top. But I never did that."

She hadn't been out of North Korea long, but she looked every inch the South Korean high roller, with her stylishly ripped jeans and her expensive-looking fur-collared coat, her suspiciously sharp cheekbones, and her black, bejeweled manicure. After she escaped to South Korea, she'd bought a huge apartment and a Mercedes-Benz and was able to indulge her young daughter's insistence on French brand clothes.

Oh used money she'd inherited from her mother's trading business to buy three fishing boats and send them out. She'd take 60 percent of their catch, and they'd keep the rest.

She'd ply the local authorities with beer and top-notch crab. They'd also get bundles of Chinese yuan, as would the border guards and customs agents who allowed her shipments to cross into China. Everyone won.

She knew that the secret to business success in North Korea came by greasing palms—a lot of them. "You have to bribe everyone to be able to do this kind of business," she told me in between answering calls from various business associates. In the South, Oh runs three factories and constantly has deals to forge or disputes to resolve.

But in the North, she had a different set of headaches: staying on the right side of the cadres and security services as she pursued her ventures.

Despite her bribes, Oh eventually ran afoul of the authorities. She spent a year in prison, where she was beaten, sexually assaulted, and told to have an abortion. She bribed her way out of prison after only a year by promising to buy motorbikes for the bosses of the local security apparatus.

Then she was back to work, and this time she was more tactical about who she bribed.

"I can't pay everybody, but I made sure I was close to the security services so nobody can touch me," she said. "A fortune-teller told me once that my mother was very talented and I was even more talented at business."

Despite the money she was making, Oh was dismayed by the system. She remained the subject of suspicion. She knew that the state narrative was all lies and decided that she didn't want her daughter—the one she'd had after refusing the abortion—to grow up in North Korea.

"They say North Korea is a socialist country, but when I gave birth, I had to bring the rubber gloves and the drip and the syringe and the meals for the doctor and everyone else on staff," she said. "It's not a socialist country. Everybody is working for the Kim regime."

CHAPTER 10

MILLENNIALS AND MODERNITY

"The capital city of Pyongyang [is] an icon of cultural efflorescence."
—Kim Jong Un visiting Mirae Science Street, October 21, 2015

EVEN AMONG THE ELITE WHO KEPT HIM IN POWER, THERE WAS one specific subset that Kim Jong Un particularly wanted to coddle. They were the millennials, the people of his generation, who, if they felt they were flourishing under his leadership, could potentially keep him in power for decades to come.

So the self-declared Brilliant Comrade set out to re-create for them the privileged enclave he inhabited during those formative years spent in Europe. Today in North Korea, there are Italian restaurants and sushi bars, pubs selling craft beer and French fries, amusement parks with rollercoasters and other gut-churning rides, volleyball and tennis courts, and Rollerblading rinks by the river. There are taxis where the meter starts at a dollar—a quarter of the average monthly wage.

The privileged elite can go riding in the faux-Swiss equestrian club, complete with imitation wood fences around the track and statues in the rose gardens. They can ski at Masik Peak, east of Pyongyang, where Kim Jong Un built a resort complete with ten slopes, Austrian chairlifts, and Italian skis for rent. There's a hotel with an interior decoration style that could be charitably described as Swiss chalet meets North Korean kitsch. It has a heated indoor swimming pool and a sauna area. There's even a bar in an ice cave.

Today, Kim Jong Un's cabal can shoot pool and sing karaoke. They can take yoga classes and drink cappuccinos with cute animal faces drawn into the foam. They can text on their smartphones and swing Christian Dior or Gucci purses.

"Some are fake, but some are real," says Lee So-hyun, who is just a few years younger than Kim Jong Un and was part of this North Korean 0.1 percent.

So-hyun and her brother, Hyun-sung, were born into Pyongyang's elite. Their father is Ri Jong Ho, who spent more than thirty years raising money for the Kim regime. (He still spells their surname the North Korean way, Ri, while the children use the South Korean version, Lee.)

They lived the good life in Kim Jong Un's Pyonghattan, a cosmopolitan capital within the capital created by the Great Successor.

Marketization may have led to a slight improvement in living standards for many North Koreans, but no one has seen an improvement like those in the rings that run closest around Kim Jong Un. It's a strategic bribe: the regime hopes that it can persuade the Pyongyang brat pack—the children of the masters of money, who know that life outside the country is much better—that for them, at least, there is no need to leave North Korea.

On my first visit to Pyongyang in 2005, I saw women dressed very conservatively and with decidedly communist aesthetics: drab browns and grays and black, long skirts, shapeless jackets, functional shoes.

By 2018, an entirely different fashion was dominant, in Pyongyang at least. North Koreans, just a few years younger than Kim Jong Un, wear clothes from stores like H&M, Zara, and Uniqlo. Women wear more colorful and fitted clothes, sparkly jewelry, and look-at-me high heels. Conspicuous consumption is clearly no longer a crime against socialism.

Young North Koreans who could travel particularly love to buy workout gear while abroad, something that was not so readily available in the capital—at least not the kind of workout gear they wanted. It's not that these millennials are exercise freaks; their love of workout gear stems from the fact that the gym is the only place they can flaunt their bodies.

"We're supposed to dress conservatively in North Korea, so people like going to the gym so they can show off their bodies, show some skin," said So-hyun, describing how women like to wear leggings and tight tops.

Those who could go abroad would shop for themselves and their friends back in Pyongyang, who provided very specific shopping lists. The sportswear brand Elle was popular among women, while men preferred Adidas and Nike. "Everyone would bring stuff like this back when they went abroad," Hyun-sung told me.

The first time I met the siblings So-hyun and Hyun-sung was at an upscale mall not far from their home in Virginia. We went to an Italian restaurant and ate pasta and steak outside on the patio. Even in the United States, they exuded privilege and ambition. I was struck by how poised and immaculately dressed they were, very neat and formal but discreet, nothing flashy. They were both impressively savvy, skillfully managing their media appearances and discussing only the things that will increase their family's standing or their chances of getting into a good university. And they were clearly used to life in the fast lane.

But while they were still part of the North Korean elite, the siblings went back and forth between Dalian in China, where they were studying while their father raised money for the regime, and Pyonghattan.

Whenever they were back home, they'd often hang out at the Kum Rung leisure complex in the middle of Pyongyang, a modern place by the standards of the capital. It has three squash courts and a gym where the treadmills show Disney cartoons on the screens. Women prance around in revealing yoga gear long after their class is finished.

Going to an indoor swimming pool is also popular—for the same reason. "It's all about the fashion," So-hyun said. In conservative North Korea, some women are even wearing bikinis, although they are very modest bikinis with a skirt for the bottom part.

Plastic surgery has also arrived. Double-eyelid operations—a relatively simple procedure to give Asian eyes a more Western look, already as commonplace as putting on makeup for young women in South Korea—are now de rigueur among the North Korean elite too. Doing your eyelids costs between $50 and $200, depending on the skill of the surgeon.

"Being beautiful and being handsome are considered a competitive advantage," So-hyun told me, sounding just like an ambitious twenty-something South Korean.

The ultimate proof of this sentiment came in the form of Ri Sol Ju, a pretty, talented singer who hailed from an elite family and literally cheered for the regime as a member of various musical groups. She has been catapulted to the top of the regime. She is Kim Jong Un's wife.

A glamorous young woman with a common touch, she has single-handedly become an aspirational figure for millennials and some-one who adds to the regime a feeling of modernity. She's the North Korean Kate Middleton, rejuvenating the monarchy and humanizing her husband.

Her arrival was designed to show that North Korea had now entered a new era, one in which young people could enjoy themselves and have ambitions—the young people who were in the elite, at least.

Ri was all smiles when she made her first public appearance as Kim Jong Un's companion in the middle of 2012. They were attending a con-cert in Pyongyang, sitting on bright-red VIP armchairs. Kim was in his standard black Mao suit, and Ri, who sported a short haircut, was wearing a fitted black skirt suit with white stitching. Both wore red Kim pins over their hearts.

They both stood and cheered at the performance of the Moranbong Band, an all-female singing group. Citizens used to musical troupes fea-turing women in tent-like dresses or in olive-green soldiers' uniforms were suddenly treated to glamorous women in tight, sparkly outfits.

The state media didn't name the woman who was at Kim Jong Il's side that night, which drove the South Korean press into a frenzy of speculation.

Was it Kim Jong Un's younger sister? Was it Hyon Song Wol, the singer in the popular Pochonbo Electronic Orchestra, best known for its hit song "Lady Riding a Fine Horse"? The majority of the South Korean press decided that it was indeed Hyon and that she was pregnant.

This was, as is often the case, completely off the mark (like the later speculation that Kim had Hyon executed).

The real story soon came out. A few weeks later, North Korean state media reported on the opening of the Rungra People's Pleasure Ground in Pyongyang, one of the new leisure complexes that Kim had ordered to show his "loving care" for citizens of all ages. Built on an island in the middle of the Taedong River, it included an amusement park, swimming pools and water slides, a dolphinarium, and a mini golf course.

Kim Jong Un attended the opening of this amusement park with a woman who was simply introduced as Comrade Ri Sol Ju. Everyone "enthusiastically welcomed them, loudly shouting 'Hurrah!'" according to the official account of the event.[1]

Kim and Ri shook hands with the foreign diplomats who'd been brought in for the opening. One, a British diplomat called Barnaby Jones, even went on one of the rides with Kim, locked into the row in front of the Great Successor.

It had never been disclosed that Kim Jong Un had married, and Ri was not officially identified as his wife. But the relationship, with Ri looping her arm through Kim Jong Un's, was clear for all to see. The public acknowledgment of a leader's wife was unprecedented in North Korea. Kim Il Sung's first wife, the revolutionary hero Kim Jong Suk, was immortalized after her death in 1949, and his second wife was already a public figure because she held political office. Kim Jong Il certainly never took any of his numerous consorts to public events.

But it wasn't just the appearance of Ri that was a break from the past; it was her whole demeanor and approach.

Ri could hardly have looked more different from other North Korean women, even from other twentysomething women in Pyongyang. That day at the amusement park, she was wearing a fitted green-and-black dress with short sleeves and a hemline above the knee, hardly considered revealing in other parts of the world but daring in North Korea and absolutely unprecedented for a political consort.

In a country where even the wives of top cadres wore the shapeless socialist outfits that made everyone equally drab, Ri cut a strikingly modern figure. She would soon go on to wear smart business suits in bold colors—even a jacket with red polka dots—and often sported a pearl brooch instead of the mandatory Kim pin worn by everyone else in North Korea. She wore platform peep-toe pumps and often carried a Chanel- or Dior-style clutch purse under her arm. Her hair changed frequently, sometimes styled short, sometimes in long waves.

But even more striking than her outfits was her demeanor. That day at the amusement park, she walked alongside Kim, smiling and twining her arm through his. She would continue to walk arm in arm with him over the coming years, a shocking public display of affection and social equality. It would have been considered embarrassing and even rash for an ordinary husband and wife to walk in the streets this way.[2]

As first lady, Ri appeared to have a moderating influence on her husband—within the constraints of his total power. The day that they went to the funfair together, one of the rides suddenly stopped while Kim and the British diplomat were on it. The stressed workers hurried to fix the problem, but the leader was furious.

The workers, shaking in terror, apologized. The diplomats looked concerned. Then Ri approached Kim Jong Un and quietly spoke to him, apparently calming him. It worked. Kim cooled down, and everyone breathed a sigh of relief.

Ri Sol Ju was not a typical North Korean. Before their marriage, she was a captivating performer in a leading artistic troupe—just like Kim's own mother.

She came from an elite family that has helped keep the Kims in power. Her father served in the air force, and Ri Pyong Chol, a former top air force general who is always at Kim's side during missile launches, is a close relative, perhaps an uncle.

Ri is five years younger than her husband and was born on September 28, 1989, according to passport information supplied when she traveled to Japan as a teenager.[3]

As a child in Pyongyang, she was sent to the Mangyongdae Children's Palace, a showcase arts school where highly made-up kids perform propaganda songs with robotic precision for foreign visitors. She attended a musical high school—photos from the school show a clearly identifiable Ri standing with her classmates, wearing a bright red-and-yellow traditional dress—and then studied in neighboring China after graduation. Communist Party–controlled China was the closest and friendliest place for North Korean students, not to mention the cheapest.

Certainly, she traveled—a privilege afforded to only the most elite North Koreans. She went to the Japanese city of Fukuoka in 2002, when she was twelve, to participate in UNESCO's East Asian Children's Art Festival.

Then, when North Korea sent a team to the Asian Athletics Championship in South Korea in 2005, Ri Sol Ju was part of the cheering squad that accompanied the athletes. They all wore the puritanical black-and-white traditional dresses of North Korea and waved flags showing a unified Korean Peninsula.

Photos from that time show Ri with short hair and a teenager's plump cheeks. She is smiling and waving to the hordes of South Korean photographers who had come to snap pictures of a squad that South Koreans called North Korea's "army of beauties."

They stayed in South Korea for six days, boosting their team and performing North Korean songs such as "Blue Sky of My Country." South Korean intelligence would have certainly been keeping close tabs on all the North Koreans who arrived for the games—as would the North Korean authorities, careful to make sure none of them had an opportunity to defect. But at the time, the South Korean spooks could not have known that they had the future leader's future wife in their midst. She was just another pretty face.

After graduating, Ri became a singer with the Unhasu Orchestra, a Western-style ensemble with singers that is a mainstay of North Korean music. They perform songs such as "Peace Is Guaranteed by Our Arms."

Ri became one of its stars. She would appear in bright traditional Korean dresses—which form a kind of tent around the body, giving no sense of shape—and with big hair and false eyelashes. At a New Year's concert in 2010, she sang a rousing revolutionary solo called "Burn High, Bonfire." The following year, the one in which Kim Jong Un would become leader, she appeared onstage in a sparkling blue dress to sing a solo of "Soldier's Footsteps." In the year between the two performances, she had had some expensive dentistry to correct her smile.

When she emerged as Kim Jong Un's wife, many North Koreans would have recognized her as the glamorous woman from the propaganda concerts.

At some stage, she appears to have caught the eye of Kim Jong Il, a man who had a habit of marrying performers. He decided Ri should marry his youngest son and heir apparent and secure a path to future dynastic succession. "Father looked at me and told me to marry that woman, so I trusted him," Kim Jong Un told the South Korean president during their first meeting some years later.[4]

As Kim Jong Il's health deteriorated, Kim and Ri tied the knot. It was an important component of the succession plan. They are thought to have two or three children, and Kim Jong Un is no doubt grooming them to be leadership material too.

From the very beginning, Kim and Ri were the epitome of a modern couple—the young dictator and his attractive wife.

During his first September as leader, in 2012, they paid a highly publicized visit to Changjon Street, an apartment complex for the elites that stood out in the capital's skyline because the buildings were rounded and lit up at night in an array of colors.

They visited Pak Sung Il, who was reported to be a worker of the City Beautification Office and who supposedly lived with his family in a five-room apartment on the second floor. It's often difficult to tell where the line between fact and fiction lies in state media reports, but in the apartment, Kim and Ri behaved as if they were long-lost relatives. Kim had one of Pak's sons in his lap, patting his cheek, while Ri presented dishes that she said she had personally cooked. At every stop in the building, there were toasts, with Kim Jong Un doing the pouring. North Korea may have its own bizarre ideology, but it still remains bound by the Confucian hierarchical order that came from China centuries ago. Those rules stipulate that junior serves to senior—and no one in North Korea is more senior than Kim Jong Un. But with Ri at his side, Kim was presenting a totally different kind of leader than his father: a tactile, warm figure with a soft side who was close to the people (at least for the duration of his carefully staged visit).

That whiff of generational change was apparent in other ways. The concert where Ri made her first public appearance with the leader seemed at first a traditional North Korean offering. It was held in the Mansudae Art Theatre in Pyongyang, one of the main venues for events celebrating the regime. Military officials in olive-green uniforms and women in black-and-white traditional dresses stood and cheered as Kim Jong Un walked in.

He shook hands but otherwise looked stern as he sat down in a prime spot with the then-unidentified woman.

When the curtains drew back, to a flash of fireworks from the front of the stage, it showed a group of women in shiny, revealing evening dresses playing electric violins and guitars. The first song may have been a traditional choice—"Arirang," the song of longing that remains emotional in both North and South Korea to this day—as were the backdrops featuring Mount Paektu and the Communist Party logo. But the performance was like nothing North Koreans had ever seen before. The tempo was fast and upbeat, and the women were doing the North Korean equivalent of rocking out to it. The show would only become more unusual.

Singers in very short, sparkling dresses and high heels sang North Korean propaganda songs, and then violinists in short black dresses performed the theme from *Rocky*, complete with a solo from a woman with a bright-red electric guitar and wearing what looked like a wedding dress.

Then things took a surreal turn. Singers performed "It's a Small World" in Korean, and out onto the stage came people in costumes: Winnie the Pooh and Tigger were there, along with Minnie and Mickey Mouse, one of the seven dwarfs, and a random green dragon. The dwarf did weird hip gyrations while Tom and Jerry cartoons played in the background. Mickey had a laugh, pretending to conduct the musicians. They played the Winnie the Pooh theme song ("Tubby little cubby all stuffed with fluff") and capped it all off with Frank Sinatra's "My Way."

The finale seemed fitting. Kim Jong Un was certainly doing things his way.

*   *   *

On one of my trips to North Korea, I set out to experience the privileged world of Pyonghattan, the world of Kim Jong Un's and Ri Sol Ju's peers.

My first stop was the Italian restaurant with the catchy name Italian Restaurant in the Mirae Scientists Street complex. The entrance was through a lobby of a shop that sold everything from liquor to power generators—although there were no customers when I visited. There was also a fancy coffee shop selling expensive mocha creations with whipped cream. It, too, was empty.

The restaurant had a few customers though, and we settled in to try the pizza, which had been cooked in an imported wood-fired oven by specially trained staff. I chatted with a North Korean who told me that the Respected Leader wanted the people of Pyongyang to be able to enjoy food from all over the world.

He probably developed a taste for pizza during his teenage years in Europe, I said mischievously. The man's head swung around. He looked at me quizzically. "You know, while he was at school in Switzerland? He took trips to Italy. He probably ate pizza." The North Korean tried to process what I had just said. Then he replied to me, very quietly, "How can you know more about our leader than we do?"

Another night, I went to a German-themed beer hall near the Juche Tower, on the southern side of the Taedong River, which bisects Pyongyang. The beer hall had exposed brick walls, dark wooden tables, and seven kinds of North Korean beer on tap lined up behind the bar. Like an American sports bar, it also had a huge television screen flickering from one wall. It was showing ice-skating.

On the menu, there was a prime steak with a baked potato for forty-eight dollars—the same price as the filet mignon at the steak restaurant in New York where the North Korean diplomats assigned to the United Nations like to go. The Weiner schnitzel was an altogether more reasonable seven dollars. But most of the North Koreans in the restaurant seemed to be opting for the local food, although at seven dollars for a bowl of bibimbap—the kind of price you'd pay in Seoul for rice mixed with vegetables and meat—it was hardly cheap.

"If it weren't for the little badges, they could be South Koreans," my dinner mate, a foreign aid worker who lived in Pyongyang, told me as we ate in the beer hall. "They're paying ten to fifteen euros for a meal," he said.

That night, the restaurant was packed with North Koreans sitting out in the open, in stark contrast to the Pyongyang pub I visited in 2005, where there were dividers between the tables for privacy and where a hush descended upon my arrival.

This time, no one batted an eyelid. They carried on drinking and laughing regardless of the Westerner in the mix. Still, some of the old Pyongyang remained. The electricity went out for a while, and we all sat in the dark as we waited for it to kick back in.

Another night, we took our minders to a barbecue restaurant over at the Sunrise complex, another new building that had popped up in Pyong-hattan. It was so new that the driver of our minivan had trouble finding the entrance, and then our minders had trouble finding the restaurant.

This restaurant was much less crowded than the beer hall, but there were still groups of North Koreans enjoying the meat that was being grilled on the table in front of them. This outfit offered a more traditional kind of North Korean discretion. A couple sitting in a booth pulled the bamboo curtain across the front of their table when they heard us arrive.

The waitress recommended cuts of meat that were fifty dollars for a single portion, the most expensive on the menu. Clearly she had been schooled in the capitalist practice of upselling. We settled on a more modest array, washed down with beer and bottles of soju.

If there's one thing I've learned from my travels in North Korea, it's that the minders never say no to a drink. Over the years, I've watched North Koreans knock back glass after glass of soju—North Koreans in North Korea, North Koreans working outside North Korea, North Koreans in South Korea. It is a coping mechanism, a way of numbing themselves to what they have to endure.

North Koreans, including the elites in Pyongyang and abroad, also always leap at the chance to eat red meat. It's a rare and expensive treat even for the 1 percent.

Across the lobby from the barbecue restaurant, the Sunrise complex has a fancy supermarket stocked with outrageously expensive imported products like Norwegian salmon, French cheese, and Swiss muesli. It was empty when I visited—at eight o'clock on a Saturday night—and local residents say they have only occasionally seen people in there. The supermarket appears to be more about propaganda than produce. But it exists.

There are other showpieces.

There's also a nascent café culture, though in a country that doesn't drink much coffee, it's more about signaling sophistication than getting a caffeine fix. At the Kum Rung leisure center, among the treadmills and yoga classes, there's a trendy café with décor and ambience that would not be out of place in Seoul or Beijing. The head barista even trained in China.

An iced mocha costs nine dollars—a price that would be steep anywhere in the world, let alone in one of the poorest countries on the planet—while an espresso is a still-astronomical four dollars, an absurdity in a country where a significant proportion of the population is malnourished.

The coffee shops don't make much money, according to Andray Abrahamian, who ran financial training courses in North Korea for the Singapore-based NGO Choson Exchange. There just isn't the customer base that likes coffee and is willing to pay such high prices.

"It's just a signifier that you're fancy and cosmopolitan," he told me. Abrahamian, a Briton who speaks excellent Korean and has visited North Korea almost thirty times, has helped train a slew of entrepreneurs, including the woman who runs the Kum Rung coffee shop.

But there are signs of a real, if fledgling, consumer class.

The supermarket in the Kwangbok department store was bustling when I visited, with locals loading imported Ukrainian candy and Japanese mayonnaise, priced much higher than the local alternatives, into their baskets. It also carried local produce. Five-liter bottles of soju liquor were on sale for only $2.60.

Huge flat-screen televisions and top-of-the-line European vacuum cleaners are on sale in jangmadang markets in the capital—if you have a few thousand dollars to drop on such things.

More than 10 percent of North Koreans now have cell phones, and there are lots of taxis on the streets, with meters that start at a dollar. Some people even have pet dogs, an unimaginable luxury just a few years ago in a country where people struggle to feed the humans in their families.

Consumerism has been experienced in varying degrees around the country, but nowhere has benefited like the capital. "Even if you don't have a great job, it's a privilege to be in Pyongyang," So-hyun told me. "So I'm sure lots of people were envious of us."

Kang Nara did not live in the capital, but she didn't do too badly up in Chongjin, the third-largest city in North Korea. It's a place that has prospered, by North Korean standards, thanks to its port and its proximity to the borders with China and Russia.

"There was nothing that we needed that we couldn't buy. They were people who were jealous and people who wanted to take some of his work," Nara told me, speaking of her father's work.

Her father was a master of money involved in the construction business. It was a booming sector to be in, and he was clearly reaping loads of cash.

She went to an arts high school where she was able to pursue her talent for music and acting, and she also had private singing lessons. "Of course there were some poor kids at my school, but I didn't hang out with them," she recalled.

She lived in a big standalone house in the center of Chongjin, where each of the three daughters had her own bedroom. Many people in North Korea still cook over fire, but Nara's family had a gas cooker and a microwave oven. They had an electric fridge and an automatic washing machine. No one in this family needed to wash clothes in the river.

She got an allowance from her father of about $400 a month—or one hundred times the amount that a state factory worker or government bureaucrat made. Not bad for a teenager.

She spent her money on clothes and pearly lip gloss from China, perfume from France, cases for their cell phones, and little stickers to decorate them. She had a baseball cap with a Nike swoosh on it, although she didn't know then that it was a Nike swoosh, just that it was cool. Everything came from a local market.

For fun on nice days, Nara and her friends would go to the skating rink in the center of Chongjin that opened in 2013, in the second year of Kim Jong Un's reign. Rollerblading had become a huge trend, and rich kids like Nara had their own skates.

"We'd carry them slung over our shoulders—it was a status symbol, a sign that you have money—when we walked to the rink," she told me. She bought her pink Rollerblades, as well as a helmet and knee and elbow pads, at the market for about thirty dollars. She shrugged. "That's unthinkable for poor kids." They had to settle for the cheap and uncomfortable rental Rollerblades if they wanted to join in—*if* they had the money even for that.

At night, Nara would go with friends to the markets, where there was now an array of cosmopolitan eateries. They could eat Peking duck or okonomiyaki, a thick, savory Japanese pancake often containing noodles and pork. There were more and more places for flashy types to entertain themselves and show off.

Other times, Nara and her friends would text each other on their smartphones and arrange to hang out at the ping-pong hall, a private operation started by a local entrepreneur. It was the cool place to be, she said. There was a bar area with stools, and the teenagers could buy beer and snacks. "Of course we didn't go there to play table tennis. We went there to hang out with boys," Nara said. "When boys came up to talk to me, I'd check out their phone. If they had one of those old-style phones with buttons, I wasn't interested." If a guy had one of North Korea's Arirang smartphones, the kind that cost $400 to buy, then she would give him a second look.

"Shoes and cell phones were the big status symbols. To be able to afford a smartphone, you had to come from a rich family," Nara told me, reminiscing about the lifestyle she once enjoyed.

"The other thing we looked at was their outfits. If they were wearing clothes made in North Korea, they were a no. We were only interested in boys wearing foreign clothes." Foreign usually meant Chinese, and that was fine. In the Western world, Chinese-made clothes might be considered cheap and inferior, but in North Korea, even Chinese clothes are a signifier of wealth and worldliness.

It was fun to be a rich kid in Kim Jong Un's North Korea. The richest kid of all was making sure of it.

CHAPTER 11

PLAYING BALL WITH THE "JACKALS"

"Dennis Rodman went up to the auditorium to bow to Kim Jong Un. Warmly welcoming him, Kim Jong Un let him sit next to him."

—KCNA, February 28, 2013

BEING AN ISOLATED AUTOCRAT CAN BE SOCIALLY LIMITING. KIM Jong Un has his brother and sister, attached to him by blood, and a wife, attached to him by his father. There is a fawning coterie who are extremely nice to him, telling him he's the best and always letting him win. But do they really like him? Or do they just fear for their lives?

Yet no amount of social deprivation can fully explain Kim's choice of celebrity friend that emerged in 2013: the six-foot-eight-inch former Chicago Bull and B-list celebrity Dennis Rodman.

That year, the one-time NBA star embarked on the first of three trips to North Korea, during which he and his entourage not only met but also partied with the leader. This nonconformist attention seeker was embraced by the leader of a country where conformity and reticence are essential for survival.

This was very annoying for the foreign policy establishment in Washington, experts and officials who had advanced degrees and language skills and had been analyzing this rogue state for their entire careers. They wanted to know everything they could about this mysterious menace, but they didn't want to ask for information from someone who was definitely not an expert, someone who they viewed as a washed-up publicity seeker.

"We're not like buddy buddies, but we do have a friendship where it's not about politics. It's about sports," Rodman said a few years later, recounting time spent with the man he calls his "friend for life." The basketballer's verdict: "To me he was just a normal guy."[1]

The trips happened because Kim Jong Un was a big Bulls fan. When he arrived in Switzerland in the summer of 1996, the Bulls had just won the NBA championship series. Michael Jordan was named MVP, but Rodman, with his knack for grabbing rebounds, was credited with a major role in securing the victory. The Bulls, with Jordan and Rodman, would go on to win the next two championships too.

When Madeleine Albright went to Pyongyang in 2000, she took a Wilson basketball signed by Jordan as a gift for Kim Jong Il. I've seen it several times, displayed in a glass case in the International Friendship Exhibition Hall north of Pyongyang, which consists of two palaces considered so sacred that visitors have to put covers over their shoes and pass through an air-blowing machine.

The idea of sending a Chicago Bull as an emissary to meet the new leader of North Korea began as a serious one. In 2009, when it became evident that Kim Jong Un had been designated his father's successor, the CIA actively discussed trying to get Dennis Rodman to go to Pyongyang. But the idea didn't go anywhere.

Then in 2012, not long after Kim Jong Un took over and before any American had met him, Barack Obama invited some North Korea experts to the Oval Office to seek their advice on how to deal with the new young leader.

One of them, an economist named Marcus Noland, who was an expert on the North Korean famine, suggested that the president conscript Steve Kerr into an unconventional diplomatic effort. Kerr had played for the Chicago Bulls during the 1990s. But more than that, Kerr had spent some of his childhood in the Middle East with his professor father, so he had some experience in tricky parts of the world.

Noland tried to convince Obama to take advantage of the new leader's obsession with the Bulls. He suggested that the president ask Kerr, who had gone on to be an announcer and coach, to go to Pyongyang. Maybe he would play H-O-R-S-E with Kim. In the worst-case scenario, Obama's advisors accompanying Kerr would get to observe the new leader.

"It was a semi-crazy idea, but it was better than Rodman," Noland said. The idea went nowhere.

Up in New York, a team of hipster television producers at Vice was having the same idea. They wanted to make a program about North Korea, and they wanted to get to the leader. How better than to tap into his love of the Chicago Bulls?

The Vice team approached Jordan's agent with the idea, but they went around in circles, and it became clear that it wasn't going anywhere. That turned out to be a problem because the Vice crew, when they had floated the idea to the North Korean diplomats in New York, had dropped Jordan's name. The North Koreans really wanted him. So Vice ended up telling them that the pro basketballer, the one forever associated with Air Jordans, was afraid of flying. It was the kind of excuse that had special resonance in North Korea, where Kim Jong Il was famously phobic about planes.

So instead they approached Rodman. The world-famous defensive player known as the Worm was also known to be up for the unusual.

He famously wore a wedding dress, complete with veil and long white gloves, and traveled in a horse-drawn carriage through the streets of the Big Apple to, as he said, "get married to the city of New York" in 1996. That just happened to coincide with the release of his autobiography, *Bad as I Wanna Be*. Nine years later, he made another strange journey, this time traveling in a hearse surrounded by black-clad beauties to participate in his own funeral. Like Lazarus on Halloween, he emerged like a zombie from a coffin liberally plastered with the logo of an online casino.

Rodman wasn't just eccentric. He also appeared to be available for hire. After retiring from basketball, he had been promoting online gambling and had also been a contestant on a range of reality TV shows, including *Celebrity Apprentice*, hosted by one Donald J. Trump.

Would he be interested in a little paid "basketball diplomacy"? Yes, he was.

The Vice crew took the news back to the North Koreans in New York that they'd secured a Chicago Bull, and the North Koreans relayed the good news up the hierarchy in Pyongyang. They got a green light.

It was only then that the North Koreans realized that Vice wasn't your average television news program, that it was staffed by millennials with tattoos who prided themselves on their disruptive approach to media.

But the North Korean diplomats couldn't go back on this deal now. The Great Successor was expecting a Chicago Bull. So they insisted on having a meeting with executives at HBO, which had bought Vice's show, to try to straighten out a few things.

There, in HBO's office in Manhattan, the North Koreans told Nina Rosenstein, the network's senior vice president, that they loved watching *Homeland*. Umm, Rosenstein responded, that's on Showtime, a rival network. She asked them if they'd seen *Game of Thrones*. They gave her a blank look. They left the meeting with box sets.

Still, the North Koreans were apparently sufficiently reassured to allow the visit to go ahead. So on February 26, 2013, Dennis Rodman and his handlers flew from Beijing to Pyongyang, accompanied by three members of the Harlem Globetrotters, a team executive, and the Vice crew. Vice wanted the Globetrotters because, with their hilarious on-court antics, they were "the most natural ambassadors of basketball in the game."[2]

It was to be a trip like no other.

This dawned on Rodman when he arrived at Pyongyang airport to find a press scrum and a motorcade. It was a world away from the dental convention where he'd been signing autographs the previous week.

"It had been a long time since anyone cared that he existed, and he was amazed and excited to find that he mattered," said Jason Mojica, Vice producer and the impetus behind the trip. Then it sank in that if they met Kim Jong Un, they would be the first Americans to do so.

"He thought he was relevant again. There were dollar signs in his eyes," Mojica told me when I went to see him in Brooklyn for a rundown of the trip.

Rodman later admitted that he loved the adulation he received. "Once I went over there and saw the respect that they gave me, whoa, I got the red carpet," he said.[3]

But the trip was not being celebrated in Washington, where the Obama administration tried to put as much distance as possible between them and Rodman.

Two months earlier, days before Kim Jong Un marked his first anniversary in power, North Korea launched a long-range rocket that put a satellite into orbit. This was a crucial technological advance for its related missile program.

Then, just two weeks before the basketball ambassadors' arrival, the regime conducted its third nuclear test. When Rodman and the delegation got to the hotel in Pyongyang that morning, they encountered a huge banner in the lobby heralding the "success" of the test and watched as thousands of people streamed toward the main square for a celebratory rally.

The trip was not universally welcomed in Pyongyang, either. Soon after their arrival in the capital, a "hard-edged" woman pulled Mojica away from the rest of the delegation and into the back of a black limousine. She told him bluntly in English that she didn't like him or his work—he'd previously reported on North Korean gulags—or Vice, for that matter. She had argued against the visit taking place but had been overruled, she told him.[4]

After Mojica told me about this incident, we went through photos from the trip so he could point out the woman. When he showed me, I recognized her instantly. She was Choe Son Hui, a very influential person in the regime.

At the time, she was head of the Americas division at the foreign ministry, haven risen from being an interpreter during multilateral nuclear talks almost a decade earlier. Her stepfather had been the state's premier, and her family was closely connected to the Kims. Within a few years, she would be a vice foreign minister. The fact that someone so senior was involved in the Rodman trip—and as an interpreter for some basketball players, no less—showed just how seriously the regime was treating the event.

Indeed, the idea of hosting the Americans in Pyongyang was a complicated one. After all, North Korea had been spewing hatred toward the United States for some seven decades.

While the war in Korea has been all but forgotten in the United States, in North Korea the memories of the devastation are kept alive and deeply engrained into the national psyche. The regime has made the United States the scapegoat for its wrecked economy and its martial law.

Elementary school kids go on field trips to the Victorious Fatherland Liberation War Museum in Pyongyang or to the Museum of American War Atrocities in Sinchon, south of the capital.

They see paintings of "cunning American wolves"—illustrated as fair-haired, pale-skinned men with huge noses—torturing and killing North Koreans in brutal ways: by driving nails into women's heads or bayonetting children, stamping on North Korean babies with their huge boots, branding them with hot pokers, and tying them up with ropes and dropping them down wells. At the Sinchon museum, these pictures are accompanied by a loud soundtrack of children screaming.

There was certainly fighting and death in Sinchon during the Korean War, but North Korea has grossly exaggerated a claim that thirty-five thousand "martyrs" were killed by US soldiers during a massacre.

Kim Jong Un has visited the museum several times since becoming leader. After one such visit, he ordered it to be expanded into "a center for anti-US class education."

The museum is a classic example of the way that the Kim regime has stoked fear of the United States to try to keep the populace cohesive: it builds from a smidgen of truth a mountain of ideologically motivated exaggeration.

So it must have been very confusing when North Koreans woke up on March 1, 2013, to see a photo of the Beloved Comrade on the front page of the *Rodong Sinmun*, the North Korean *Pravda*, sitting with an American—and one who had the temerity to wear a hat and sunglasses in the presence of their leader.

Rodman and his entourage had arrived in Pyongyang on a freezing day at the end of February 2013, in the fourteenth month of Kim Jong

Un's reign. They had plans to lead a basketball camp—a bunch of kids in a high school gym, they thought—and play in an exhibition game.

They arrived at a ten-thousand-seat stadium in Pyongyang to find the under-eighteen national team waiting for them. The bleachers were empty, but this was clearly going to be no casual pickup game.

The following day, Rodman and his Globetrotters turned up at the stadium for the exhibition game. This time the stands were not empty. Thousands of people sat waiting patiently. Then, all of a sudden and almost in unison, everyone leapt to their feet and started clapping and cheering "Manse!" or "Live for ten thousand years!"

There he was.

"I'm sitting there on the bench and all of a sudden, he walks in. This little short guy," Rodman said, recalling that moment. "And I'm like, wait a minute. Who is that? That must be the president of the country. And he walks in with his wife and all his leaders and stuff like that."[5]

Kim Jong Un, in a black Mao suit, was coming down the stairs into the VIP section of the stadium with his wife, Ri Sol Ju.

Rodman was waiting for the leader in the VIP section, where they would watch the game in armchairs together. The Worm, wearing dark sunglasses and a black cap with "USA" on it, his ears, nose, and bottom lip glinting with rings, approached Kim and shook his hand.

The crowd continued to applaud. "The players and audience broke into thunderous cheers, greatly excited to see the game together with Kim Jong Un," the state news agency reported, adding that Kim "allowed" Rodman to sit next to him.

The North Korean basketballers were clapping too, but they looked quite nervous.

"Every North Korean person is in awe of the Marshal and wants to meet him," Pyo Yon Chol, a player on the North Korean national team, said afterward, referring to Kim by his official military title. "To be in the same place as the Marshal, it's impossible to describe the feelings with words. To play with them in attendance, I had a desire to play a better game. I cannot want anything more."[6]

The teams were picked, playground style, so each contained both Americans and North Koreans. Then it was game on.[7]

As the play progressed, everyone began to loosen up a bit. The Globetrotters did their party tricks, standing on the basket or hanging upside down from it, to hoots and cheers.

At one stage, Mark Barthelemy, a fluent Korean speaker and friend of Mojica's from their days playing in punk bands in Chicago, pointed his camera at Kim Jong Un. To his shock, the young dictator was staring directly into the lens. Barthelemy looked out from behind his camera, and Kim gave him a little wave. Then Kim nudged his wife, and she waved at Barthelemy too. It was, he told me, a most bizarre moment in a day full of bizarre moments. The dictator was being playful.

In the fourth quarter, though, the game got serious. Kim was talking intently with Rodman, discussing the play-by-play through an interpreter, nodding, gesturing, and looking like a couple of awkward old friends at a Knicks game.

Incredibly, the game ended in a 110–110 tie, with no overtime permitted—an adroit diplomatic result.

Then Rodman stood to give a speech, telling Kim what an honor and privilege it was to be there. Kim sat expressionless, looking around at the crowd as if concerned about what the guest might say next.

But Rodman did the diplomatic thing: he regretted that their countries were not on good terms before offering himself as a bridge: "Sir, thank you. You have a friend for life," he said, bowing to the dictator.

Finally, after two intense hours, Kim left the stadium. Everyone exhaled.

But the adventure was far from over. The delegation's handlers hurried Rodman and his entourage out of the stadium, telling them they had an important event on their schedule.

One minder brought the Vice team an invitation on a thick white card, announcing a reception. No details were printed. But the guests were told to dress properly and that they could take nothing to the party: no phones, no cameras, no pens, nothing. It could mean only one thing.

They were driven through the streets of Pyongyang, out past a wooded area, up a road with unnecessary hairpin turns, to a large white building. They went through airport-style security, with metal detectors and wands, and entered a large white-marble room with white tablecloths and white chairs.

Kim Jong Un was waiting to greet everyone personally in a receiving line. It was like a wedding.

Rodman was still wearing his sunglasses and baseball cap, but he had put on his version of a tuxedo: a gray T-shirt with a black suit vest over it. A hot-pink scarf tied around his neck accessorized his pink and white nail polish.

Everyone was smiling broadly as they sat down at the tables, which were decorated with elaborate vegetable sculptures: large flowers carved out of pumpkins, birds crafted from some kind of white vegetable perched upon whole watermelons. Dinner stretched to ten courses, including caviar and sushi. There was wine from France and Tiger beer from Singapore. Coca-Cola, beverage of the imperialist devils, was also served.

Kim started the evening's proceedings with a toast, clinking small glasses of soju with Rodman. Ri apparently thought better of drinking the firewater. She kept to red wine.

Then Rodman delivered a long and rambling toast, which concluded, "Marshal, your father and your grandfather did some fucked-up shit. But you, you're trying to make a change, and I love you for that."

Everyone held their breath. Then Kim Jong Un raised his glass and smiled.[8] Phew.

Soon after, the man on the other side of Ri stood up and gave a toast about how they were all going to get to know each other. Kim Jong Un rolled his eyes as if to say, "Not that old windbag again," recalled Mojica. Checking photos from the event, Mojica confirmed what I'd suspected. That old windbag was Uncle Jang.

But it was all smiles and happiness that night. There was round upon round of toasts. Mojica, feeling emboldened by the soju, invited Kim Jong Un to make the return journey to New York. He then raised his glass—a tumbler of Johnnie Walker Black that the waiters had been filling throughout the night as if it were wine—and took a sip. All of a sudden, the young dictator was yelling and gesturing at him. For a second, Mojica wondered if he'd committed a grave error. Then the translator kicked in with a "bottoms up!"

"It was a command performance," Mojica told me. "The evil dictator was demanding that I chug my drink. So I chugged my drink."

He was woozy, but he still had the mic. He slurred, "If things carry on this way, I'll be naked by the end of the night." Madame Choe had a look of complete disgust on her face, but as the translator, she relayed the remark to Kim Jong Un, who broke out into laughter.

It was party time.

A curtain went up, and on the stage was the Moranbong Band, sometimes called the North Korean Spice Girls. The women, wearing white jackets and skirts that were scandalously short by North Korean standards, hitting above the knee, broke into the theme from *Rocky*. They had electric guitars and electric violins, a drum set, and a synthesizer.

The soju was working. Kim's face grew progressively ruddier, and his smile grew broader, revealing the discolored teeth of a heavy smoker. Mojica estimated that the Great Successor had at least a dozen shots of soju. Everyone was, in the Vice producer's words, "wasted."

At one point, the Globetrotters were onstage, hand in hand with the Moranbong band members. Later, Rodman had the microphone and was singing "My Way" while Barthelemy played the saxophone, leaning back with his eyes closed like he was channeling Kenny G.

Rodman sent his sidekick over to Mojica to tell him to tone down their raucous behavior. That's when Mojica realized how out of hand things had become. You know it's wild when an internationally notorious bad boy is telling you to cool it.

Everything else is hazy. "If I was being my best journalist, I would have stayed sober and committed everything to memory," said Mojica. "But we all really got caught up in the spirit of the evening."

After several hours, Kim Jong Un stood to give the final toast. He said that the event had helped to "promote understanding between the peoples of the two countries."

Footage not broadcast on North Korean television shows Rodman and Kim hugging, the leader patting the basketballer on the back, a big smile on his face. He got his Bull.

Remarkably, Dennis Rodman remembered his promise to the Great Successor made during the drunken romp in Pyongyang.

Seven months later, he kept it. Rodman returned to Pyongyang, this time with an even more unusual posse. His muscular personal assistant, Chris "Vo" Volo, was at his side, and they were joined by a Columbia University geneticist called Joe Terwilliger, a man who prides himself on being idiosyncratic. He plays the tuba professionally, does Abe Lincoln impersonations, sometimes sports an Amish-style beard, speaks Finnish, and is a champion hotdog eater.

As a geneticist, Terwilliger had studied the Korean diaspora. He'd learned some Korean and had been teaching at the Pyongyang University of Science and Technology, a private institution run by Korean American Christians.

So when he heard that Rodman was interested in returning to Pyongyang, he bid $2,500 at a charity auction and won the opportunity to shoot hoops with him. While they were on the court, Terwilliger pitched himself as a Korea expert who could help the basketballer. He made the team.

The problem was that the team couldn't find a way to get back to Pyongyang. So Terwilliger called a guy he'd met in Pyongyang one time: Michael Spavor, a Canadian living in northern China who escorted academic and business-related delegations into North Korea.

In September, the four of them arrived in Pyongyang. They were put on Kim Jong Un's private helicopter, decked out with easy chairs and a wooden table for his ashtray. They were to travel to Wonsan, the seaside resort, where the helicopter landed right in the royal compound.

Rodman liked the VIP treatment. "Everything is just like five-star, six-star, seven-star. It's just a great day every day. There was so much entertainment, so much fun, just so much relaxation. Everything was just so, so perfect."[9]

This time, there was no televised basketball, no formalities. It was all about having a good time at the palatial waterfront compound.

Kim Jong Un took Rodman and the entourage out on a 150-foot wood-paneled sailboat that had belonged to his father. The son had his own boat, too, a $7 million ninety-five-foot-long yacht, but that stayed in its special covered dock at the Wonsan compound.

They drank Long Island iced teas on the deck. They raced Jet Skis along the coastline. Kim Jong Un always won because he had the most powerful machine. The young leader liked to zoom close to the shore and jump the waves.

Kim's wife was there with their chubby baby daughter, Ju Ae. His siblings were there too. His older brother, Kim Jong Chol, spoke English with the guests and jet-skied with them out to the two-hundred-foot-long floating pool boat, complete with water slides, moored offshore.

His younger sister, Kim Yo Jong, was there too. She had just graduated with a degree in engineering, they were told. In the years ahead, she would take an increasingly prominent role in her brother's regime, acting as his most trusted advisor and general fix-it woman. But on this day, she was sitting on the beach in a red bathing suit, watching the shenanigans. The women from the Moranbong Band were also there, cavorting on the beach in a way that did not go unnoticed by the male guests.

Another day, Kim Jong Un and the Rodman crowd went horse riding together. A photo shows Rodman on a white steed. He is not wearing shoes. Instead, his pink-socked feet sit in the stirrups.

Afterward, there was more lavish dining, drinking, and carousing. The women of the Moranbong Band were still around. Hyon Song Wol, the glamorous head of the band who'd been reported dead in the South Korean press just the previous month, was there and very much alive.

The band broke out their instruments, and Terwilliger sang a North Korean song, "My Country Is the Best." Rodman, in a gray suit vest with his tattoos on full display, belted out his karaoke favorite, "My Way." Kim Jong Un, for his part, tried to sing "Get on Up," by James Brown, according to Rodman.

It was during that visit that Kim told Rodman that he had hated the showiness of the Harlem Globetrotters. He was serious about basketball and wanted to see a serious basketball game. So Rodman said, "Let's put on a real basketball game." When he realized that it would be the leader's birthday in January, Rodman thought it would be the "perfect" date for a competitive game.

Plans were quickly put in motion. Rodman and his crew returned in December to pick the North Korean team that would play against a team of former NBA stars. Their timing was terrible.

Not even a month before, Kim Jong Un had ordered the execution of his uncle, Jang Song Thaek. So while the outside world was reacting to the brutality of a man who'd kill his own family member in his quest to retain power, Rodman and his team were having fun at the Golden Lanes bowling alley in Pyongyang and viewing the wrecked American planes at the Victorious Fatherland Liberation Museum.

The backlash in the United States grew. Paddy Power, the Irish gambling company that had planned to sponsor the event, pulled out. Some of the NBA players thought about doing so too. The trip went ahead, but it was a disaster from the outset.

Rodman, who has battled alcoholism for years, started drinking on the flight from Beijing to Pyongyang and, it seemed, didn't stop.

The other NBA veterans were clearly growing concerned. Word from home reached them that there was a lot of criticism about the fact that they were playing in a game to celebrate the birthday of a dictator. The game hung in the balance.

But in the end, they decided to proceed. They'd come all that way, after all.

On January 8, 2014, the day that Kim Jong Un turned thirty, the former NBA players were on the court. Rodman came out, sans cap, and took off his sunglasses. He bowed from the waist to Kim Jong Un, sitting in the stands.

Then he took the microphone and noted that people in the outside world had expressed "different views" about the trip and about the Marshal himself. This was probably one of the most treasonous statements ever made in public in North Korea, a country where people can have only one view about the Marshal: that he is a demigod.

Kim Jong Un was leaning back in his armchair, surveying the stadium, apparently wondering what on earth was coming next. Rodman proceeded. "Yes, he's a great leader. He provides for his people here in his country. And thank god the people here love the Marshal." Then he broke out into a memorably weird rendition of "Happy Birthday."

The North Korean state news agency made the event suitably staid, reporting that Rodman had said that "he felt the Korean people were respecting Kim Jong Un" and "sang a song reflecting his reverence for Kim Jong Un, touching the spectators."

There were more surprises to come. The Americans had gone into the game assuming that, even if they were older and more out of shape than they had once been, they would ace the contest.

But the fit and fast North Koreans showed they could not be underestimated, outsmarting and outmaneuvering the Americans throughout the first half of the game. The score after the first two quarters was 45–39 to the North Koreans. The wily underdogs had outfoxed the supposedly superior Americans.

After the first quarter, Rodman had bowed out of play and sat next to his imperious friend. They engaged in an enthusiastic play-by-play throughout the second half. Kim leaned in and seemed to hang on Rodman's every word. He was smiling and laughing, and his mood extended through to the end of the game, when the crowd broke out into a song celebrating the leader while he stood center stage, waving at the adoring masses.

As he chilled out in a side room afterward, Rodman, leaning back in his chair, was high on the atmosphere. "I just sang 'Happy Birthday' to the fucker." He laughed, apparently astonished at himself.

But his behavior would have serious repercussions for him.

During the game, Kim Jong Un had invited Rodman and the core part of his delegation to spend the weekend with him at the Masik Pass ski resort he'd had developed. When they arrived, members of Kim's family and other senior regime figures were already there. Spavor, who grew up near the Rockies, hit the slopes with Kim's brother and sister. Terwilliger spun out of control on an inflatable tube and wiped out several North Koreans. Luckily, he came to a halt before going over a cliff.

Inside at the resort, Hwang Pyong So, a top military official, spent long periods of time sitting in his undershirt and boxer shorts at the analogue phone in the corridor of the VIP floor. It was the phone that went straight to the leader.

Kim Jong Un did not show up that weekend. The friendship for life was on ice.

PART THREE

THE CONFIDENCE

CHAPTER 12

PARTY TIME

"I will fight on undauntedly, offering myself without regret in the sacred struggle to hasten the final victory of the cause of the Juche revolution pioneered in Mt. Paektu."

—Kim Jong Un, May 10, 2016

KIM JONG UN MAY HAVE OFFICIALLY BECOME LEADER OF NORTH Korea in December 2011, when his father died, but he really, truly became the leader in early May 2016. That was when the Great Successor delivered a show of force and confidence that left no doubt he was in absolute control.

The occasion was the Seventh Congress of the Workers' Party of Korea, the highest-level meeting of the Communist organization through which the Kim family has kept a grip on the state for three generations.

The last congress had been in 1980, while his grandfather was still leader, four years before Kim Jong Un was even born. His father never convened one. But the new leader wanted to bring together the cadres who kept the regime together. This time it was his party.

I arrived in Pyongyang three days before the congress opened. My regime-appointed guides for this trip were waiting for me. There were two midranking officials: Mr. Jang, who played the role of bad cop, thwarting my every attempt to break out of the prearranged schedule, and Mr. Pak, a jovial good cop. Throughout the trip, Mr. Jang complained that I asked too many questions and tried to move me along through hospital wards and snail farms—these were the stops on our itinerary—while Mr. Pak smiled and took pictures of the sights on his smartphone.

There was a lot to photograph. Pyongyang was in celebration mode. The newspapers were full of reports about the "70-day speed battle" that had been unleashed to prepare for the event. Waves of cadres in dark suits and military officials in olive dress uniform from around the country were flooding out of Pyongyang Station.

Along country roads and city streets, at farms and in factories, banners heralded the congress, and red flags bore the golden hammer, sickle, and brush of the Workers' Party. The April 25 House of Culture, the colonnaded and distinctively socialist-looking building that would host the congress, had been wrapped up in red like a present.

The official slogans rolled out for the event sounded just as strange in Korean as they did in the English-language versions distributed by North Korea's news agency. "Make the whole country seethe with a high-pitched campaign for producing greenhouse vegetables!" "Let's give a decisive solution to the problem of consumer goods!" "Let's dynamically wage this year's general advance in the same spirit as shown in succeeding in the H-bomb test!"

There was no doubt who was at the center of all the celebrations. The slogans called on North Koreans to devote themselves to fighting for the "Beloved Supreme Commander Comrade Kim Jong Un" and to make themselves into his "unfailingly faithful young vanguard."

On the second day of the congress, I was sitting at my computer in a press center the North Koreans had set up for us at the forty-seven-story Yanggakdo Hotel, a place they like to keep journalists in because it's on an island in the middle of the river that runs through Pyongyang. Journalists call it "Alcatraz."

The North Koreans want to make sure visitors have no reason to try to leave. There's a casino in the basement and a restaurant at the top that, once upon a time, used to revolve. Now you must walk around it to get the 360-degree view because its motors are defunct. The convenience store array includes surprisingly good local beer, biscuits that may or may not be made of sawdust, and boxes of North Korea's own Neo-Viagra.

On the big screens set up in the middle of the press center, I watched as Kim Jong Un walked out onto the stage of the congress hall, which was decked out in glorious socialist red: red seats on the stage for Kim Jong Un and his cronies, red seats for the audience, red flags with the Workers' Party insignia, and red banners declaring "single-hearted unity."

Kim Jong Un wore a dark Western-style suit and gray tie, the same outfit that his grandfather was wearing in the portrait that formed—together with one of Kim Jong Il—the backdrop to the stage. They were lit up like a sunrise. An old day was dawning.

Every one of the 3,467 delegates in that hall, many of whom were twice his age, stood to cheer Kim Jong Un for what seemed like hours. The military top brass wore medals down to their waists. On the stage, Kim Yong Nam, the eighty-eight-year-old premier and a man who had been deputy prime minister of North Korea before the Great Successor was even born, turned to applaud him.

Kim Jong Un tried to shush them with hand gestures as if to tamp down their enthusiasm for him, but the delegates knew better than to stop cheering and clapping.

He was just thirty-two. And he was now confident enough and secure enough to stand up there in front of all of them and lap it up. He delivered a fourteen-thousand-word speech in which he boasted about a nuclear test done a few months before.

He laid out a five-year economic plan that would now be directly associated with him—and which he would be personally responsible for putting in place. He highlighted North Korea's food and energy shortages—something already well known to people around the country, but notable because he acknowledged it—and pledged to lead the drive to address them.

He repeated his promise from that very first speech he made back in 2012 to improve people's lives. And he took a swipe at China, decrying "the filthy wind of bourgeois liberty and 'reform' and 'openness' blowing in our neighborhood."

To no great surprise, Kim Jong Un was reelected as leader of the party. But his title was upgraded from first secretary to chairman. He was restoring the party to pole position in North Korea, returning it to the vaunted status it held during his grandfather's years, before it ceded some ground to the military during his father's years.

It could have been a risky move, causing the kind of resentment that has sometimes led to military coups in other countries. But as with the "byungjin" policy of simultaneously pursuing economic development and nuclear weapons, Kim Jong Un wasn't demoting the military as much as elevating the party.

The Great Successor would find ways to keep the military happy and stave off a putsch—mainly by pouring scarce resources into the nuclear and missile programs and turning the generals in charge into North Korean celebrities. They also had the memories of the former defense minister, the one reduced to a pulp with an anti-aircraft gun after he fell asleep in a meeting, in the backs of their minds.

Throughout the pageantry of the congress, I was struck by how remarkably self-possessed Kim Jong Un was. He was not a man worried about his job. He had proven the skeptics on the outside—and on the inside, if there were any—wrong. He had demonstrated an aptitude for purging and executing rivals.

He had shrewdly promoted economic development and nuclear development at the same time. The detonation a few months earlier was North Korea's biggest nuclear test to date. The economy wasn't going gangbusters, but it was ticking along at 4 or 5 percent growth—the highest it'd been in years.

The following month, Kim Jong Un scrapped the National Defense Commission, which had been established in 1972 by his grandfather as the state's highest institution for military and national defense. He established the State Affairs Commission as North Korea's supreme power and policymaking organization and appointed himself its chairman. This formally made him the Supreme Leader of North Korea.

Everything Kim Jong Un had done since taking power, ruthless as much of it had been, was done in a calculating way.

Contrary to the popular perception of the younger leader as a madman, all the evidence suggested that Kim Jong Un was a "reasonably psychologically stable individual," said Ian Robertson, a clinical psychologist and professor of neuroscience at Trinity College Dublin and someone who had also been trying to penetrate Kim Jong Un's psyche. The author of a book about the psychology of winning, Robertson has been closely following the young leader's movements ever since he took power.

I asked Robertson what he could glean about Kim Jong Un's state of mind, and the psychologist pronounced him a classic narcissist.

"Most people who don't get scared off by their conscience or the stress of being a leader develop narcissism," Robertson told me. Because it's an acquired narcissism, it's a personality distortion rather than a personality disorder.

But there's a chemical component too. Becoming leader of North Korea could have actually changed Kim Jong Un's brain. "Power is possibly one of the most profound causes of major biological and psychological change in the human brain," Robertson said.

It turns out there is some scientific basis to the thought encapsulated by the nineteenth-century British politician Lord Acton, who said "power corrupts; absolute power corrupts absolutely." He was referring to absolute monarchies, such as those run by godlike Roman emperors and Napoleon Bonaparte, but it could equally apply to the Kims.

This kind of power releases dopamine, the neurotransmitter linked to the brain's reward and pleasure centers. It's the chemical that regulates how we perceive and experience pleasure—from eating ice cream to having sex—and makes us want to do it again. Dopamine is often linked to addiction.

In a leader like Kim Jong Un, the rush he gets from exerting his power makes him crave another fix, Robertson said. Very few human beings can resist this chemical effect and stay balanced if they hold enormous power for long periods of time.

But there's a very unpleasant flipside: the more the ego swells, the more vulnerable it is. Many tyrants develop an eggshell-thin skin that can be pierced by the tiniest infraction. In Kim Jong Un, that vulnerable ego erupted in alarming ways.

Kim Jong Un, having asserted himself at home, was ready to up the ante abroad. He needed to prove to his detractors in the outside world that he was no joke.

His nuclear program would be a key part of that.

As he was celebrating his fourth anniversary in power, he went to a former munitions factory in central Pyongyang, the place where grandfather was said to have test fired a submachine gun soon after the division of the Korean Peninsula. He dropped a proverbial bombshell.

Standing outside, Kim said that North Korea had become "a powerful nuclear weapons state" and was ready to detonate a hydrogen bomb to "defend its sovereignty and the dignity of the nation."

"If we struggle in the same spirit with which the workers produced submachine guns by their own efforts just after the liberation of the country, when everything was in need, we can further build up our country into a powerful one no enemy dares provoke," he reportedly said. Aides in military uniform took down his every word in their notebooks.

I visited the site a few months later and wandered through the gallery of photos commemorating Kim Jong Un's visit. Every site in North Korea that has been blessed with a royal visit has an exhibition like this. I asked my guide, a fiftysomething woman in traditional dress, if she'd been working on the day that the Marshal came by. It turned out she had. But when I tried to ask her about him, she stormed off, raising her hand over her face to try to block me out.

Kim Jong Un's claim was treated with skepticism in the outside world. Since he took power, Kim Jong Un had presided over just one nuclear test, at the start of 2013, only the country's third in its history. A relatively small, simple atomic bomb was detonated, which didn't seem to indicate much improvement in North Korea's technical abilities.

Intelligence agencies and nuclear experts wrote off the claim of a hydrogen bomb as typical North Korean exaggeration, dismissing the suggestion that Kim Jong Un's regime could make a thermonuclear device, which would require both fission and fusion technology.

Their doubts seemed justified a month later, when Kim Jong Un ordered the second nuclear test of his reign. The regime claimed it as a hydrogen bomb. Looking at the seismic waves it caused, outside experts said that it appeared to be an ordinary, vanilla atomic bomb. It had a yield of about six kilotons, making it about the same size as North Korea's 2013 atomic test.

The Little Boy atomic bomb that the United States dropped on the Japanese city of Hiroshima in 1945 had a yield of fifteen kilotons, while the Fat Man dropped on Nagasaki a few days later had a yield of twenty kilotons.

But such mockery of the bomb's small size missed the point. The statement was an aspiration. Kim Jong Un was working on a hydrogen bomb.

At the same time, the Great Successor was nurturing an entirely different kind of army: one of cyber warriors. Just as North Korea was considered inept at making nuclear weapons, it was thought of as second rate when it came to hacking.

North Korean hackers had been tinkering around the internet for years but without causing much alarm. In 2009, a group called the DarkSeoul Gang attacked South Korean banks and television stations, sometimes with the aim of collecting information but usually just to cause chaos.

But the state's hacking activities have grown exponentially under Kim Jong Un. South Korea is hit by about 1.5 million North Korean hacking attempts every day—that's seventeen every second—according to southern officials.[1]

Pyongyang used cyberattacks to mount asymmetric warfare, the American military commander in South Korea said.[2]

At the end of 2014, North Korea provided a stunning illustration of this theory. The first target was Sony Entertainment, revenge for the film *The Interview*, which ended with a Kim Jong Un character exploding in a fireball to a Katy Perry soundtrack.

When news of the film emerged in June 2014, Pyongyang was incensed that the studio would dare imagine an assassination attempt on the North Korean leader. It vowed "merciless countermeasures" if the movie was released.

A month before the planned release date, Christmas Day, a group that called itself the Guardians of Peace sent malware to Sony employees, some of whom clicked. The resulting hack was embarrassing for Sony, wiping computers, releasing salary details, and disclosing nasty emails between executives. The group then threatened "9/11-style" terrorist attacks on movie theaters that screened *The Interview.* All the major chains dropped the film.

The Federal Bureau of Investigation said that there was clear evidence pointing to North Korea as the perpetrator of the attack. The Justice Department brought charges against a North Korean man it said had orchestrated the hack for the Reconnaissance General Bureau. The RGB, an elite spy agency run by the military, has a unit of computer hackers called Bureau 121.

Kim Jong Un's regime denied any involvement but called the hack a "righteous deed."

North Koreans were also accused of being members of the Lazarus Group, which was behind two audacious hacks.

The first involved a plan to steal $1 billion from Bangladesh's central bank in 2016 by posing as bank employees to order money transfers through the global electronic system called SWIFT. A spelling error disrupted the attack but not before the hackers had stolen $81 million. The FBI called it the largest cyberheist in history.[3]

Then in 2017, the hackers launched WannaCry 2.0, a computer virus containing ransomware that infected more than 230,000 computers in 150 countries. It encrypted data on victims' computers and demanded money to restore access. Among the victims was Britain's healthcare system, which was crippled by the attack. The United States and the United Kingdom both accused North Korea of being behind it, but North Korea again denied any involvement. Yet technical experts say the hackers left plenty of evidence behind, in the form of source codes, IP addresses, and email accounts, to prove that North Koreans were the culprits.

North Korean hackers went on to steal a huge amount of data—some 235 gigabytes' worth—from a South Korean military network. These included classified wartime contingency plans and a "decapitation" plan for removing Kim Jong Un. Then, at the beginning of 2018, they were suspected of stealing $530 million worth of digital tokens from the Japanese cryptocurrency exchange Coincheck.

At every turn, the hackers showed themselves to be increasingly sophisticated and wily.

By one estimate, RGB hackers have attacked more than one hundred banks and cryptocurrency exchanges around the world since 2016 and pilfered more than $650 million in the process.[4]

The North Korean regime is actively cultivating elite hackers to join the RGB's Bureau 121. Students who show potential—some as young as eleven years old—are sent to special schools and then on to the University of Automation in Pyongyang, North Korea's military college for computer science. For five years, they are taught how to hack and how to create computer viruses. They compete in "hackathons," solving puzzles and cyberattack problems under extreme time pressure. "For six months, day and night, we prepared only for this contest," said one former student.[5]

Throughout 2018, North Korean students based in Pyongyang were regularly scoring in the top ranks, and sometimes winning, in competitions run by CodeChef, an Indian software company.

Hacking is the country's strongest weapon, said another former student. In North Korea, it's called "the Secret War," he added.[6]

American intelligence agencies say North Korea has a total of more than one thousand cyberoperatives living and working abroad, where there is better access to the internet. Most are in China, but some are in Russia and Malaysia.

They have one purpose: to earn money for Kim Jong Un's regime however they can—malware, ransomware, spear-phishing, sneaking into gambling and gaming sites—as long as they meet their targets. The good ones can make $100,000 a year—$90,000 for the regime, $10,000 for themselves.[7]

These kinds of funds would become increasingly important for the Great Successor as revenues from more legitimate businesses were cut off by international sanctions. If he couldn't earn, he would steal.

Kim Jong Un had been working on another way to get the attention of the outside world and, in particular, of the people the North Korean regime calls the "cunning American bastards."

It was time to take some more hostages—some more US hostages. It had proven to be a good way of focusing American minds in the past.

Many of the people North Korea had previously detained were Korean Americans doing missionary work on the borders or using business activities as a cover for proselytizing.

A year into Kim Jong Un's tenure, his regime had arrested Kenneth Bae, a Korean American missionary who was trying to spread Christianity in North Korea. He was accused of setting up bases in China with the aim of trying to overthrow Kim Jong Un's regime and was sentenced to fifteen years of hard labor. He spent two years in detention, some of it working in the fields, some of it in the Friendship Hospital in the diplomatic quarter of Pyongyang being treated for various medical complaints. It's the only place where foreigners are allowed to be treated.

Then the regime seized Matthew Miller, a troubled young man from California who had ripped up his passport on arrival at Pyongyang and asked for political asylum. He was taken into custody, apparently part of a plan to get arrested so he could document what life was like in a North Korean prison. He spent eight months in detention.

Next came Jeffrey Fowle, a fifty-six-year-old bespectacled road maintenance worker from Ohio. He traveled to North Korea as a tourist, packing into his luggage a basketball that he bought at a Harlem Globetrotters' exhibition game in Dayton. He got the players to put their autographs on the ball, and as they were signing it, Fowle told them that he hoped to take it to North Korea.

In his imagination, he wanted to present it to Kim Jong Un himself. He also took with him a turquoise-covered Bible in Korean, which he left behind in a toilet in the Chongjin Seaman's Club in the hopes that a secret Christian would find and share it. The North Korean who found it turned it in immediately, starting a process that would see Fowle spending almost six months in a North Korean detention center.[8]

Christians were unwelcome in a country with room for only one deity—Kim Jong Un himself. Korean American Christians were particularly unwelcome because they could speak the language and were traitors to the Korean people, in the eyes of the Kim regime. So they were prime targets for detention.

The regime had a well-established pattern. It would generally keep the detainees until a sufficiently senior envoy from the United States came to free them. Former presidents Jimmy Carter and Bill Clinton were among those who had previously traveled to Pyongyang to spring American detainees. These visits could be heralded in the North Korean media as signs of important people coming to pay homage to and curry favor with the all-powerful North Korean leader.

But at the end of 2015, a young American college student did something that, at a frat party in the United States, might have earned him a reprimand from the campus police. But in North Korea, it turned out to be a deadly mistake.

Otto Warmbier had just turned twenty-one. He was an all-round good student from the suburbs of Cincinnati, a guy from a well-off family, someone who had a penchant for whacky thrift-shop shirts. He was an economics major at the prestigious University of Virginia, embarking on a study-abroad trip to Hong Kong. He'd seen a little of the world—going to Cuba with his family, London to study, Israel as he explored his Jewish faith—and decided he would go to North Korea on his way to Hong Kong.

Initially, three Warmbiers—father Fred and sons Otto and Austin—were going to go to North Korea with Koryo Tours, the most established of the Beijing-based travel companies that cater to foreign tourists. Independent travel in North Korea is not allowed, but the Brits who run Koryo had established a good reputation.

In the end, only Otto went. He joined Young Pioneer Tours, aimed at people of his age, an outfit that takes its name from the Soviet Union's Communist youth league and markets tours to "destinations your mother would rather you stayed away from." I'd encountered this tour group during one of my trips to Pyongyang. At about eleven o'clock one morning, I'd been walking through the café area at the water park, when I saw them ordering pints of beer. The tour leader was flirting wildly with a North Korean woman who was present. I remember thinking at the time that this was a recipe for disaster.

That December 29, Otto flew from Beijing to Pyongyang on a five-day, four-night New Year's Party Tour. For the first few days, everything was normal. Otto posed for photos with his tour mates in front of the seventy-foot bronze statues of Kim Il Sung and Kim Jong Il in the center of Pyongyang as locals trudged through the snow to pay their compulsory respects. He went to the weird musical performances that North Korean children put on for outsiders. A big smile on his face, he threw snowballs with some local kids in a freezing parking lot.

On New Year's Eve, the tour group traveled down to the demilitarized zone that separates the two Koreas, another regular stop on the North Korean tourist itinerary. When they got back to Pyongyang, they went for dinner, had some beers, and headed into Kim Il Sung Square for a huge firework display. The group kept on drinking, as twentysomethings are wont to do on New Year's Eve.

It was after midnight when things started going wrong for Otto Warmbier. We may never know what happened in the hours between midnight and 4:00 a.m., when Otto's roommate, Briton Danny Gratton, returned to their room and found the American man asleep in bed.

Kim Jong Un's regime says that, in the small hours of the morning, Otto went to a staff-only floor in the hotel and is alleged to have pulled down a large propaganda sign that read "Let's arm ourselves strongly with Kim Jong Il's patriotism!" The regime labeled this a "hostile act" against the state and stopped Otto at Pyongyang airport on January 2 as he went to board his flight out.

But it wasn't until three weeks later—after a nuclear test and a long-range missile launch—that the regime announced it had Otto. And it wasn't until the end of February that he was seen. The distraught young man was brought before the cameras in Pyongyang to deliver a bizarre confession that had all the hallmarks of being written for him.

He said that his family was cash strapped—they weren't—and that he'd been asked by a member of his Methodist church in Ohio—he's Jewish—to steal the sign as a "trophy" in return for $10,000. He also said that the Central Intelligence Agency and a secret student group at the University of Virginia called the Z Society were behind his gambit.

Otto looked extremely shaken and, after saying he had made the "worst mistake of my life," bent at his waist into a deep and awkward bow of apology.

Did Kim Jong Un know what was going on with Otto? Probably not at the beginning. Regime officials don't require his permission to defend the leader's honor. But at some stage after Otto's arrest, Kim would have been informed about the new hostage—a white American, an important fact because North Korea makes a distinction between white and ethnically Korean Americans. Kim Jong Un would have known that this young man could become a crucial bargaining chip heading into a presidential election year in the United States.

Two weeks after that first bizarre display, Otto appeared before the cameras again. On March 16, he was led, handcuffed, into a courtroom for an hour-long show trial. At the end of it, he was sentenced to fifteen years in prison with hard labor. It was an unimaginable prospect for a twenty-one-year-old man who had already spent ten weeks alone in North Korean detention.

The following day, the regime released a grainy security camera video with a timestamp on the video: 1:57 a.m. on New Year's Day. It shows a tall figure—his face cannot be made out—walking into a hallway and taking a sign down from the wall. The person puts the sign on the floor in front of him, and the video cuts out. It's impossible to say whether the person is Otto, and everything about the video is strange: the way the person walks directly to the poster without looking around to see if anyone is there, the way he places it straight on the floor, the fact that the lights were on in an electricity-starved country. I've never been in a building with the lights on unnecessarily. In fact, I've been in many buildings in North Korea where the lights should have been on but were not.

By the time the North Korean regime released that video, Otto had already suffered the injury that would lead to his death, for something happened to the student on the night of his sentencing. The North Koreans said that he had a case of botulism after eating spinach and pork and had a bad reaction to some medicine they gave him. Some observers think that the young man, in his distress, might have tried to kill himself in his cell and was discovered too late. It is unlikely that we will ever know for sure what happened to Otto that night.

What is not in doubt is that he fell into a coma. He was taken to the Friendship Hospital, where Kenneth Bae had also been treated. For all their depravity and provocations, the North Korean regime does not want American blood on its hands. Previously, with elderly or ill detain-ees like Bae, it has freed them or treated them in the hospital. A dead prisoner is a useless bargaining chip.

But in this case, the security services appear to have panicked and tried to cover their tracks. Instead of informing the relevant authorities of Otto's condition and allowing him to be returned home for medical treatment, they hid it. Maybe they thought he would recover. Maybe they realized too late that he wouldn't.

When I arrived at the Yanggakdo Hotel six weeks after his sentenc-ing, I immediately requested an interview with Otto. I thought this might be possible, given that previous detainees had been trotted out for visiting journalists. I also asked whether I could see the floor where he had allegedly gone to steal the poster. I got neither.

Weeks turned into months, and there was still no sign of Otto Warm-bier. The North Korean foreign ministry officials stopped responding to Swedish diplomats in Pyongyang, who represent the United States there in the absence of diplomatic relations.

An intermediary told me the North Koreans had declared Otto and three other men being held, all Korean Americans with missionary links, to be prisoners of war. But he also told me that the North Korean diplo-mats seemed to be completely cut out of the loop.

With the US presidential election approaching, there was specula-tion that the hostages were being held as pawns until after the vote. Perhaps they would be released to the next administration as a way to embarrass President Obama, in the same way that the Iranian students snubbed Jimmy Carter by releasing the American embassy hostages just hours after Ronald Reagan was inaugurated in 1981.

But the election came and went. Donald Trump was sworn in as the new president of the United States, yet still there was not a peep about the hostages. Things would not start to change until early in May 2017, some sixteen months after Otto was detained.

Madame Choe, the foreign ministry official, was traveling to Nor-way for talks with former American officials, a not irregular type of meeting at which the North Koreans ask about US policy and the Amer-icans encourage them to behave better.

Joseph Yun, the US State Department's point man on North Korea, obtained permission to travel to the talks in Oslo specifically to ask about getting the four Americans freed. During the talks at a fjord-front hotel, Yun convinced Choe to allow consular access to the four men, none of whom had been seen in months, as a gesture of goodwill.

Choe flew back to Pyongyang and told the security services about the agreement she'd reached. It was only then that she discovered there was a very big problem. The security services told her that Warmbier was in a coma and had been in that condition for fifteen of the seventeen months he'd been held.

Choe immediately grasped the gravity of the problem. She alerted a North Korean diplomat at the United Nations, who delivered the news to Yun. This led to a frenzied effort to medically evacuate the young man. At President Trump's direction, Yun prepared to travel to North Korea with an American doctor.

The North Koreans wanted a decoy to distract the media. They clearly realized how serious this was going to be. Relations between the two countries reached a nadir. There was strong concern in Washington and in Seoul that the war of words could escalate into actual military conflict.

Into all of this walked Dennis Rodman.

The NBA champion had become strangely relevant since his last drunken trip to North Korea. In the intervening months, the former host of *Celebrity Apprentice* had become president of the United States; Dennis Rodman had twice appeared on *Celebrity Apprentice*. That made him the only person in the whole world who knew both Trump and Kim.

This time, Rodman's appearance was even more bizarre than usual. He arrived in Pyongyang wearing a T-shirt for the marijuana cryptocurrency PotCoin, his latest sponsor. There was speculation that he was going to North Korea as a presidential envoy. He even took a copy of Trump's *The Art of the Deal* with him.

It turned out that Rodman had been invited to North Korea at precisely the same time as the American diplomatic team was going in to retrieve Warmbier. The basketballer had been trying to return to

Pyongyang that summer, but the North Koreans delayed the trip by a few weeks so that his visit exactly coincided with the secret American delegation. It appeared that the North Koreans wanted Rodman to unwittingly stage a diversion.

With Rodman putting on the sideshow, Yun and the doctor went into hours of meetings and eventually to the hospital where Warmbier was being held. He had a feeding tube in his nose and was not responsive. After arguments and going through the motions of having his sentence commuted at his bedside, the doctor readied Otto for the long trip home. But before they let Otto go, the North Koreans presented Yun with a bill for Warmbier's medical treatment. It was for $2 million.

Kim Jong Un's regime—having taken a healthy young man hostage over a minor infraction and rendered him brain dead and then having held on to him for well over a year, denying him proper medical treatment—now had the audacity to expect payment for his "care."

Yun called the then-secretary of state, Rex Tillerson, from the hotel phone. Tillerson called Trump. They instructed Yun to sign the piece of paper agreeing that he would pay the $2 million. The first priority was getting the young man home.

Otto Warmbier died six days later in a hospital in Cincinnati, not far from the leafy suburb where he grew up. The $2 million hospital bill went to the US Treasury Department. And there it stayed—unpaid.

CHAPTER 13

THE UNWANTED BROTHER

"Kim Jong Un is still just a nominal figure and the members of the power elite will be the ones in actual power. The dynastic succession is a joke to the outside world."

—Kim Jong Nam, 2012

AUTOCRATS ARE A PARANOID BUNCH BY NATURE. BUT NO ONE makes an autocrat more paranoid than his brother. After all, the brother shares the same background and the same blood; he is, by definition, a leader in waiting.

Since Romulus killed Remus to found Rome, since Cain killed Abel in a pique of jealousy, and since Claudius killed King Hamlet, brothers have found themselves on the chopping block. The Ottomans codified fratricide: Mehmed the Conqueror passed a law allowing whichever of his sons who ascended to the throne to "kill his brothers for the common benefit of the people," a way to stave off power struggles. The recommended method was to have them strangled with silk cords by men who were deaf and mute.[1]

Kim Jong Un, having already ruthlessly dispatched his uncle, decided to take the Conqueror's advice and get rid of his older half brother, Kim Jong Nam.

Their father had felt the same way about his own half brother. When he was becoming heir to the throne, Kim Jong Il felt threatened by his younger half brother, Kim Phyong Il, who was said to hold sway within the military.

In the late 1970s, as he was being groomed as their father's successor, Kim Jong Il had his younger brother sent on what would become a four-decade-plus diplomatic posting. Kim Phyong Il has been ambassador in various countries in eastern Europe—Yugoslavia, Hungary, Bulgaria, Poland, and now the Czech Republic. He remains in Prague to this day.

Kim Jong Nam, the firstborn son in a culture that prizes firstborn sons, posed a greater threat to the Great Successor. It didn't matter that he'd been living outside North Korea in a kind of exile for some fifteen years. Kim Jong Un clearly did not want the First Son, a man who also had mythical Paektu blood coursing through his veins, to be part of North Korea's story.

On February 13, 2017, just before 9:00 a.m., Kim Jong Nam became the target of a most audacious public assassination.

He was at the Kuala Lumpur International Airport's terminal for budget airlines, a seething mass of humanity and overstuffed bags. He was checking himself in for a flight to Macau, his main base for the previous fifteen or so years, on AirAsia, the EasyJet of the region. He had no luggage, just a backpack, and no entourage. For a man with a reputation as a high-rolling international playboy, the balding forty-five-year-old looked decidedly ordinary.

As he stood at the kiosk, a young Indonesian woman approached him from behind, reaching up to cover his eyes and then wiping her hands down his face and over his mouth. As she ran off to wash her hands, another woman, this one from Vietnam and wearing a white top with LOL across it, came up and repeated the action before she rushed to the washroom and then out of the airport.

They had smeared him with two chemicals that, when combined, formed the deadly nerve agent VX, an internationally banned chemical weapon. Kim approached the airport staff for help and was escorted to the airport's medical clinic. There, he slumped in the chair with his belly exposed and soiled his pants.

The chemicals were seeping through his mucous membranes. They caused his muscles to continuously contract, starting with his heart and lungs. He died in the ambulance on the way to the hospital, barely fifteen minutes after he was attacked.

In one of the many mysteries surrounding his death, it later emerged that Kim Jong Nam was carrying twelve vials of antidote for poisons— including VX—when he was killed.[2] Why he didn't use one of them will never be known.

Instead, he suffered an excruciatingly painful death, and it all happened in full view of airport security cameras.

Initially, I was skeptical that the North Korean regime was behind this. North Korea had assassinated people before but never in such a brazen manner and never using foreigners. It also struck me as strange that the women, Siti Aisyah and Doan Thi Huong, who were quickly picked up and charged with the murder, had lived to tell the story.

They said they had been tricked into carrying out the killing, told they were appearing on a TV prank show and promised one hundred dollars for their work. They faced the death penalty.

But I was thinking of the old North Korea. This North Korea, Kim Jong Un's North Korea, was deliberately sending a defiant public message to defectors: wherever you are, we can get you—and it will hurt.

He was also laying down the gauntlet to the outside world. He had his own flesh and blood killed with a chemical weapon in a crowded public place. So what? The verbal condemnation was swift, but there was little other real effect on Pyongyang.

The Trump administration, in office for barely a month when the attack took place, had been on the brink of allowing North Korean diplomats to travel to New York for the first direct talks in years. Those plans were torn up when the administration blamed the attack on the Kim regime. There are few actors with access to this kind of chemical weapon, and even fewer with the motivation to use it. But apart from canceling the meeting and issuing a couple more sanctions, there was nothing more the United States could do.

The North Korean agents in charge of the operation had fled Malaysia immediately, taking a circuitous route—Jakarta, Dubai, Vladivostok, Pyongyang—to avoid going through China. They knew that the government in Beijing, which had protected Kim Jong Nam and was thought to be keeping him in reserve in case they needed to install a new leader next door, would be apoplectic.

The North Korean ambassador was expelled from Kuala Lumpur, his ignominy compounded by photos showing he flew out in a middle seat in economy class. But efforts to hold other North Koreans accountable failed after the North Koreans took Malaysian diplomats and their families in Pyongyang hostage.

Soon the countries were back to business as usual. Mahathir Mohamed, a man who'd long taken a soft approach to North Korea, was elected prime minister and showed no interest in pursuing the case. Lots of states kill, he said at a conference in Tokyo. Look at Israel and Palestine. What's the big deal?

Kim Jong Nam was born in Pyongyang on May 10, 1971, the outcome of his father's relationship with a very famous and very married actress, Song Hye Rim. Kim Jong Il made the actress divorce her husband, but he still kept the relationship secret from his father.

In North Korea, it was not the done thing to have a child out of wedlock with an older, divorced woman who hailed from an aristocratic southern family, especially not if you had designs on taking over a socialist revolution. The little boy never met his grandfather.[3]

Despite the secrecy, Kim Jong Il was besotted with his son for the first ten or so years—until Kim Jong Un and his siblings came along.

"Words cannot describe how deeply Jong Il loved his son," Song Hye Rim's sister wrote in her memoir of life inside the royal court.[4] "The young prince rocked his fretting son on his back to sleep, carried him until he stopped crying, and mumbled to the baby the way mothers calm a crying baby."

The child had everything he could ever want—everything except friends and freedom. He lived in walled-off compounds in Pyongyang, cared for by his maternal grandmother, his aunt, and a huge retinue of household staff, including two grown men—one of whom was a film technician, the other a painter—who were supposed to be his playmates. He called them "the clowns." They were apparently appointed just as the sushi chef was assigned to Kim Jong Un.

His mother was mostly absent. She was depressed and anxious after giving up her glittering acting career only to be treated as a shameful secret. Such was her descent into mental turmoil that after she went to Moscow for medical treatment when Kim Jong Nam was three, she never really came back.

Kim Jong Nam stayed in the compound with his grandmother and the household staff. The little boy "was being raised in an abnormal way, totally secluded from the world outside the fence, without even one friend, and not knowing the joy of playing with friends," his aunt wrote.[5]

When the boy reached school age, his aunt moved into the house to become something of a Victorian-era governess, teaching him Korean, Russian, math, and history. She brought her own two children: a boy who was ten years older than Jong Nam and a girl who was five years older. They couldn't believe the contrast with their life in ordinary Pyongyang.

The older boy soon left for university, leaving just Jong Nam and the girl, whose name was Nam Ok. They had a very lonely childhood together, prohibited by Kim Jong Il from leaving the compound.

They also had a ridiculous number of toys. The pair, who essentially became siblings, could watch movies and shoot guns and careen around in golf carts. They lived in a weird alternate universe.[6]

More than a decade before Kim Jong Un had his ostentatious eighth birthday party, Kim Jong Nam had a similarly extravagant one of his own. There he was presented with a custom-made child-sized military uniform, which carried the rank of marshal. He bragged to real soldiers that his uniform was better.

The little boy was soon being referred to as Comrade General—the name his youngest half brother would receive more than a decade later when he was in the ascendency and Jong Nam was falling from favor. The First Son's birthday would be celebrated with an ostentatious firework display and the words "Happy Birthday, Comrade General" written in the sky in gunpowder.

For other birthdays between the ages of six and twelve, Kim Jong Il would send a gift-purchasing team overseas to buy presents for his eldest son. They went to Japan, Hong Kong, Singapore, Germany, and Austria, spending $1 million a year on gifts for the little princeling. He had every electronic game that a child could want and a toy gun plated with gold.[7]

His grandmother worried about the "unfortunate circumstances" of the boy's birth. So as he approached the age of nine, she raised the prospect of them all going to Moscow, ostensibly so the boy could visit his mother. But she wanted to lay the groundwork for them all to move there so that the boy could have a relatively normal life.

Off they went in the fall of 1978: grandmother, sister/cousin, and the youthful Comrade General. Leonid Brezhnev was at the helm of the Soviet Union, but it was a period of deep economic malaise, sometimes referred to as the Era of Stagnation.

It was a rough period for Jong Nam too. The boy, unused to being around other people, did not enjoy life in the last days of the Soviet Union. One day at school, he had refused to use the bathroom because it was so dirty and eventually wet his pants. His pants then froze as he walked home in the subzero temperature.

The Kims went home to Pyongyang.

As 1980 dawned, Jong Nam's grandmother came up with plan B. Over a New Year's Day feast so elaborate that the staff wondered if the table would buckle under the weight of all the food, she raised the prospect of sending the children to Switzerland. The country's neutrality and discretion would provide a level of protection, she said, plus the bathrooms would doubtless be cleaner.

Kim Jong Il's sister and brother-in-law were enthusiastic about the idea, so Kim Jong Il summoned a French-speaking foreign ministry official called Ri Su Yong. He introduced eight-year-old Jong Nam as his son—the first time he'd ever done so—and told the diplomat to go to Geneva immediately to check out the International School of Geneva, a private institution that teaches in both English and French. Notable alumni include the Hollywood actor Michael Douglas and the former prime minister of India Indira Gandhi, as well as several Thai royals.

Uncle Jang went along too. When they returned, they declared it suitable. Plan B was put into action.[8]

The unusual family moved into a huge villa, complete with swimming pool and sauna, on the shores of Lake Geneva. That house cost

North Korea $2 million. Kim Jong Il gave the group $200,000 in spending money initially, and from then on, they had to make do with $50,000 a month.[9]

Ri was appointed to the number-two position in the mission, and Jong Nam and his sister/cousin were registered as his children, Ri Han and Ri Ma Hy, or Henry and Marie. They studied in the French side of the school, mostly to keep away from the South Koreans, who flocked to the English-language stream.

Foreshadowing the experiences that Kim Jong Un would later have in Bern, Kim Jong Nam struggled to interact with other children. That was partly due to his inability to speak the language, but it was also because he hated other children. "He was accustomed to adults that flattered him, saying, 'Comrade general, was it this? Comrade general, was it that? Yes sir. Yes sir,'" his aunt wrote. He didn't want to play with the other students. At recess, he stayed inside and drew cartoons of "American bastards," just like those he'd seen back home.

But Jong Nam's guardians were always terrified that something might happen to the boy. They put his sister/cousin into the same class as him, even though she was five years older. They rented a fifth-floor apartment across from the school so they could surveil it, and they tailed him on school field trips.

They stayed only a couple of years in Geneva before Ri Su Yong, who was called Ri Chol in the Swiss years of his career, thought it was too dangerous for the children. So the group returned to Moscow, where the two would attend a French school so as not to lose the language they'd acquired in Geneva.

Meanwhile, the diplomat Ri noticed that the royal winds were shifting, and he deftly switched his affiliation to the Kim Jong Un branch of the family. He was appointed ambassador to Switzerland and moved to Bern, where he remained throughout Kim Jong Un's school years. It was a decision that paid off for him. He has flourished under Kim Jong Un, becoming his foreign minister in 2014 and then being promoted to even higher positions in the Workers' Party.

The secret family stayed in Moscow for a few years. Then they returned to Geneva so Nam Ok could attend university and Jong Nam could finish his high school years there. By then, Jong Nam simply called himself Lee—a variation of his adopted surname, Ri—and said he was the son of the North Korean ambassador. No one paid him much attention. As Kim Jong Un would experience at private school in Bern, in that melting pot of diplobrats, everyone was from somewhere else, and everyone spoke a bunch of languages. Plus the European kids didn't differentiate between North and South Korea.

Kim Jong Nam fell in with a teenage jet set that populated nightclubs. They included rich Arabs, Hilton hotel heirs, and the children of Charles Aznavour, the "Frank Sinatra of France."

He never dealt well with authority, said Anthony Sahakian, a Swiss businessman who went to school with Jong Nam. "Rules weren't for him. I'm not saying that he was an anarchist, but he would skip a lot of classes, and he was driving before he was legally allowed to."

There were some things about "Lee" that stood out. He didn't just drive around Geneva; he drove a Mercedes 600, the huge sedan that was a favorite among dictators. "At the time, all we wanted to do was drive, so we were very jealous. We'd skip class and go somewhere else during the day to drink coffee," Sahakian told me.

It was a life of paranoia and privilege, secrecy and subterfuge. But Lee managed to enjoy being a teenager in Europe, going skiing with his friends, buying booze with his fake ID, and joyriding in the Merc.

It came to an end in 1989, however, when Jong Nam was eighteen. He returned to Pyongyang and to a life that could hardly have been more different from his freewheeling youth in Europe. Jong Nam had talked to his school friends in Geneva about "life in the palace" being oppressive. "He had everything he could possibly desire, but he was in a black depression there," another old school friend told me.

Making matters worse, much worse, he discovered that the affection his father once had showered upon him was now directed at a new family. It included two little boys called Jong Chol and Jong Un. The younger boy was five by then.

Now his father hardly ever stayed at the compound where the Jong Nam branch of the family lived. The household pulsated with rivalry.

They were convinced that the other woman, Kim Jong Un's mother, was a manipulative shrew who was poisoning Kim Jong Il against them. They talked about whether the other woman was fat—unlikely, since she'd been a dancer—and derided her as "half Jap." They nicknamed her Pangchiko, a pejorative mash-up of the words for "hammer nose" and pachinko, the gambling business in Japan that was dominated by Koreans.[10]

By the early 1990s, it was clear to Nam Ok—as it was to the Japanese sushi chef—that Kim Jong Il favored his youngest son, Kim Jong Un.

Rejected by his father, cooped up in the compound, and unable to imagine what kind of life he would lead, the First Son became unbearable, his sister/cousin Nam Ok would later say. He began to sneak out of the compound at night and to drink and sleep around. He made matters worse by showing himself publicly. In this way, he was defying his father's ground rules, opening a window onto the Dear Leader's private life.

"The more time [Kim Jong Il] spent with the other family, the more things became difficult with my brother," Nam Ok said in a memoir that was never published. "It became easier for Papa to stay with the other family."

Jong Nam and Nam Ok lived in luxury in comparison to the rest of North Korea, which was tipping into the famine, but they felt like they were in a "high-class prison" and that they would be prisoners for life. So when Kim Jong Il offered a deal to his eldest son—if he got married and had a child, he could leave North Korea—Kim Jong Nam accepted with gusto.

Kim Jong Nam married by 1995 and had a son, Han Sol, and then a daughter, Sol Hui. The family moved to Macau and occupied two villas in an exclusive gated community.

Then he took up with another North Korean woman and had three children with her. They were installed in an exclusive gated community in Beijing.

In 2011, he had another child with a third woman, his associates said. Like father, like son.

* * *

Even after the embarrassment of being caught at the airport in Tokyo and being deported in full view of the cameras, or perhaps because of it, Kim Jong Nam became an object of fascination. He was the only member of the North Korean royal family who was out and about in the world and who was recognizable.

The South Korean press was full of experts, defectors, and government officials who spoke with misleading certainty about Kim Jong Nam's role in the regime. He was a high-ranking military official. Or a Worker's Party official. Or head of the half-billion-dollar Korea Computer Center in Pyongyang, the headquarters for computer hacking.

There were reports that the younger brothers banded together to dispatch their rival, arranging a plot to have Kim Jong Nam assassinated while he was visiting Austria at the end of 2002. Two years later, there were rumors about another assassination attempt, this time in China. Then another and another.

After his death, the head of South Korea's intelligence service told lawmakers that Kim Jong Nam had contacted his younger brother, pleading to be spared. "We have nowhere to go and nowhere to hide. Our only escape is suicide," he is said to have written.[11]

Kim Jong Nam and his aunt, Kim Jong Il's sister, were said to have long, drunken phone calls lamenting the state of the country. Other experts said that Kim Jong Il was sending his eldest son out into the world to test his abilities. As late as 2007, there were reports that he had returned to Pyongyang and was working at the Organization and Guidance Department of the Workers' Party.

Much of Kim Jong Nam's life remains shrouded in mystery. What is known is that he lived in the shadows amid gamblers, gangsters, and spies. He appeared to keep some links to the regime at the same time as living outside it.

Kim Jong Nam used multiple aliases, including Kim Chol, and had several passports, including two North Korean passports and a Portuguese one. A former business acquaintance said he had a Chinese passport too. As well as Korean, he spoke Chinese, passable Japanese, English, French, and Russian.

But throughout these years, Kim Jong Nam had used his unique skill set to his own advantage—in dangerous ways that would have angered the regime back home and contributed to his demise.

Kim Jong Nam became an informant for the CIA, an agency with a track record of trying to bring down dictators it didn't like. His brother would have considered talking to American spies a treacherous act. But Kim Jong Nam provided information to them, usually meeting his handlers in Singapore or Malaysia.[12]

After that last fateful trip, security camera footage showed him in a hotel elevator with an Asian-looking man who was reported to be an American intelligence agent. Kim Jong Nam's backpack from the airport contained $120,000 in cash.

It could have been payment for his intelligence-related activities. Or it could have been earnings from his casino businesses.

For at least a decade before he died, Kim Jong Nam was running gambling websites across Southeast Asia, including Malaysia, according to a former business associate turned friend who began working with him in 2007.

I first talked to the business associate on the day Kim Jong Nam died. We'd been put in touch by a mutual acquaintance. He was on a plane, and he was terrified. He was crying down the line to me, barely intelligible as we talked on FaceTime over in-flight Wi-Fi. He told me about additional questioning at immigration points and strange people hanging around his office.

I know the man's name, his nationality, and where he lives. He told me a few vague details about his work. Like so many people involved in this murky underworld, he was extremely cagey.

But he wouldn't let me use any of these details, so I'll call him Mark here.

Mark is a specialist in internet security. One day, at the upscale Shangri La hotel in Bangkok, he was introduced to a man who called himself Johnny Kim and needed an IT specialist to help him keep his servers secure.

Mark had no idea who the man was or even where he was from, but he knew he was a bit dodgy. The work he was doing was "not legitimate." He was running gambling websites, a lot of them. Casinos in general, and online casinos in particular, are well-known ways to launder ill-gotten money.

One day in 2009, when they were watching TV, Johnny turned to Mark and said, "I want to tell you who I am. I'm the son of Kim Jong Il. My name is Kim Jong Nam." Mark wasn't sure how to respond. He didn't know much about North Korea. They carried on working together, as before, on the many online gambling sites that Johnny ran.

There were two North Korean cyberspecialists who worked with Kim Jong Nam a lot, Mark said. In Macau, he had close dealings with two titans of the gambling scene: Stanley Ho, the "King of Gambling" who owned about twenty casinos in Macau and even one in Pyongyang, and Chan Meng Kam, a former legislator who also owned casinos. Kim Jong Nam liked to hang out at the Lisboa, one of Ho's casinos in Macau, or at Chan's casino, the Golden Dragon. They ordered vodka and whisky by the bottle, Mark said.

"He knew a lot of influential people," Mark told me. "Chinese, English, Portuguese, Americans, Singaporeans. Everyone in Macau knew him."

Macau was the optimal place for Kim Jong Nam to launder the counterfeit one-hundred-dollar bills that North Korea was mass producing in the early 2000s, Mark said. One time, Kim Jong Nam even paid Mark with these fake Benjamins, called "superdollars" because they were so well forged. The US government sanctioned a Macau bank, Banco Delta Asia, in 2006, accusing it of helping the North Korean government launder money and distribute counterfeit American currency.

In Macau, the First Son enjoyed being a man about town, going to gentlemen's clubs and drinking heavily. He had girlfriends all over Asia. He had huge dragon and koi tattoos on his body in a style common in organized criminal gangs in Asia. And he had a "fascination" with the Japanese mafia, called the yakuza, and the Chinese triads, Mark said.

Throughout his time in quasi-exile, Kim Jong Nam maintained links to the regime. He remained particularly close to his uncle, the economic reformer Jang Song Thaek, and talked to him often.

He went home infrequently. He flew to Pyongyang in 2008, when his father had a stroke. He also went to France to find out about medical treatment for his father. During that trip, he also met Eric Clapton, Kim Jong Nam told Mark. It seems that the love for Clapton runs strong through the whole Kim family.

He visited North Korea again in the weeks after his father died, although he didn't see his younger half brother, by then the Supreme Leader, or go to the funeral.[13]

"He was a bit concerned about what would happen to him" after his brother took over, Mark said, adding that Kim Jong Nam never talked about wanting a role in North Korea. "He was happy living the life that he was living. He was happy that his children and wives and mistresses were not in North Korea."

When he met old school friends in Geneva and Vienna, he told them he was in town on business. That business, he said, was consulting for very wealthy Asian clients in Europe, like Chinese nouveaux riches who wanted to spend $30,000 on wine or buy property in Switzerland. "Things like that. Nothing sordid," said Sahakian, his old classmate at the International School of Geneva.

Kim Jong Nam enjoyed drinking wine and smoking cigars. He was a bon vivant who wore expensive watches. But Sahakian said he never saw the alcoholic/playboy/gambler of his reputation.

His friend didn't pry, but he had the sense that Kim Jong Nam was really working for a living, that his brother had cut him off. On his last trip to Geneva, Kim Jong Nam stayed in an Airbnb, not at the Four Seasons.

Sahakian sent me a selfie they took together in Geneva. It showed two aging men with stubble, sunglasses tucked into their shirts, smiling into the camera in front of a gourmet hotdog joint called Mischa.

Both friends said that the First Son was always very security conscious. He would make sure that all the web cameras on computers were covered, and he often had offices and his homes swept for bugs, Mark said.

He knew secret pathways between buildings where there were no security cameras, enabling him to duck about town undetected. He would spot Japanese people and steer clear of them in case they were reporters. He was especially paranoid in Beijing, Mark said. He used a very old Nokia phone from the early 2000s, a cell phone that couldn't be used to track his location.

But for someone so secretive, Kim Jong Nam was also surprisingly open.

All the while he was in exile, he maintained a Facebook page under the name Kim Chol, one of his aliases. He freely posted photos of himself there, including a whole slew of him outside various Macau casinos. "Living Las Vegas in Asia," he captioned one.

When the Facebook account was revealed, I immediately sent messages to all 180-odd of his friends. That's how I found Sahakian. I would also later discover that I had contacted Kim Jong Nam's brother-in-law.

The First Son also talked an awful lot to reporters. Japanese journalists waited for him at the Beijing airport, thrusting their business cards at him. In 2004, when there had been no public declaration about the succession, Kim Jong Nam emailed a few of them to say that his father had the "absolute right" to choose whomever he wanted.

With his father getting noticeably frailer, Kim Jong Nam, wearing sweatpants, was dismissive to a Japanese TV crew that tailed him in Macau in 2009. "Would I be dressed like this if I was the successor?" he responded.

Later, after his father chose Kim Jong Un, the jilted older brother said that he was opposed in principle to third-generation leadership, but he wished Kim Jong Un the best. "I hope my brother does his best to make the lives of North Koreans better," he said, adding that he was happy to offer his help from abroad.[14]

Later, he became even more critical, calling the disastrous currency denomination of 2009 a "mistake" and saying it was time for North Korea to "reform and open up" like China.

His sharpest critique came at the start of 2012, just a month after his younger half brother had become the leader of North Korea. "I have my doubts about whether a person with only two years of grooming as a leader can govern," Kim Jong Nam wrote to Yoji Gomi, a Japanese reporter who met the First Son on two occasions and exchanged more than 150 emails with him.

That kind of criticism would not be tolerated by the Great Successor.

*   *   *

A year after Kim Jong Nam's death, I found his sister/cousin, Nam Ok. It had been a quarter century since she'd escaped from the clutches of Kim Jong Il, the man she called Papa, boiling with frustration over the way her life had been sacrificed for her "brother." She hadn't had a proper schooling because of him. She couldn't go to university because of him. She was punished because of him, punished because he—as a twenty-year-old—was drinking and sleeping around.

Nam Ok slipped away. She became French, married a Frenchman she'd met at the Lycée in Moscow, and had two good-looking, fun-loving French sons.

She is still living a life of privilege, but it is a different kind of privilege. She and her husband have started a successful business, in no small part due to her good political connections. They have a very comfortable lifestyle. Her paperwork says she was born in Vietnam. She tells people her background is simply "Korean."

She is intensely private. There are no photos of her on the internet from recent decades. There are still photos of her with her "brother" from those years they lived together. She's in a mink coat or traditional Korean dress. Or they are in matching sailor suits in Wonsan. Or out shooting, at the beach, or in the swimming pool in North Korea.

Those photos come from a memoir that she worked on with Imogen O'Neil, a British-French writer whom she met through old Lycée connections. O'Neil had completed the book, which was to be called *The Golden Cage: Life with Kim Jong Il, a Daughter's Story*. But Nam Ok got cold feet, and the book was never published.

I had tracked her down to the city where she lived with her husband and left a letter for her at her company. Her husband agreed to meet me and tried to explain why Nam Ok couldn't and wouldn't talk to me herself. She had to remain quiet about the North Korean regime for her safety, her husband told me.

Her real brother had been killed by the regime, shot in the head and chest in his apartment building outside Seoul. He'd defected to South Korea and had lived a secret if troubled life there, untouched by the regime. Then, bankrupt, he published a book about the royal court. He was dead a few months later.

Afterward, "Uncle" Jang, the man who arranged for her to go to school in Switzerland and had been one of the few figures of fun when she was cooped up in Pyongyang, had been publicly humiliated and sent to his death.

And most recently, her adopted brother had just been killed by the regime in a grisly and public way. She couldn't risk speaking out and suffering the same fate, her husband told me.

I didn't entirely believe this explanation for Nam Ok's reticence. There were plenty of signs that she still had links to the regime, that she was still benefiting from being North Korean.

I wrestled with my discovery of Nam Ok. I could have published a story disclosing her new name and where she lives and her businesses and why I think she's still in cahoots with the regime or at least the regime's supporters. It would be a bona fide journalistic scoop. In twenty-five years, no one has found her.

But just as I honor ordinary escapees' requests for anonymity to protect their families, I chose to preserve Nam Ok's. Her children have done nothing to deserve the kind of attention that this disclosure would bring them, the hordes of South Korean and Japanese reporters who would follow them to their universities or on their ski trips.

Out of this whole dysfunctional greater Kim family, she was the only one who'd managed to make a normal life. I didn't want to be the one who blew that apart.

The person most obviously at risk after Kim Jong Nam's death, however, was not his sister/cousin, but his outspoken son, the only one of his children with any kind of public profile.

Han Sol, who uses the English name Donald, had also been surprisingly critical for a member of the North Korean royal family. Although he was born in Pyongyang, he grew up in Macau, living a variation of the wealthy-expat-kid life that his father had experienced. It was one that looked happy. He went to a private school and spoke perfect, slightly British-accented English. He bleached his hair, pierced his ear, wore a cross around his neck, and had a pretty girlfriend named Sonia.

He had posted photos on Facebook and comments on YouTube videos. "I know my people are hungry," he wrote in a comment on a YouTube video showing starving North Koreans. "I'd do anything to help them." But he also revealed on another post that he was "related" to the ruling family. "LONG LIVE DPRK," he wrote on another video, using the official abbreviation for North Korea.[15]

In 2011, just months before his uncle took over the running of North Korea, Han Sol moved to Bosnia to attend the United World College in Mostar. He lived in relative isolation for a few months before South Korean media found him and started tailing him.

He gave an extraordinary interview to the former Finnish defense minister and one of the founders of the college. It aired on Finnish television and showed a cosmopolitan young man trying to lead a normal life despite his abnormal family.

He said he didn't know how his uncle became the "dictator" of North Korea but, like his father, said he hoped things would improve. "I've always dreamed that one day I would go back and make things better and make things easier for the people back there. I also dream of unification," he said. He also said he went back to North Korea every summer "to keep in touch with my family."

After Bosnia, Han Sol's next stop was France, where he enrolled at the Le Havre campus of Sciences Po, the elite university, in the fall of 2013. When Uncle Jang was executed at the end of that year, he'd been placed under the protection of the French police.

He has reason to fear. He is male, and he is a direct descendent of the fictional Paektu bloodline. That gives him the same birthright as Kim Jong Un and could make him a rival—in the leader's mind, at least.

Han Sol was reportedly in Macau when his father was killed. While I was in Kuala Lumpur and the Malaysian police were insisting on a DNA sample before releasing Kim Jong Nam's body, there was intense speculation that Han Sol would come to provide it. Television crews swarmed every twentysomething Asian man with geek-chic glasses coming off the AirAsia flight from Macau.

But he never arrived. He, his mother, and his sister instead embarked on a frantic escape, first to Taiwan, where they spent thirty hours awaiting visas for their onward travel, with the help of the United States, China, and the Netherlands. Several parties reportedly tried to interfere with the evacuation, attempting to stop a young man with Paektu blood from escaping into anonymity and potentially continuing to criticize Kim Jong Un—or, even worse, to plot against him.[16]

Once they were all safe, Han Sol released another extraordinary video. "My father has been killed a few days ago. I'm currently with my mother and my sister," he said, wearing a black sweater and sitting against a white backdrop that could be anywhere in the world. He held up his North Korean passport as proof of identity, although the information page was blacked out. Still, he didn't need proof. He was the spitting image of his father.

In the video, he thanks a number of people for his family's safety, including the Dutch ambassador to Seoul. That sparked speculation that he was in the Netherlands. But there were also rumors about France, China, and inevitably the CIA.

The video was stamped with the seal of the Cheollima Civil Defense, a group that appeared to be established for the purpose of airing the video—perhaps by South Korea's intelligence service. It took its name from a mythical Korean horse but pointedly used the South Korean spelling.

Han Sol ended the video with the words "We hope this gets better soon."

There is, however, one direct male descendent of the Paektu line who appears to be safe, thriving even.

Kim Jong Chol, the leader's older, full brother, appears to be living within the cloistered walls of the royal compounds. He is someone that Kim Jong Un knows well and clearly trusts. Plus, the brother, who's been described as "effeminate" and even "bosomy" over the years, doesn't seem to pose any kind of threat. He just wants to play guitar. So he gets to live.

One day in 2015, Thae Yong Ho, then the deputy ambassador in London, received an encrypted message from Pyongyang telling him to buy tickets for Eric Clapton's Seventieth Birthday Celebration Tour concert at the Royal Albert Hall.

He wasn't told who they were for, but he didn't need to be told. Everyone knows who's the biggest Eric Clapton fan in North Korea.

The VIP would be coming to London for four days and three nights, arriving on an Aeroflot flight from Vladivostok via Moscow.

Thae had readied a two-bedroom suite in a five-star hotel—the Chelsea Harbor Hotel, where the penthouse suite costs more than $3,000 a night—for his charge, who seemed to be quite sick. He traveled with a doctor, who needed to stay close, and took a big pile of pills three times a day, Thae said, cupping his hands.

A nervous Thae had also prepared a list of top sightseeing places to go to and, like a good North Korean official, learned lots of facts and figures about each place. A visitor can't go anywhere in North Korea without a guide describing how many bricks were used to build a tower or when the Great Leader first visited. So there Thae was, brimming with trivia about the Tower of London and Parliament Square.

But all Kim Jong Chol wanted to do was look at guitars on Denmark Street, a row of specialist stores in London's Soho, that is renowned among guitar enthusiasts.

There, in the shops, Kim Jong Chol tried out guitars. He was very serious and intent, Thae said, and impressed the store owners with his skills. He had calloused fingertips on his left hand, a sign of how much he played.

But none of the shops had the specific guitar Jong Chol wanted, so Thae was dispatched to locate one that did. He found another specialist dealer in a small town about twenty-five miles outside London, and off they went.

They had the guitar, and Jong Chol bought it. It cost about 3,000 pounds, or $4,500 at the time. Thae kept his distance while the transaction was taking place. Jong Chol's English was good enough for the job. "He was mad about that guitar," Thae recalled.

Then Jong Chol went to see Clapton at the Royal Albert Hall not once but two nights in a row. Photos show him wearing a black leather jacket and sunglasses, accompanied by Thae, another man, and a woman. She was also dressed to rock, in a green leather jacket and sunglasses. She wasn't his girlfriend or his wife, Thae said. She was a guitarist from the Moranbong Band.

Despite the throngs of journalists and cameras waiting for him on the second night, the North Korean VIP was in his element at the

Clapton concerts, which featured hits from throughout Slowhand's career, including "Layla," "Tears in Heaven," and "Wonderful Tonight."

"He was having a great time, singing along to all the words," said one fellow concertgoer.[17]

Thae said that Kim Jong Chol seemed to be overtaken by the music, standing up, clapping wildly, and raising his hands in the air. He snapped up T-shirts and other souvenirs. Back at the hotel, still on a high, the North Koreans emptied their minibars.

Outside the concerts, Thae arranged for his VIP visitor to enjoy the best of London.

"I took him to a fancy restaurant in the Shard, but he didn't eat much," Thae told me some years later, referring to the landmark London tower. "So I asked him what he wanted to eat, and he said McDonalds. So we went to McDonalds, and he ate. He particularly loved the French fries."

But even at the concerts or eating fries, Kim Jong Chol didn't seem happy for long, Thae said. "He seldom smiled. He was so silent."

Kim Jong Un seemed to have his full brother where he wanted him, close enough to keep an eye on him and see that he harbored no illusions about who was the rightful heir to their father's throne. Kim Jong Chol didn't sneak around and embarrass his younger brother, and he certainly didn't offer any criticisms to journalists.

Except for those Eric Clapton concerts, he was never seen publicly. He didn't appear next to his brother at military parades, at on-the-spot guidance sessions, or during the nuclear tests and missile launches that were about to become increasingly frequent.

CHAPTER 14

THE TREASURED SWORD

"We will continue to build up our self-defense capability, the pivot of which is the nuclear forces, and the capability for preemptive strike as long as the United States and its vassal forces keep on nuclear threat and blackmail."

—Kim Jong Un, January 1, 2017

THE GREAT SUCCESSOR WAS HAPPY—VERY HAPPY. HANDS-ON-hips, open-mouthed-smile, applauding-himself happy.

In September 2017, nearly six years into Kim Jong Un's reign, North Korea was proclaiming it had just dealt "a merciless sledge-hammer blow to the U.S. imperialists and their vassal forces."

The country's scientists had built a hydrogen bomb, and they had just detonated it underneath Mount Manthap in the north of the country. The explosion was so huge that earth-observation satellites showed the 7,200-foot peak visibly subsiding immediately after the blast.[1]

With that test, North Korea had become the newest—and very unwelcome—member of the H-bomb club, a club that until that day had officially included only the United States, the United Kingdom, Russia, China, and France.

We are now armed with a "powerful treasured sword for defending peace," Kim told the North Korean power players while declaring that no more nuclear tests would be needed.[2] It was his signal that North

Korea had achieved the technological capacity that it wanted. It didn't need to do any more tests because it had perfected "the bomb."

Kim Jong Un was already head of an army of 1.2 million soldiers, making it the fourth largest in the world. Now, at thirty-three, he was the world's youngest nuclear-armed leader too. He wanted to make it clear that this was his program. He was pictured at missile launches and engine tests, inspecting the peanut-shaped hydrogen bomb and signing the order to detonate it.

Kim had pledged to develop the economy and the nuclear program in parallel, but in reality it was more of a staged process. Although he had taken the shackles off the economy and allowed the markets to flourish, the economic growth experienced during those early years was more a result of benign neglect, of inattention, than anything else.

For Kim's attention was on the nuclear program. To bolster his claim to lead North Korea—and to make the outside world think twice about challenging him—Kim Jong Un poured all his state's resources into the nuclear and missile programs.

For a while, the world sniggered at North Korea's self-proclaimed military prowess. The "genius strategist" Kim Jong Un was lampooned for looking through upside-down binoculars shortly before he became leader and afterward for riding through the water in a clearly rusted submarine while supposedly commanding the navy. When Kim Jong Un appeared with what North Korea said was a miniaturized nuclear weapon, it was mocked as looking like a disco ball. The internet exploded with memes.

But the Great Successor wanted to prove he was no joke. As he settled into his new role, he wanted to show clear progress. He needed to make good on his constant refrain that North Korea was a "strong and prosperous country" and quickly homed in on the nuclear weapons program as a way to do it.

The first advancement was a paper one. In the middle of 2012, Kim Jong Un revised the country's constitution to elevate his father and celebrate his nuclear achievements in black and white. For the first time, the word "nuclear" was put into the constitution. Kim Jong Il had turned North Korea "into an invincible political ideological state, nuclear-armed state and undefeatable militarily strong state," the revised document said.[3]

With his first nuclear test in February 2013 and his early missile launches, it looked like Kim Jong Un was making the same unsubstantiated boasts that his father had made, talking up his state's technical abilities and using the program for political purposes.

The North Korean regime likes to time its provocations for maximum impact, and in the month around that February nuclear test were three events that he could mark with an ostentatious display of North Korean bravado: Barack Obama had started his second term as president of the United States just a few weeks earlier, and the conservative Park Geun-hye would be sworn in as president of South Korea a few weeks later. In between was the anniversary of his father's birthday, a day celebrated in North Korea as the Day of the Shining Star.

From a technical standpoint, Kim's first nuclear test wasn't much of an advance from the previous ones. The timing seemed designed to show that the young dictator had found his feet. The missiles launched in 2013 and 2014 were not particularly impressive either, a rat-a-tat of short-range missiles that North Korea was already known to possess.

All that started to change in the middle of 2016. In January of that year, Kim Jong Un's propagandists claimed they had tested a hydrogen bomb. The explosion did not have the yield of a hydrogen bomb. Then, within days, they released footage of what they said was a ballistic missile being launched from a submarine, something that could be a significant advance if true.

It turned out the video had been digitally manipulated so that North Korea could grossly exaggerate its abilities again and seem like it had made more progress than it actually had. More laughter ensued around the world at the tin-pot regime that couldn't even master Photoshop. How could they be taken seriously as a threat?

But this was another case of North Korea signaling its intentions. Kim Jong Un didn't have an H-bomb, nor could he fire ballistic missiles from under the water, but he wanted to be able to. And soon he would.

To mark Kim Il Sung's birthday in 2016, North Korea fired a Musudan, an intermediate-range ballistic missile technically capable of reaching all of Japan and South Korea and even the American territory of Guam in the middle of the Pacific. The launch was a failure. A week later, another submarine-launched ballistic missile resulted in another failure. At the end of May, another Musudan failed.

But in June, two more tests showed the North Koreans were learning from their mistakes. One test was successful, the other not. While the outside world scoffed, North Korea was making progress, and it was all due to "the Ever-Victorious, Iron-Willed Commander."

"We have the sure capability to attack in an overall and practical way the Americans in the Pacific operation theater," said an elated Kim Jong Un, who'd supervised the successful launch. He was pictured sitting at a table, holding binoculars and with a map in front of him, while all around him were ecstatic military men cheering and throwing their hands in the air.

The missiles were being fired from mobile launchers, converted trucks that could be wheeled out from any hangar or tunnel in the country. They were no longer coming off fixed test stands that were easy for satellites to monitor. This ought to have alerted the rest of the world that North Korea had upped the ante.

By August, the laughter that had followed the failed submarine launches had faded. A ballistic missile unleashed from a submarine off North Korea's east coast flew right into Japanese-controlled waters. From then on, the failures became fewer, and the successes became more frequent. The missiles flew farther. It wasn't just the progress that was alarming; it was the sheer number of launches. It showed that North Korea had missiles to burn.

In 2017, two nuclear tests took place, including one that really was a hydrogen bomb. For good measure, they also launched three intercontinental ballistic missiles, the first on America's birthday, July 4, for maximum effect. That one could theoretically reach Alaska. Kim Jong Un's regime called it "a gift to the American bastards."

Next time it was launched, at the end of the month, the missile showed it could reach Denver or Chicago. By the end of November, Kim Jong Un had supervised another launch, but this time the missile's range demonstrated that it could technically reach anywhere in the United States, including Washington, DC.

He hadn't yet proven the regime's ability to combine the two components: delivering a nuclear-tipped warhead to a target is a very difficult feat, one that requires the nuclear device to withstand severe vibration and huge extremes in temperature. But few analysts doubted that Kim Jong Un would soon, with time and more testing, be able to achieve that.

For Kim, developing a credible nuclear weapons system was a way to fend off the United States while he consolidated his grip on the regime. Indeed, despite the highly provocative nature of the nuclear tests and missile launches, the leader emphasized that he would only use his nuclear arsenal in defense. We "will not use nuclear weapons first unless aggressive hostile forces use nuclear weapons to invade on our sovereignty," he said at that first-in-a-generation congress in 2016.

Kim saw his nuclear program as an insurance policy against the kind of fate that had befallen Muammar Gaddafi. Using it preemptively would be suicidal, guaranteeing an American response that would be impossible for the Kim family to survive. But having a few nuclear-tipped missiles that can reach Washington could help deter the United States from attacking North Korea. Nothing says "take me seriously" to the outside world like an H-bomb and the potential to deliver it.

The tests and launches also carried an important domestic message. To the people of North Korea, Kim Jong Un was saying, "Look what a strong and advanced state we're becoming under my great leadership."

Channeling precious resources into the nuclear program was a way to placate the military—the institution that might be the least impressed with the unqualified "marshal." In a country that has so little else to celebrate, the nuclear program is a great source of pride, even among those who bucked the system.

"I remember one day when we were taught about nuclear technology," Man-bok, the science student who escaped, told me when I asked him about his course work. "I remember being really impressed that my country had been able to make these advances and become a nuclear power."

Nuclear weapons and missiles have been built into lessons at school, with little children taught to have pride in the programs and older ones taught about the physics involved. An elementary school "socialist ethics" textbook published in 2013 shows a man, a boy, and a picture of an

Unha-3 rocket. "Is it true that you gave joy to the Respected Leader?" the child is asking his father, who appears to be an engineer.

Kim Jong Un has lavished praise and luxuries on scientists of all stripes since he became the state's leader.

"Boundless is Kim Jong Un's loving care for the scientists and technicians, who have played a big role in improving the people's livelihood and beefing up the defense capabilities," state media reported when the Great Successor visited Kim Chaek University of Technology—the MIT of North Korea—in 2013. One of the most surprising images of Kim Jong Un's tenure that did not involve Dennis Rodman came after the ground test for a new rocket engine in March 2017.

The Respected Marshal, in a brown overcoat and with a broad smile, gave a piggyback ride to one of the key men involved in the project. The clearly anguished rocket scientist, who is decades his senior, bounced around on Kim's back as other officers, all decked out in olive-green military uniforms, laughed and cheered.

The act recalled a Korean tradition of symbolic piggybacking. Young men carry their parents on their backs to show how grateful they are. And in Korean wedding ceremonies, the groom hoists his bride on his back to show his strength and that he intends to carry her, if not exactly literally, for the rest of their lives.

So Kim's message was clear: he was showing his unprecedented gratitude and his love for these rocket experts.

When North Korea's state media issued photos of the young emperor inspecting a nuclear device one Sunday morning near the end of his sixth year in power, the reaction from the outside world was to chuckle.

The photographs showed Kim craning over a device with a silver metal casing, a small bulge at one end and a larger bulge at the other. It was immediately nicknamed "the peanut." The internet laughed at the funny dictator looking at the funny bit of kit the size of a large barbecue.

Five nuclear scientists, all dressed in dark Mao suits identical to Kim Jong Un's, pointed out the finer details of the device to the leader. And they all took notes in little notebooks, apparently jotting down the leader's thoughts, although they were nuclear scientists and he was not.

In case there was any doubt about what Kim Jong Un wanted to do with this device, it was positioned behind the nose cone of an intercontinental ballistic missile. Reinforcing the message, there was a chart on the wall behind showing how the warhead would fit into the cone.

It seemed like classic North Korean hyperbole. It was not.

A few hours later, seismic sensors recorded an artificial earthquake in the north of the country with a magnitude of 6.3. It was a thermonuclear blast from a bomb exponentially more powerful than the devices they'd set off before. The waves showed that the device had a yield of as much as 250 kilotons, making it about 17 times the size of the American bomb that destroyed Hiroshima in 1945.

The scientific evidence seemed beyond question. Intelligence agencies and nuclear experts around the world generally conceded that the size of the blast was consistent with a thermonuclear test.

Kim Jong Un made sure to take full credit for this development. A television special showed him signing the authorization for the test. Everyone had to know that these achievements were all his glorious doing. This bomb was his baby. The celebrations continued for more than a week in Pyongyang.

The following weekend, the nuclear team posed for a commemorative photo in front of the Kumsusan Memorial Palace mausoleum, the kind of photo that looks like a joke because there are so many people arranged underneath pictures of the two dead leaders. It's impossible to make anyone out except for the large man in the black Mao suit center front. But that's the point: Kim Jong Un wants to show that a domestically produced nuclear weapon is made through the hard work of very many North Koreans, and that the effort is inextricably intertwined with the vision of the Eternal President and the Dear Leader.

Later, at a huge banquet at a palatial guesthouse in the middle of Pyongyang, cadres pledged with "revolutionary enthusiasm" to defend North Korea "with the strongest nuclear bombs in the world." They vowed their loyalty to Kim Jong Un.

The sequence of celebrations was topped off by a concert in Pyongyang, where a jubilant Kim Jong Un walked into the theater with his wife and his two top nuclear scientists to the resounding applause of the awaiting cadres. The concert included snappy numbers such as "Glory to General Kim Jong Un" and "We Will Go Along the Road of Loyalty." When the young leader's picture was displayed on the huge screen, the audience broke into "enthusiastic applause with excitement," the state media said.

"Our H-bomb with super explosive power is certainly the H-bomb of Kim Jong Un, produced by his ardent love for the country and the people," Ri Man Gon, the director of munitions industries and one of the people most responsible for the nuclear program, said at the concert. It was Ri and the other nuclear scientists who'd done all the work, but they knew to whom they had to give the credit.

Lights shone around the theater, glinting off the medals that covered many of the chests in the crowd. The applause and adoration were guaranteed. Everyone chosen to be in that audience knew what was required of them, but there can be no doubt that it was also partly genuine. After all, it was universally acknowledged that North Korea had achieved a spectacular feat.

Outside, there was widespread shock that a state so primitive in most of its technology and unable to provide basic sustenance and services to its people had made *the bomb* and that it had managed not only to master the technology but also to circumvent the decade of sanctions meant to cut off its ability to get the money or the necessary parts.

Siegfried Hecker, however, was not shocked. North Korea had been telegraphing its intentions every step of the way. The problem is that very few people were taking the regime seriously.

"They have been showing us since the 1980s that they were working on this," he told me shortly after the detonation. Hecker is a renowned nuclear scientist who had been the director of the Los Alamos National Laboratory, the birthplace of the atomic bomb, before moving to Stanford University. But he has also had an unparalleled view of North Korea's nuclear program. When North Korea wanted to show off its achievements, they called Hecker.

When he was invited to North Korea in 2010, while Kim Jong Un was doing his dictator's apprenticeship, Hecker expected to see fifty-year-old technology as he had on previous visits.

Instead, he was taken into a modern uranium enrichment facility, where he saw two thousand current centrifuges all lined up neatly. Hecker was astonished. That's when he realized it: "We are not going to get them to give up the bomb."

The centrifuges that Hecker saw that day were housed in a building with a bright blue roof that was clearly visible from the sky.

Since Kim Jong Un took charge, that blue-roofed building has doubled in size. No one knows exactly how much fissile material the regime has. Some experts say enough for fifteen bombs; US intelligence says perhaps enough for sixty or even seventy. Hecker thinks the Kim regime is producing enough material for six or seven bombs a year—every year.

In many ways, it doesn't matter how much nuclear material North Korea has. One fact is incontrovertible: North Korea now has the bomb. "People are surprised that this backwards country can do this," Hecker told me. "But in this business, they are not backwards."

With the hydrogen bomb test and the concurrent development of the ballistic missile program, Kim Jong Un had made his grandfather's dream an undeniable reality.

From the earliest days of North Korea's existence, Kim Il Sung had been thinking about getting nuclear weapons. His obsession with them stemmed from seeing the devastation that the United States wreaked on Hiroshima and Nagasaki in 1945 and the way two bombs forced imperial Japan's immediate surrender.

Then came the American threat during the Korean War to use nuclear weapons against the North. The warnings had the desired effect—the two sides called the war to an end with an armistice. But the effect on Kim Il Sung's thinking cannot be overstated. The danger that the United States might use its nuclear weapons against the North has been a central principle in the regime's strategic thought and actions ever since.[4]

Kim Il Sung wanted the same weapons. Just a few years after North Korea emerged from the Korean War, Kim Il Sung sent his nuclear scientists to study and receive practical training at the Soviet Union's preeminent Joint Institute for Nuclear Research in Dubna, outside

Moscow. It wasn't long before the North Korean leader saw exactly why he needed his own nuclear capability, illustrated all too alarmingly by the Cuban missile crisis.

In 1962, the Soviet Union and the United States were locked in a thirteen-day standoff over the installation of nuclear-armed Soviet missiles in Cuba, less than one hundred miles from the US coastline. For those two weeks, the world teetered on the edge of nuclear war. But the conflict was resolved diplomatically when Soviet leader Nikita Khrushchev agreed to remove the missiles as long as President John Kennedy agreed not to invade Cuba. A deal was done.

Kim Il Sung viewed this deal as a capitulation by the Soviet Union to the United States, a sign that Moscow was willing to sell out an ally for the sake of its own security. The Great Leader apparently learned from this that North Korea should never entrust its national security to any other government.

This injected new momentum into his drive for nuclear independence. Within a few months, Kim Il Sung's regime had started to explore the possibility of developing a nuclear deterrent of its own. The leader who had espoused a need for a stronger agricultural policy was soon standing before the cadres in Pyongyang to hammer home the importance of putting equal emphasis on economic growth and national defense. This was the first "simultaneous push" policy. The proportion of the national budget devoted to defense rose from only 4.3 percent in 1956 to almost 30 percent within a decade.[5]

The nuclear scientists who returned home from the Soviet Union set about building, about sixty miles northeast of Pyongyang, a similar complex to the one they'd worked at in Dubna. This would eventually become the Yongbyon Nuclear Research Complex.

More impetus came in the early 1970s, when it emerged that North Korea's other main ally, China, had secretly started to forge relations with the United States, an effort that led to President Richard Nixon's historic visit to Beijing in 1972.

Meanwhile, in South Korea, the strongman Park Chung-hee, a general who'd seized the presidency through a military coup, was secretly pursuing nuclear weapons of his own. When this news emerged, it was an unbearable blow to Kim Il Sung's personal vanity and sense of national pride.[6]

Another key factor that must have been weighing on Kim Il Sung's mind was his own mortality. He was in his sixties by this time and was starting to prepare his son to take over. He thought that having nuclear weapons would make it easier for his son to keep a grip on the state. In lieu of charisma, Kim Jong Il should at least have nukes.

In the late 1970s onward, the North Koreans had built more than one hundred nuclear facilities at Yongbyon alone.[7] American intelligence agencies were alarmed. In the space of about six years, a country with no previous experience had built a functioning nuclear reactor. Three years later came unambiguous proof that the reactor's purpose was military, not civilian; the country had built a major reprocessing facility that would enable it to turn the fuel from the reactor into fissile material.[8]

But its efforts were not going unnoticed among allies either. The Soviet Union pressured Kim Il Sung into signing the Nuclear Non-proliferation Treaty at the end of 1985. It took seven years for North Korea to allow in the inspectors required under that treaty, and when they got in, they found numerous signs that the regime was secretly working on the very kind of nuclear program it had pledged against. In 1993, Kim Il Sung threatened to withdraw from the treaty, triggering an alarming standoff. North Korea and the United States came the closest to war in forty years.

Talks to resolve the impasse were ongoing when Kim Il Sung suddenly died in the summer of 1994, propelling both sides into unknown territory. They did, however, manage to sign a landmark nuclear disarmament deal called the Agreed Framework, under which North Korea agreed to freeze and eventually dismantle its nuclear weapons program and a US-led coalition agreed to build two civilian nuclear reactors that could be used to generate electricity for the energy-starved country.

Pyongyang had no intention of abiding by this agreement either. Signing the deal was all about buying the Kim regime time to work on its program while maintaining the appearance of cooperating.

North Korea had developed a close relationship with Pakistani nuclear scientist Abdul Qadeer Khan. In the 1990s, while North Koreans were dying of starvation and while Kim Jong Un was watching Jackie Chan movies in Switzerland, the regime was building a uranium-enrichment program. Uranium enrichment wasn't technically covered under the Agreed Framework. And North Korea loves technicalities.

George W. Bush's administration declared in the summer of 2002 that Pyongyang had a dedicated program, helped in no small part by A. Q. Khan. Thereafter, the Agreed Framework was dead.

As Kim Jong Un was preparing to mark his fifth anniversary in power, an event happened half a world away that would upend North Korea's way of dealing with the United States. Celebrity businessman Donald J. Trump was elected president. Officials in North Korea, as in many other countries, initially struggled to anticipate what this new president's approach would be.

But as Kim Jong Un's weapons program became more and more credible during the first year of Trump's presidency, the new American commander-in-chief used increasingly blunt language. Republican leaders quickly labeled Kim Jong Un a madman. Donald Trump called him a "total nut job." Trump's first ambassador to the United Nations, Nikki Haley, said he was "not a rational person." The Republican senator John McCain called him a "crazy fat kid."

Since his first days in power, Kim Jong Un's state of mind has been the subject of intense speculation.

Many leaders over the centuries have realized that, as Machiavelli also wrote, it can be wise to pretend to be mad. Sometimes leaders want their enemies to think they're crazy as a way to force them into action they would not otherwise take.

President Richard Nixon offered a textbook example of this during the Vietnam War. He even called it his "madman theory" of coercive diplomacy. During the arms race between the Soviet Union and the United States in the 1960s and then through the Cuban missile crisis, the prospect of nuclear action led both sides to exercise restraint in issuing nuclear threats.

"With the prospect of mutually assured destruction, the leaders in Moscow and Washington avoided making explicit threats, exerted tight central control over their nuclear forces, and used direct communications to defuse tensions that could escalate into a military confrontation neither side desired," scholars Scott D. Sagan and Jeremi Suri have written.[9]

Nixon believed his predecessor, President Dwight Eisenhower, had convinced North Korea, China, and the Soviet Union to end the Korean War in 1953 by threatening to use his nukes.

In 1969, Nixon was unable to win domestic support for his preferred option of launching a massive bombing campaign against the North Vietnamese. So Tricky Dick wanted to use Eisenhower's tactics. He was going to pretend to do what he knew he couldn't do. He would send a secret nuclear signal to try to convince the Soviets that he was going to launch a major bombing attack, perhaps even a nuclear attack, against North Vietnam.

"I call it the Madman Theory," he told his chief of staff. "I want the North Vietnamese to believe that I've reached the point that I might do anything to stop the war. We'll just slip the word to them that 'for God's sake, you know Nixon is obsessed about Communism. We can't restrain him when he is angry—and he has his hand on the nuclear button'—and Ho Chi Minh himself will be in Paris in two days begging for peace."[10]

During 2017, many wondered who was playing the madman in the war of words between Trump and Kim. Some said Trump was trying to convince the North Koreans he was volatile enough to do what presidents before him had not—even if it meant sacrificing Seoul. Yet all the while, Trump was accusing Kim Jong Un of being the crazy one.

The North Korean leader was a "maniac" and "obviously a madman" who "doesn't mind starving or killing his people," Trump said in 2017. (For what it's worth, North Korea fired back by calling Trump an "old lunatic.")

The American president's remarks might make ideal soundbites for cable news, but are they actually true? Does a person have to be clinically insane, a verifiable psychopath, to be so cruel to his own people? Can a person succeed against the odds if he doesn't have all his mental faculties?

These are questions that occupy psychological profilers in spy services around the world.

For decades, the CIA has been trying to build profiles of world leaders to figure out what makes them tick and to predict how they might act, especially during negotiations and crises.

As far back as 1943, the Office of Strategic Services, the precursor to the CIA, was trying to figure out Adolf Hitler's psychology and personality using "psycho-biographical techniques." Since the 1970s, the CIA has built profiles of world leaders to assess their political behavior, their cognitive styles, and their decision-making processes. But it also looks at the culture in which the leader operates to assess what other factors might have an influence.[11]

Contrary to Trump's assertions, American intelligence analysts described Kim Jong Un as a "rational actor" who is operating in accordance with fulfilling his one goal in life: staying in power.

"There's a clarity of purpose in what Kim Jong Un has done," Yong Suk Lee, a top official in the CIA's Korea Mission Center, said in rare public remarks in 2017, as the young leader was firing a barrage of increasingly high-tech missiles. Kim Jong Un is not going to wake up one morning and decide to nuke Los Angeles, because he knows that this would lead the United States to reciprocate. "He wants to rule for a long time and die peacefully in his own bed," Lee said.

In fact, it would be mad for Kim Jong Un not to pursue nuclear weapons. For a small country with few resources and a constant fear of being annihilated by the United States, North Korea gets a lot of firepower by investing in nuclear and missile technology. Even Kim Jong Un knew his conventional weaponry was no match for American military might, but the prospect of mutually assured destruction, which had worked so well during the Cold War, could help him stave off any US attack.

But in the White House, Kim Jong Un's actions were depicted as those of a certifiable madman.

After the intercontinental ballistic missile launches of July 2017, the American president threatened to rain down "fire and fury like the world has never seen" on North Korea. The US military was "locked and loaded," he said. After the nuclear test in September, Trump took the podium at the UN General Assembly and said that he would "totally destroy North Korea" if necessary to defend the United States. Although this had been the United States' policy for decades, no president had ever said it quite as bluntly as Trump.

At the same time, the American president mocked his adversary as "Little Rocket Man." "Rocket Man is on a suicide mission for himself," Trump declared to a stunned UN audience.

Kim Jong Un was not deterred. In fact, he was emboldened. "I will surely and definitely tame the mentally deranged US dotard with fire," he said about Trump, sending people the world over scrambling for their dictionaries. The statement was not just the normal North Korean bluster—this time the threat was attributed directly to Kim Jong Un himself, an extremely rare event that underlined the gravity of the situation.

This was a primitive alpha male contest like no other.

Trump's threats helped Kim bolster his claim that he was protecting the North Korean people from the evil Americans. This state was founded on the premise that the United States was a hostile power out to destroy it. Trump's words seemed to confirm that.

Coincidentally, the American and South Korean militaries were starting their huge annual drills. Amphibious craft began practicing beach landings, while fighter jets dropped bombs on a training range in South Korea, just a few dozen miles from the border with the North.

White House national security advisor H. R. McMaster was threatening "preventive war" if the North Koreans continued to rapidly accelerate their nuclear weapons program. He defined that as "a war that would prevent North Korea from threatening the United States with a nuclear weapon."

McMaster spoke in language that recalled the lead-up to the invasion of Iraq. "I think it's impossible to overstate the danger associated with a rogue, brutal regime, [a man] who murdered his own brother with nerve agent in an airport," he said.[12]

The South Korean and American militaries began actively practicing conducting "decapitation strikes" on the North Korean leadership. South Korea set up a dedicated "decapitation unit" of elite soldiers called Spartan 3000. During that tense period, Kim Jong Un often changed his itinerary at the last moment to keep people guessing, according to South Korea's intelligence agency.

In response, North Korea threatened to "envelop" the American territory of Guam with missiles to "tame the Americans with fire." It also threatened to "take our hand closer to the 'trigger' for taking the toughest countermeasure," a North Korean official declared, hinting at a nuclear strike.

There was a very palpable concern in northeast Asia—and in parts of Washington, DC, too—of a real prospect of conflict with North Korea.

Japan held drills to prepare for incoming missiles for the first time since World War II. South Koreans worried about the unpredictable and inflammatory new American president. In Hawaii, authorities reactivated a network of sirens dating back to the Cold War.

In Washington, even cautious analysts were putting the chances of conflict at higher than 50 percent.

This fear was only heightened when McMaster and other Trump administration officials suggested that deterrence—the bedrock of American nuclear policy throughout the Cold War—could no longer work with North Korea.

Instead, Trump launched a campaign of "maximum pressure" on North Korea, pushing for even tougher sanctions.

Whereas sanctions had previously targeted industries and money flows linked to the nuclear and missile programs, they now began to look like a trade embargo. Seafood, coal, and garment exports were banned. The sanctions were accompanied by a travel ban that required every American citizen to get special permission to travel to North Korea—and humanitarian workers found that their reasons for visiting were not accepted by the State Department. The Global Fund, a multilateral global health agency, suspended funding for malaria and tuberculosis projects in North Korea, leading doctors to warn of a major public health and humanitarian crisis that could take decades to reverse.

The US State Department estimated that the sanctions had blocked more than 90 percent of North Korea's exports, not including labor, which, for good measure, was also banned. In total, the sanctions were estimated to cut North Korea's hard currency earnings by one-third—or by $1 billion.

That was a huge number, but the game-changing actions were happening on North Korea's border. China enforced the sanctions like never before.

Previously, Beijing had done the bare minimum, fearing the collapse of North Korea much more than any rogue missile. But now, it seemed like Trump might be serious about conducting strikes on the North, and Beijing found the prospect of war much more alarming than the prospect of instability.

Beijing cut off trade. The seafood and the coal stopped arriving in China. Many of the thousands of North Korean laborers working in China were sent back. A palpable chill settled over Dandong, the commercial gateway to North Korea. I got kicked out of a North Korean restaurant in Dandong at 7:30 p.m., barely having finished my last mouthful of dinner. In this kind of environment, everything was being closed down.

China needed to show the United States that it was taking action with sanctions to make sure that Washington did not take military action. Stability was better than instability, but instability was better than an invasion.

Experts also openly worried about miscalculation leading to war, that one side might misread the delicate dance of signals and maneuverings that had been carefully choreographed between them over the years and react impulsively. After all, the leaders of the two countries had only seven years of political experience between them. Six of them were on Kim Jong Un's side.

The chances for misunderstanding seemed to grow greater by the day.

There was talk about the Trump administration hatching a plan to give Kim Jong Un a "bloody nose." The idea was to conduct a limited, surgical strike on a North Korean nuclear site or missile facility and, in doing so, force the young leader to think twice about his provocative actions and return to talks about getting rid of his nuclear program.

The regime in Pyongyang didn't know what to make of this new American president. Was he doing a Nixon and playing a madman? Or was he serious?

North Korean officials began asking former American officials to decipher Trump's tweets for them. They read *The Art of the Deal*. They read *Fire and Fury*, an explosive book about the chaos inside the White House. They asked about the United States' nuclear attack protocol. They asked if Trump really had the sole authority to push the nuclear button.

Kim Jong Un's regime was taking the challenge from Trump extremely seriously. Officials began asking foreign diplomats and other intermediaries what they thought would happen if North Korea did go ahead and lob a missile near—or even onto—Guam. How would Trump react? They didn't quite know where the red line was.

Meanwhile, posters went up throughout Pyongyang showing a North Korean missile targeting the US Capitol building and an American flag, entitled "North Korea's Response."

As 2017 turned into 2018, with two historic antagonists led by two bold and relatively inexperienced leaders who liked to boast about their nuclear buttons, the fragile peace on the Korean Peninsula seemed to be holding by a thread.

CHAPTER 15

THE CHARM OFFENSIVE

"We will open our doors to anyone from South Korea . . . for dialogue, contact and travel, if they sincerely wish national concord and unity."

—Kim Jong Un, January 1, 2018

KIM JONG UN HAD DONE ALL THE THINGS HE NEEDED TO DO TO consolidate his rule. He had obtained a credible nuclear deterrent. He had dispatched with rivals, real or imagined. He had created a group of people who had a strong interest in keeping him in power.

Now it was time for the cruel, threatening, nuclear-armed tyrant to begin his metamorphosis into misunderstood, gracious, developmental dictator. In phase two, Kim Jong Un would seek to shore up his rule by improving relations with the outside world.

To start this process, he unleashed his secret weapon: his younger sister, Kim Yo Jong. She would attend the opening of the Winter Olympics in South Korea at the beginning of 2018, marking the first time since the Korean War that a member of the ruling Kim family had gone south.

It was a masterful decision from Kim Jong Un's perspective. His younger sister has the same incentive as he does to ensure that the regime remains in power—she also wants to keep the family at the helm—but she doesn't have his cartoonish qualities. In fact, she was almost entirely silent during the three-day trip south.

Kim Yo Jong arrived in South Korea on February 9, 2018, the day that the Olympics was scheduled to open, wearing a Mona Lisa–type smile. South Korean television stations broadcast live coverage of her brother's jet, Air Force Un, landing at Incheon airport outside Seoul. The North Koreans appreciate the power of symbolism. When Kim Jong Un's jet arrived in the South with his sister onboard, it carried the flight number 615. The South Korean government took this as a sign of good intent. The first inter-Korean summit, held in 2000, had concluded on June 15, or 6/15.

TV crews followed in a throng as the North Korean princess— together with the ninety-year-old Kim Yong Nam, the senior official who was technically the head of the delegation—came off the plane and glided into a VIP room to be welcomed by senior South Korean officials.

From that moment on, the First Sister was an object of fascination among the South Korean public. She was demure and discreet. She wore plain black outfits and minimal jewelry and drew her hair back in a no-nonsense style. Young South Koreans, used to seeing their celebrities laden with bling and enhanced with plastic surgery, were surprised at how understated this princess was.

She was so "humble," the papers noted after she gestured to Kim Yong Nam to sit first, in line with Confucian hierarchical rules, even though she's North Korean royalty. "Look at her posture," the commentators observed. She sat so upright—maybe she'd been a dancer like her mother. Kim Jong Un could hardly have created a more mysteriously alluring goodwill ambassador for a country that has no goodwill.

Kim Yo Jong cheered on the joint Korean team at the opening ceremony of the Olympics, where American vice president Mike Pence pointedly ignored her, making him look petty. She stood for the South Korean national anthem, an act that is a political crime in North Korea. She cheered on a combined North-South Korea hockey team at a game the next night.

At that game, I snuck down from my seat in the press section above where the VIPs were sitting so that I could get a better look at her. She seemed a picture of decorum, in stark contrast to the image of her brother. She smiled politely and made chitchat when spoken to but otherwise remained an enigma.

The next day, she went to South Korea's presidential Blue House to deliver a message from her brother. The last time North Koreans had gotten close to the Blue House was in 1968 when a group of commandos tried unsuccessfully to assassinate the South Korean president.

This time, they came through the front door, arriving in a government-provided luxury Hyundai Genesis car. Kim Yo Jong wore a pin of her father and grandfather over her heart, and she was carrying a blue folder that contained an invitation: Would the South Korean president, Moon Jae-in, like to meet with her brother?

Just eight months before, Moon had been elected president after his hard-line conservative predecessor suffered a shocking fall from grace that landed her in prison, potentially for the rest of her life. Moon was the polar opposite in terms of temperament and policy. While his predecessor had been trying to strangle North Korea with sanctions, Moon wanted to engage. He had taken office pledging to talk to the North Koreans to try to broker an end to the tense standoff that has paralyzed the peninsula. Kim Jong Un realized that an opportunity had presented itself, and he sent his sister to capitalize on it.

The signs had been there for a couple of months. On November 29, when the Kim regime conducted another intercontinental ballistic missile launch, it indicated it was ready to talk. "We have now completed our rocket program," it said. That was the signal. Having amassed its bargaining chips, North Korea was now ready to play.

This became clear on New Year's Day, when Kim Jong Un stood up to give his annual address to the people, the North Korean equivalent of the American president's State of the Union.

"We should work together to ease the acute military tension between the North and the South and create a peaceful environment on the Korean Peninsula," he said, urging South Korea to "respond positively to our sincere efforts for a détente."

Complicating matters was the fact that Kim had also used the speech to declare that North Korea would begin "mass production" of nuclear weapons and missiles in the year ahead. But for Kim, there was no contradiction: his messages were for different audiences, and they could point in different directions.

Moon chose to ignore the nuclear bombast. He was poised for talks; his team had been secretly meeting with North Korean officials for several months, including on the sidelines of soccer matches in China, to lay the groundwork for North Korea attending the Olympics.

Just as ping-pong diplomacy between China and the United States in the 1970s paved the way for a normalization of relations between those two adversaries, sports were now being used to provide an apolitical way into highly political talks.

South Korea had dubbed the Olympics the "Peace Games," a nod to the roots of the games in ancient Greece but a clear encouragement to the northern regime, especially since the venue stood in a province that straddles the border between North and South Korea. Athletes from the two sides marched into the opening ceremony together, wearing uniforms that said simply "Korea" and waving flags that showed a unified peninsula.

To make the symbolism even more perfect, the International Olympic Committee was led by Thomas Bach, a former Olympic fencer from the once-divided, now-united country of Germany. During the opening ceremony, he heralded the cooperation of the two Koreas as a great example of the unifying power of the games.

"I hope Pyongyang and Seoul will become closer in the hearts of Koreans and will bring unification and prosperity in the near future," Kim Yo Jong wrote in the guest book at South Korea's presidential Blue House. The seduction continued.

Although she said nothing in public, in private Kim Yo Jong struck her hosts as refreshing and frank. "I never expected to come here on such short notice to be honest, and I thought it would be strange and different but it's not," she said when asked to make some remarks at a private farewell dinner. "There are many things similar and the same. I hope we can quickly become one and meet these good people again in Pyongyang."

The First Sister mesmerized the South Korean press, who called her "the Ivanka Trump of North Korea." She was the approachable, moderate face of an oft-pilloried, immoderate male relative. Furthermore, just as Kim Jong Un had sent his sister to the opening ceremony of the Olympic Games, President Trump was sending his daughter to the closing.

But the North Koreans made sure to give only what they wanted to give during this trip, both in terms of politics and intelligence. Kim Yo Jong had stayed in the presidential suite of a five-star hotel, but she had brought her own cot to sleep on. When she checked out, her room was left spotlessly clean. She left behind not a single fingerprint, not a single strand of hair. South Korean intelligence would not be getting any Kim family DNA.

As one of the few people who Kim Jong Un trusts, Kim Yo Jong has come to play a crucial role in her brother's regime, acting as a kind of chief of staff, protocol officer, and executive assistant all in one. She is his right-hand woman and gatekeeper.

In this way, the siblings are following the example set by their father. Kim Jong Il was very close to his younger sister, Kim Kyong Hui, the one who married Uncle Jang. He adored her, one family member would later say.[1] After he sent his half brother into exile, she was really the only family he had. She played a crucial advisory role to her brother and held important positions within the Workers' Party right up to her disappearance at the time her husband was executed by Kim Jong Un.

The two women were seen together at Kim Jong Un's equestrian center at the end of 2012, both of them wearing brown jackets and riding white horses. Kim Kyong Hui appeared to be grooming her niece for the role of First Sister, just as Kim Jong Il had groomed his son.

Kim Yo Jong is several years younger than her brother; exactly how many years is anyone's guess. The South Korean intelligence service says she was born in 1988; the US government thinks it was 1989. When she joined her older siblings in Bern, registered as Pak Mi Hyang, her birthdate was declared as April 28, 1991. That seems too late and may have been changed to get her into a younger class in Switzerland as she learned a new language.

A photo from this time shows a girl of about eight or nine with a bright smile and chubby cheeks that are a stark contrast to her angled face of today. She is wearing a choker necklace, the kind that was fashionable in the late 1990s, and a red dress. Like her mother, she loved to dance.

She led a cloistered life, growing up in the royal palaces of North Korea. Her father called her "sweet, sweet Yo Jong" and "Princess Yo Jong" and thought she was quick-witted and possessed good leadership skills. Kim Jong Il identified both Kim Jong Un and Kim Yo Jong as having an aptitude for political life.[2]

She was also sent to Switzerland to join her brothers in Bern. She stayed there until late 2000, having completed the American equivalent of sixth grade. She is thought to have finished her schooling with a private tutor and then to have studied at Kim Il Sung University.

We didn't see her again until it was time for her brother to take the reins. She appears in the grainy family photo taken under the tree in Wonsan in 2009, and she was at the same Workers' Party conference in 2010 where her brother emerged as their father's successor. She stood alongside Kim Jong Il's fifth "wife," who worked in the leader's personal secretariat. This suggested that the First Sister was working in the secretariat too.

Then she was seen at her father's funeral, a gaunt figure in a black dress, her face down as she walked behind her brother toward their father's body. But so little was known about her that no one was sure who she was, leading to the speculation that she might be Kim Jong Un's wife. At that stage, no one knew about First Lady Ri Sol Ju.

From the earliest days of her brother's leadership, Kim Yo Jong has been there, supporting him.

While the glamorous Ri Sol Ju is at Kim Jong Un's side to make him appear a more modern leader and convey a sense of aspiration, Kim Yo Jong is working. The first lady may swan about in bright outfits and clutch her husband's arm, but the First Sister is usually seen in the background, making sure everything goes smoothly.

She could be seen popping out from behind a pillar on a balcony overlooking a huge military ceremony in Pyongyang in 2017, bringing documents to her brother that were apparently related to the spectacle taking place in the square and sky in front of them. At the opening of a flagship residential district in the capital, she was there on the stage, making sure that the photographers were in place and everything was ready before her brother arrived. She's often checking her phone.

She has accompanied Kim Jong Un to on-the-spot guidance visits at military sites, factories, and museums. She often has a smile on her face and a notebook in her hand, like the other cadres. She is always dressed like a functionary.

She has been elevated up the Workers' Party ranks since her brother took over.

Toward the end of 2014, Kim Yo Jong was made vice director of the Workers' Party's Propaganda and Agitation Department. The department controls all the media in North Korea, deciding what airs on television and over the radio waves, which stories appear in the newspapers, and which books are fit for publication. It is the guardian of the personality cult.

Within the department, she controls Documentary #5 Office, the propaganda unit that produces reports and photos about the Supreme Leader's activities that are then used in state media. Her father undertook the same role for his father.[3]

Kim Yo Jong's title in the propaganda department is somewhat misleading. She is no deputy. She was put in that position to ensure that her brother, like their grandfather, comes across as a benevolent leader to be adored. She took over from an eighty-nine-year-old who had been such a key figure in the regime that he had walked alongside the hearse during Kim Jong Il's funeral, a man who suddenly disappeared in mid-2016. But the First Sister was suddenly everywhere.

In 2016, she was made a member of the Central Committee of the Workers' Party. The next year, she became an alternate member of the Worker's Party politburo, taking her aunt's position there. The photo of the new politburo shows Kim Jong Un at the center, flanked by dozens of men old enough to collect their pensions and one waiflike woman in her twenties.

She's never been revealed as the leader's sister, but it doesn't take a genius to figure it out. Even among the North Korean elite, there's no clear path for a young woman to rise so rapidly up the ranks of power. Plus, Korean naming conventions—they both have a "Jong" in their given names—suggest that she's closely related to Kim Jong Il and Kim Jong Un.

She became prominent enough to earn herself a place on American sanctions lists. In 2017, she was accused of human rights abuses because of her role in enforcing a system of rigid censorship in North Korea. Being on the list blocks American citizens from doing business with her, and her assets were frozen in the United States—a symbolic designation since she doesn't do business with or own anything in that country. But it underlines her role at the center of the regime.

It made no difference to her. She continued to gain influence in North Korea and make her way up the communist hierarchy, just like Kim Jong Il's sister before her.

There is no obvious heir to Kim Jong Un. If he has a son, he is still a very young child. That has led to speculation that he might be grooming his sister to take over in case anything should happen to him.

One day, I met a South Korean expert on North Korea's leadership and asked him if Kim Yo Jong could be in line to succeed her brother. He looked at me like I was crazy. "She can't be leader. She's a female," he responded. He politely left off the "duh!"[4]

He has a point. It would be exceptional in highly chauvinist North Korea for a woman to play anything other than a supporting role. Most likely, a man in the family would take over. Maybe their unseen-in-North-Korea brother, Kim Jong Chol. Kim Yo Jong would turn her formidable skills to promoting him as the rightful heir to the family dynasty while continuing to pull the strings from behind the scenes.

The First Sister also appears to have been working on creating the next generation of Paektu offspring. She has been seen with a band on her wedding ring finger and is reportedly married to the son of Choe Ryong Hae, her brother's chief lieutenant. Her husband is said to work in Office 39, the Workers' Party unit that raises money for the leader's slush fund.

When Kim Yo Jong visited South Korea for the Olympics, some noticed that she had a slight belly on an otherwise slender frame and wondered if she might be pregnant. Southern officials later disclosed that she'd given birth a few months earlier.

The First Sister's visit to the South triggered a frenzy of contacts between the two Koreas. Officials started laying the groundwork for a summit that would take place in Panmunjom, the truce village in the middle of the DMZ, within two months.

But first, there was some very surprising soft power. A huge South Korean artistic troupe went to Pyongyang to perform for Kim and his cadres in a concert called "Spring Is Coming."

The troupe included a whole raft of singers whose music was officially banned in the North, including K-pop stars like Red Velvet, a girl group whose members sport dyed hair and revealing outfits. They sang hits including "Bad Boy" in the presence of the ultimate Korean bad boy. "Every time I come around, another bad boy down. Got 'em like ooh ooh," they sang, their choreography less provocative than usual.

Kim and his wife, a former member of North Korea's answer to these manufactured K-pop groups, clapped throughout, and the final standing ovation lasted ten full minutes. It was like nothing the North Korean elite had ever seen before—at least, not officially.

South Korean musicians had previously performed in North Korea but never in the presence of a leader. This was all part of the Great Successor's effort to look like a more modern ruler. He even adjusted his schedule so he could make it to the first concert and see Red Velvet, he told the singers, thanking them for their "kind gift" to Pyongyang's citizens. But the group's toned-down performance was apparently still too risqué for general consumption. They were cut from the footage of the concert shown on North Korean state television.

Still, Kim met with them afterward and even posed, with his wife, for a photo with all the performers: the South Koreans with blond hair, women with short shorts and over-the-knee boots, the YB rockers in their white suits, and Kim in the middle in his Mao outfit.

This photo appeared on the front of the *Rodong Sinmun*, a staggering move for the main state newspaper. South Korean music was banned in North Korea; being caught with it was a political offense that could have serious consequences. Yet here were these southern infidels with their questionable morality posing with the man who enforced the ban.

North Korea didn't acknowledge any contradiction. "Our dear leader comrade said his heart swelled" while he was listening to the performance, the state media reported, adding that he was happy to see his people develop a deeper understanding of South Korean pop culture.

Kim Jong Un was very friendly in person, said Choi Jin-hee, a South Korean singer in her sixties, who met him after the concert. "Of course I know that he killed his uncle and did all those terrible things, but he was very eloquent and gave a good impression," she told me when I went to visit her afterward.

Choi is famous for the hit song "The Maze of Love," said to be a favorite of Kim Jong Il. She thought that would be an obvious number for her to perform in Pyongyang, but once she arrived, she was asked to sing "Belated Regret," a South Korean ballad from 1985 that she had never performed before. She was puzzled, but it transpired that the leader himself had asked for the song.

"Kim Jong Un actually approached me and told me that he really appreciated me singing the song," Choi said. "I got the backstory from the North Korean singers later. Apparently when his mother was sick with cancer, she used to listen to 'Belated Regret' a lot."

Kim Jong Un had not traveled outside the country during his first six years in power. He'd been busy at home.

Now, with his sister having made the arrangements, he was ready to portray himself as a responsible and respected global leader. During this transformation, he showed himself to be a crafty tactician capable of moving the pieces around the chessboard of international diplomacy.

He had invited the South Korean president to a summit. But he proved himself to be clever in getting the South Koreans to act as intermediaries in setting up a summit between himself and Donald Trump. The South Koreans had an incentive like never before to make this work.

At the beginning of March 2018, less than a month after the Olympics opened and Kim Yo Jong delivered the first invitation, the South Korean president's envoys traveled to Washington for meetings at the White House. They thought they would talk with officials first and perhaps meet Trump the following day.

Instead, Trump walked into the first meeting, surprising the South Korean delegation, and then, surprising them again, instantly agreed to the summit with Kim Jong Un. In fact, he wanted to hold the meeting at once.

The South Koreans were flabbergasted. They asked, Shouldn't the South Korean president meet him first and find out what he wants? Trump reluctantly saw the sense in what they were saying.

Trump's national security staff asked him to delay the announcement. He gave them an hour or so. They scurried to call the Japanese prime minister's office and warn the conservative ally about what was coming. Then the South Korean envoys walked out into the West Wing driveway and announced the summit. From a diplomatic perspective, it was highly irregular: a foreign government had just made an announcement on behalf of the American president.

Somehow, Kim Jong Un, who had been an international pariah up until then, had managed to set off a competition among leaders to be the first to meet him, for it wasn't just Trump who wanted to make history.

In Beijing, President Xi Jinping was watching. The Chinese leader had made it clear that he had no time for the young punk next door. Bucking seventy years of history in which China and North Korea were supposedly "as close as lips and teeth," Xi and Kim had not met even once in the almost five years they'd both been in power.

Kim Jong Un had never made the ritual trip to pay homage to the great Communist benefactor and protector across the border. And Xi Jinping, who rose to the presidency at the start of 2013, showed no interest in engaging with him. After all, the very same year that Xi took over, Kim Jong Un had executed the North Korean who was arguably the closest to China, Uncle Jang.

China was not impressed by Kim Jong Un's restless pursuit of nuclear weapons and missiles. When North Korea fired three medium-range ballistic missiles on the very day that Xi was hosting leaders of the world's twenty largest economies in the eastern city of Hangzhou, the Chinese were clearly angry. Another salvo the following year ruined Xi's opening of the Belt and Road Forum, a huge spectacle that was meant to be

China's answer to Davos. The brash North Korean had embarrassed the Chinese president.

These provocative moves showed jaw-dropping audacity from the young North Korean leader. It was one thing to refuse to kowtow to the president next door but an entirely different matter to actively try to humiliate him.

But the events of early 2018 changed the calculus: suddenly Xi had an urgent interest in talking with Kim. Or, rather, he didn't want to be the only one not talking to him.

So for the first stop in his coming-out parade, Kim Jong Un and Ri Sol Ju boarded the leader's special train, with its stuffed pink armchairs, bound for Beijing. Kim was going to personally give Xi an update on the recent developments, Chinese state media reported.

This leader who'd been shunned by Xi for so long was given a red-carpet welcome—literally. There was a red carpet on the platform at Beijing Station. Later, Xi and Kim walked along the red carpets, inspecting a military guard, and posed for happy photos. Xi's wife, Peng Liyuan, is a famous opera singer in China, so the women added a heavy dose of glamor to the events.

Dinner was a jolly affair. Black-and-white footage of the good old days was played across large screens. There was Kim Jong Un's grandfather meeting Mao Zedong and hugging Deng Xiaoping and Jiang Zemin. There was Kim Jong Il hugging Jiang and his successor, Hu Jintao, three times in the socialist tradition.

Then at the end, Xi and Peng, holding hands, waved and smiled as the young couple departed in a black car. It was like newlyweds leaving their first Thanksgiving with the groom's parents.

It was a startling sign of both sides' recognition that they had much to gain from being close and harmonious friends. Kim Jong Un knew he needed the man who was still, despite their strained relations, his closest ally.

And now that Kim Jong Un had started talking, China didn't need to worry about the "maximum pressure" campaign anymore. The specter of war on the Korean Peninsula had subsided, so Xi Jinping could revert to his usual concern: ensuring there was stability in North Korea. North

Korean seafood began returning to the markets in Chinese border cities, and North Korean workers began venturing back out to factories. The international sanctions, while still technically in place, no longer needed to be fully enforced. Xi didn't need to stave off an invasion anymore.

When Kim Jong Un got home, North Korean state television aired extensive coverage of the visit. It transpired that the young leader had arranged for every moment of his trip to be filmed. There were even cameras installed overlooking the bridge between China and North Korea to film Kim Jong Un's train rolling across.

The Great Successor wanted his subjects to see every second of it. He wanted them to see the two leaders standing literally shoulder to shoulder in front of Chinese and North Korean flags, their glamorous wives at their sides, Kim Jong Un and Xi Jinping looking like equals.

A month later, Kim Jong Un waddled up to the concrete curb that marked the dividing line between the estranged Koreas for sixty-five years. South Korean president Moon Jae-in, whose parents were evacuated from North Korea during the same war, was waiting on the southern side of the Joint Security Area, the part of the DMZ where the armistice agreement that ended the war was signed in 1953.

Kim Jong Un approached, his arm outstretched to shake hands with the smiling Moon for an inordinately long time while the cameras caught the historic moment.

Then the young North Korean showed who was in control. After crossing the line to the southern side and posing for more photos, he invited the South Korean leader to cross back into the North with him. Moon accepted, and, holding hands, the two men stood in what is technically North Korea. The South Korean reporters gasped. Kim Jong Un was writing this script.

April 27, 2018, proved to be an extraordinary day that produced an agreement under which the two leaders pledged to work toward formally ending the war and improving relations. They also declared that the Korean Peninsula should be nuclear-free. This was treated in parts of Washington—specifically the White House—as though Kim Jong Un was laying the groundwork to give up his nuclear weapons. "Good things are happening," Trump tweeted when he woke up to read the summit news.

In fact, the wording of "Korean Peninsula" hinted at potential problems. North Korea has long insisted that the United States remove its nuclear capability from the southern half of the Korean peninsula as part of any deal. Although the United States removed nuclear weapons stationed in South Korea as part of a deal in 1991, it regularly sends nuclear-capable strategic jets and ships to the south. For the United States and its military alliance with South Korea, this had always been non-negotiable.

That day in April, I watched disbelieving as Kim and Moon strolled along a boardwalk in the DMZ specially built for the occasion. For half an hour, on park benches in the sunshine, they talked one on one about topics ranging from the United States, the United Nations, and North Korea's nuclear program to Donald Trump personally, according to lip readers who analyzed the footage. Moon appeared to be explaining how the American president would approach his own meeting with Kim.[5]

This was the first of three meetings that would take place between the two leaders over the next few months. The second was a hastily arranged gathering when it looked like the planned summit between Kim Jong Un and Donald Trump was going off the rails, and the third was when Moon made the return visit to North Korea.

The diplomacy produced some astounding outcomes. Kim Jong Un allowed the South Korean president—a man who held a position that North Korea considers entirely illegitimate since the Kims are supposed to be the only legitimate leaders of Korea—to stand in a stadium in front of 150,000 North Koreans and deliver a heartfelt speech. By the end of 2018, the two sides had started pulling down guard posts in the DMZ.

Kim also ordered the shuttering of North Korea's nuclear test site under a mountain in the north of the country. He didn't need it anymore—he'd achieved the technical capability he wanted, and the mountain was severely weakened anyway—but it was a spectacular way of making it look like he was giving up his nuclear program without actually giving up any weapons. Explosives were detonated in the portals to the test site, and the footage was broadcast around the world. It was a classic North Korean move: Kim Jong Un looked like he was ceding something, but it was just—in this case, literally—a smokescreen.

The staged encounters with Moon may have been relatively superficial, but they still offered a treasure trove of information. Each rendezvous offered glimpses into how Kim Jong Un operated.

The North Korean leader, more used to issuing incendiary threats and weapons of mass destruction, showed himself to be capable of acting like an international statesman, being affable and even self-deprecating.

When Thomas Bach, the German who was president of the International Olympic Committee, went to North Korea in March of 2018, Kim Jong Un took him to a soccer game afterward at Pyongyang's huge May Day Stadium.

During the match, Kim repeatedly talked about the importance of sport in the North Korean education system and for the general well-being of the population. Sport was a priority, the leader said.

The irony of a clearly obese person talking about the importance of sport was not lost on Kim Jong Un, and he showed a surprising ability to joke about himself. Such a joke would be treasonous if made by anyone else in North Korea.

It may not look like it, he more or less told Bach, but I love sport, and I used to play a lot of basketball. Much laughter ensued.

Indeed, the meetings offered unfiltered insights into what may be Kim Jong Un's biggest risk factor: his health. The young leader looks like a heart attack waiting to happen and has clearly had health problems. That period at the end of 2014 was an early indication. He was still thirty when he disappeared for six weeks, apparently the consequence of severe gout, and returned with a walking stick.

Four years later, when the two Korean leaders shoveled dirt onto the base of a pine tree during their first meeting, the sixty-five-year-old South Korean president did it with ease. The thirty-four-year-old North Korean, however, could be seen huffing and puffing. His face was red after the smallest exertion. At an earlier meeting, Kim Jong Un's wife told the southern envoys that she couldn't get him to give up smoking.

Then, when they all went to Mount Paektu together in September, Kim Jong Un was panting heavily. He observed that Moon didn't seem out of breath at all. Not for a walk as easy as this, responded the South Korean, who loves to hike.

The North Koreans guard details of the leader's health closely. For all his meetings outside North Korea—including in Singapore—they travel with a special portable toilet for him to use so that he won't leave any samples from which health information could be extracted.

But with all these meetings, there was plenty of uncensored footage of Kim Jong Un out and about, and medical experts were able to draw certain conclusions from it.

First, they classified him as severely obese. Kim Jong Un is five feet, seven inches tall, and his weight is estimated to be about three hundred pounds. That means he has an extremely high body mass index of 45 or 46.

It affects the way he walks—with his toes and arms out. Doctors speculated that he snores heavily. In poring over the footage of Kim, they had even counted his breaths. He'd exhaled thirty-five times on a forty-two-second walk with Moon during the first summit. Either he was very nervous, or his lung capacity was reduced from lack of exercise.

They noted that there seemed to be something wrong with his right ankle—consistent with the reports from 2014, although not proof that it was the result of excessive cheese consumption—and that he could be wearing a brace.

They speculated that the Great Successor was binge eating as a result of the stress of the job and opined that his health prospectus was dire. "Generally, such obesity, coupled with smoking, will reduce one's life expectancy by 10 to 20 years," said Professor Huh Yun-seok of Inha University Hospital, postulating that the young leader already had diabetes.

His "waddling" was also an indication of a weak physical state. Another doctor noted that a severely obese person is four times as likely to develop arthritis.

It wasn't just the Great Successor who was in poor shape. He knew his country was too.

Kim Jong Un was surprisingly frank during his meetings with the South Korean president about shortcomings in the supposed People's Paradise north of the DMZ. He warned his southern counterpart that when he came North, he'd find the transportation system "deficient and uncomfortable" compared to the South's high-speed rail.

He capped off the day by speaking live to the world for the first time. He stood in front of a podium next to an elected head of state and read a statement to reporters just like a regular leader.

His wife also knew how to play the part. At the dinner that night, the South Koreans brought in a magician to break the ice. But it was the North Korean first lady who got everyone laughing first. "Am I going to disappear?" Ri Sol Ju asked jokingly, immediately lightening the atmosphere.

The magician went around the room, collecting money from attendees and turning big bills into small ones. Then he turned a ten-dollar note into a hundred-dollar note, which he handed to Moon. The two leaders laughed uproariously, Moon holding up a Benjamin and an ebullient Kim waving his hand in the air. Someone yelled out, "No more exports necessary from North Korea. You can create money just like that with magic!"

They drank plentifully. The South Koreans had laid out a super-premium brand of soju, alcohol content 40 percent, and Kim Jong Un did not once refuse an offer of the liquor during the almost three-hour-long dinner banquet.[6]

After the dinner was over, North Korean staff swept through and collected all the glasses and cutlery that Kim Jong Un and his sister had used at the meetings, washing them forensically clean.

Throughout these encounters, Kim Jong Un had proved he could crack a joke, that he could turn on the charm, and that he could stroke a rival president's ego. In every respect, he proved that he was no madman but a calculating leader with a strategy that was proceeding according to plan.

With the dress rehearsal complete, Kim was ready for the main event.

CHAPTER 16

TALKING WITH THE "JACKALS"

"The meeting of the century, pioneering a new history in US-North Korea relations."

—*Rodong Sinmun*, June 13, 2018

THE MUCH-LAMPOONED AND UNDERESTIMATED MAN WAS ABOUT to rack up his biggest triumph yet: the leader of a tiny country that was technically still at war with the United States was going to sit down with its president. Such a meeting would give Kim a worldwide veneer of legitimacy and respectability. And, if it went well, it could pave the way for the removal of crippling sanctions and even, in the future, American investment.

On June 12, 2018—less than nine months after the North Korean threatened to "tame the mentally deranged US dotard with fire"—Kim Jong Un and Donald Trump walked onto a platform at the secluded Capella Hotel in Singapore. In front of carefully arranged North Korean and American flags, they smiled at each other and shook hands for what felt like minutes.

It was astounding. Even for the Great Successor himself.

"Many people in the world will think this is from a science-fiction movie," the North Korean leader told Trump through his interpreter as they walked into the room where their delegations were waiting.

Gone was "Little Rocket Man." Gone was the "total nutjob." Kim Jong Un was demonstrating that he was indeed the "smart cookie" that Trump had once called him.

Kim Jong Un achieved something that his grandfather and father had tried but failed to accomplish.

In the last years of his life, Kim Il Sung was exploring the possibility of a "grand bargain" with the United States. He twice met with the American evangelist Billy Graham. For their first meeting in 1992, Graham carried a personal message from President George H. W. Bush.

Kim Jong Il invited Bill Clinton to Pyongyang as the American president was approaching the end of his second term. Clinton sent his secretary of state, Madeleine Albright, on an exploratory mission, and there were hopes that this was the start of improved relations. Instead, Clinton chose to spend his final months in office dealing with another intractable problem: Israel and Palestine.

But Kim Jong Un was the one to make it happen.

In Washington, DC, talking heads had been tearing their hair out. This isn't the way diplomacy is done, they said. Summits come at the end of a process, not the beginning, they wailed. He's taking a page from his father's playbook, they raged. The United States won't get North Korea to give up its nuclear weapons this way.

But from my perch in Singapore, I felt optimistic about the process. I didn't for a second think that the Great Successor was going to give up his nuclear weapons. They were his security blanket, and he needed them. The fate of Muammar Gaddafi was still in his mind.

But he might be willing to give up some of his missiles and nuclear warheads to get sanctions relief and to normalize his leadership in the eyes of the world. Kim Jong Un wouldn't make it easy, but he appeared willing to play ball.

And maybe it was time to try something different. For a quarter century, the conventional way of doing things hadn't worked. Maybe these two unconventional leaders were just the right people to try something unorthodox.

Kim Jong Un had shown he was not his father. He was much bolder and more audacious. And Trump was unlike any president the United States had ever seen.

Since taking office, Trump had adopted an unusual practice in his meetings with other world leaders. He liked to meet with them alone, sometimes with only one translator between them. That was a sign of his conviction that he could build a personal rapport with his counterpart and hammer out a good deal.

This approach suited Kim Jong Un. And personal relationships are extremely important when doing any kind of business in Asia, particularly when that business is difficult. This is even more the case in autocracies run by strongmen.

When the United States and China were normalizing their relationship in the early 1970s, then secretary of state Henry Kissinger spent hundreds of hours in meetings with the Chinese premier, Zhou Enlai. In a similar way, Secretary of State Pompeo spent hours with Kim Jong Un and his top aides both before and after the summit, in Washington, New York, and Pyongyang.

By holding this summit, Kim Jong Un and Donald Trump were taking a personal stake in this process. Both would have an incentive to make it work.

Plus, for all their differences, Kim Jong Un and Donald Trump have a lot in common. Both were born into a family empire. Neither was the oldest son, the automatic heir. But both proved to their fathers that he was the right man to inherit the dynasty. And both love a grandiose construction project.

My optimism about the summit stemmed most of all from the fact that Kim Jong Un had delivered a very clear but widely overlooked signal that he was now pivoting 100 percent to the economy.

Just a week before his summit meeting with South Korea's President Moon, Kim Jong Un delivered a speech to a Workers' Party meeting in Pyongyang in which he declared the "byungjin" or "simultaneous advance" policy to be over. He no longer needed to pursue nuclear weapons—he had achieved them. He declared an immediate end to nuclear tests and intercontinental ballistic missiles launches.

Having proven his military credentials and gotten rid of detractors and potential rivals, he was ready to move ahead with the deliberate changes that would enable economic growth.

From now on, Kim Jong Un said, he would be focusing on a "new strategic line." He would be concentrating on the economy. And for that, he would need an "international environment favorable for the socialist economic construction."

It was a tectonic shift. In 2013, he had boldly elevated the economy to level pegging with the nuclear program after decades of "military first" policy. Five years later, almost to the day, he was unequivocally making economic development his top priority.

But he couldn't achieve his strategic vision for economic development while the American-led sanctions, which were so sweeping they threatened to strangle the economy, remained in place. Nor could he achieve his diplomatic goal to be seen as the respectable and responsible leader of a normal state without the American president's seal of approval.

Kim Jong Un's contrived metamorphosis into cosmopolitan global statesman was apparent the moment he departed North Korea.

His father, who had been was terrified of flying, always took his armored train when he went to Beijing or Moscow. The Great Successor didn't have this fear, but he didn't have a particularly trustworthy plane, either. So he sponged one from his benefactors next door—an Air China Boeing 747 that was usually occupied by Beijing's premier. It was an American plane with a big Star Alliance logo by the door.

Kim Jong Un didn't even try to disguise the fact that he had a borrowed ride. The photos of him boarding the Air China jet appeared in full color on the front page of North Korea's main newspaper, almost as if it was a point of pride that powerful China had loaned him the jet.

The First Sister traveled on a separate North Korean plane. The Kims apparently didn't want to risk spilling too much Paektu blood at once if something untoward happened.

The logistical preparations were exhaustive. Kim had never been that far from home since becoming leader. The Supreme Guard Command, the leader's personal security entourage that is estimated to comprise as many as 120,000 soldiers, left nothing to chance.

North Korean guards monitored the security check at the entrance to St. Regis Hotel, where Kim Jong Un and his sister would be staying. Incidentally, their now-deceased half brother Kim Jong Nam had liked to stay at the very same hotel.

The top three floors had been reserved for the North Koreans, including the $7,000-a-night presidential suite on the twentieth floor.

(Singapore picked up the bill for the hotel accommodation and meals.) The guards were stationed in the elevators around the clock to make sure that no one tried to go above the sixteenth floor.

The guards had wanted to check all the rooms in the hotel, but the management refused to allow access beyond the top three floors. They swept those hotel rooms, along with the meeting rooms at the summit venue, for explosives, eavesdropping devices, and anything else that might harm or offend their leader.

None of the rooms would be released until two days after Kim Jong Un had left Singapore. The North Korean staff had a lot of cleaning to do before they could hand the rooms back to the hotel management, free of Kim family DNA.

Kim and his sister had stuck to their rooms while in the St. Regis. They ate specially prepared meals cooked with ingredients brought in from Pyongyang, transported on a separate cargo plane, and delivered in refrigerated trucks that were waiting at Singapore's airport. The same plane carried Kim Jong Un's limousine as well as authorized weapons and other supplies.

Once he arrived safely in Singapore, Kim Jong Un was at his most winning.

On the first day, he met with Singapore's prime minister, the son of the island-state's founding leader, Lee Kuan Yew, a strongman who'd ruled for some five decades. The prime minister later declared that the thirty-four-year-old was a "confident young leader."

There was another official handshake photo to add to Kim Jong Un's legitimacy album.

That night, after dark, he went on an unannounced tour of Singapore's most spectacular sights. Guided by Singapore's foreign and education ministers, Kim Jong Un, his sister, and a huge posse of bodyguards and North Korean cameramen walked along the glittering waterfront. They admired the flowers at Gardens by the Bay, a spectacular futuristic park. And they did what millions of tourists before them had done in that spot: posed for selfies. Kim smiled into the foreign minister's camera, his cheeks ruddy in the sweltering humidity.

They walked over a bridge and around to the Marina Bay Sands Hotel, an architectural wonder comprising a giant concrete boat resting atop three skyscrapers. Incidentally, it is owned by Sheldon Adelson, the casino magnate who backed Trump in the 2016 election and whose properties in Macau were a regular haunt for Kim Jong Nam.

They ascended to the Sky Park, an open-air bar area with an infinity pool on the fifty-seventh floor. Kim Jong Un stood on the deck for about ten minutes, looking out over the skyline with its skyscrapers topped by illuminated Citibank and HSBC signs.

Everywhere he went, the North Korean leader drew huge crowds. Hordes of tourists and locals wanted to get a glimpse. They lined the streets, straining at the police barriers, as he arrived at his hotel. They flocked to the waterfront area to snap photos for their social media pages as he walked along the esplanade. They stood on tiptoes in the lobby of the Marina Bay Sands complex to try to see him over the mob. Swimmers, some in skimpy bikinis, got out of the infinity pool to snap him as he walked past.

It was all perfect fodder for Kim Jong Un's personality cult. Just as crowds assembled in North Korea to demonstrate their devotion to him, here were throngs of foreigners flocking to see the Beloved and Respected Supreme Leader. Photos of all this would be splashed across North Korean newspaper and television screens. "See?" his propagandists could say to the North Korean people. "Kim Jong Un is revered abroad too."

Singapore was the ideal destination for the summit for many reasons. A steady stream of North Koreans and North Korean businesses had passed through the city over the years. They hadn't even needed a visa to enter the country, making it one of the few places North Koreans could travel to easily. Singapore was the standard bearer for the wider sentiment in Southeast Asia that engagement was the way to lead rogue states down a better path. It was a very different approach from the sanctions and isolation favored by the United States.

This was not the first time an Asian leader had come to Singapore for inspiration.

China's economic visionary Deng Xiaoping had visited in 1978. He toured the city with Lee, who explained how he'd done it. Deng was hugely impressed. Five years later, he introduced socialism with Chinese characteristics. So Singapore hoped to inspire another Asian country desperately in need of economic transformation but mortally afraid of political change.

Kim Jong Un was receptive. Extraordinary proof of this came through the North Korean state media the very next day, when the main newspaper ran photos on its front page showing Kim's walk through Singapore, complete with the boat on skyscrapers.

It was complemented with an eye-popping forty-two-minute television documentary entitled *The Epochal Meeting That Pioneered a New History between North Korea and the United States*, which showed every part of Kim's trip. The most surprising aspect was that the official film showcased how dazzling, clean, and beautiful Singapore was, from the plush presidential suite rented for Kim at the St. Regis to the many magnificent and unique buildings the city boasted.

It showed his motorcade driving down Singapore's most famous shopping street, past the Rolex and Prada stores, and strolling along the magnificent waterfront.

"The Great Comrade Leader said," the narrator relayed in the documentary, "that we will study Singapore's excellent knowledge and experiences in various fields from now on."

After the summit, a Pyongyang economist said that if the sanctions were lifted and the political climate improved, North Korea could emulate countries like Singapore and Switzerland, "which have few resources and little territory but have used their geographical location to their greatest advantage."[1] The economist had clearly never been to Singapore or Switzerland and seemed to have little grasp of the unlikeliness of this happening any time soon. There were a few other hurdles in the way, to put it mildly. Like a democracy and a rule of law.

Kim Jong Un was signaling to the outside world—but, most importantly, to his own people—that this was his vision. It was the clearest indication yet that the North Korean leader didn't want to be a dull Stalinist dictator. He wanted to be a developmental dictator of the kind that has flourished in other parts of Asia.

*   *   *

The big day had arrived. The day he would come face to face with his archnemesis. The stakes were incredibly high for Kim Jong Un—both in terms of politics and his security. A paranoid dictator lives in constant fear for his life.

When Kim Jong Un left his hotel to go to the summit venue that morning, he was surrounded by more than forty agents from the Supreme Guard Command.

Entrance into the elite squad is extremely selective, with the best conscripts from the military put through a series of tests regarding their health, personality, height, appearance, and—most crucially—family background. Those charged with guarding the Brilliant Comrade must have excellent political credentials and come only from the most loyal classes. One former bodyguard wrote that getting into the leader's security detail was "harder than passing through the eye of a needle."[2]

But once they're in, they live a good life in North Korea. Kim Jong Un certainly doesn't want unhappy men with guns around him.

Twelve of the bodyguards briefly became internet celebrities when they were filmed running alongside Kim Jong Un's limousine in black suits, even in the Singapore humidity. It seemed to encapsulate the absurdity of the North Korean leadership.

Kim got the idea for this human shield from Clint Eastwood. As a boy, he'd seen the movie *In the Line of Fire*, in which Eastwood plays a US Secret Service agent who had been guarding John F. Kennedy when he was assassinated in 1963. Eastwood's character and other agents run alongside the president's car.[3]

The car itself was also notable. Kim Jong Un arrived in a Mercedes-Maybach S 600 Pullman Guard, a twenty-one-foot-long saloon that had gone on sale less than a year earlier. It retails at a cool $1.6 million.

Mercedes markets the "highly exclusive vehicle" to "heads of state and other individuals at particular risk." It features a "generously sized and tastefully appointed club lounge in the rear," according to the company, but it's the array of security features that no doubt made it appeal to Kim.

It is fully armored and can withstand machine-gun fire; it has blast protection underneath to stop explosive devices and a steel bulkhead behind the rear seats to shield the passengers' heads from anything that might come through the back window. This also helps make the car weigh in at five tons. Its doors are so heavy that they have their own motors to help them open and close.

After their initial hand-gripping encounter in front of the cameras, the two leaders went into a one-on-one meeting, or rather two-on-two, since they both had interpreters. At the outset, Kim Jong Un said, "Nice to meet you, Mr. President" in English. I've asked a dozen or so English and German speakers who've met him if Kim Jong Un ever gave them so much as a hello in those languages. He did not, but he made an extra effort for Trump.

Throughout the five-hour-long encounter, Kim proved that he knew exactly how to handle the American president.

He entered the hotel first, in line with traditional Korean rules about respecting one's elders. Trump was more than twice Kim's age, meaning he had the higher status and should enter last. The Korean language has complex levels of politeness, and Kim Jong Un made sure to use the most honorific terms when speaking to Trump, something he knew would be appreciated by the American president. Trump's interpreter told him that the North Korean leader was using very deferential language.

It wasn't the first time Kim Jong Un had played to the American president's famous ego. In the weeks leading up to the summit, he sent a top aide, Kim Yong Chol, to the White House with a letter for Trump—not just any letter but one in an envelope so enormous it bordered on comic. The White House released photos of a grinning Trump holding the missive, immediately inviting comparisons on the internet to the giant checks that game-show contestants win.

At the summit, Kim didn't appear to be nervous. He was engaging. He told jokes. He showed that he knew how to impress but also that he cared about how he was seen by others. He wanted to be viewed as gracious.

As the American president introduced the North Korean leader to his team, the tone was light. Referring to Trump's previous assertion that he'd be able to get a read on him within a minute, Kim asked the president how he was doing. Trump responded that he'd found his counterpart to be strong, smart, and trustworthy.

Not missing a beat, Kim Jong Un turned to John Bolton, Trump's hawkish national security advisor, who, just a few months before, had written a column laying out the legal arguments for missile strikes against North Korea.[4]

North Korea and Bolton had a history. When Bolton was part of the George W. Bush administration, Pyongyang's propagandists had derided him as "human scum" and a "bloodsucker." For his part, Bolton had a joke he liked to deploy: How do you tell when the North Koreans are lying? Their lips are moving.

But in Singapore, after Trump had complimented Kim, the North Korean leader asked Bolton what he thought. The national security advisor paused for a second and then responded diplomatically. "My boss is the best judge of character."

When the two leaders sat down in armchairs for a scripted exchange in front of the media, Kim Jong Un told Trump that he was very happy to have the meeting. "It was not easy to get here," he said. "The past shackled us, and old prejudices and practices worked as obstacles on our way forward. But we overcame all of them, and we are here today."

Trump gave Kim his trademark thumbs-up.

The man who wrote a book called *The Art of the Deal* was charmed. Trump said that the North Korean leader was "very talented," "very smart," and a "very good negotiator." He added that Kim had proven to be "one out of ten thousand" for the way he'd inherited the country in his twenties and has been "able to run it, and run it tough." He said the two of them had forged a "very special bond." He said he trusted Kim.

Both before and after the summit, Kim wrote letters to Trump, short, one-page letters in Korean—with an English translation supplied by the North Korean side—that were masterclasses in rhapsodic flattery.

Kim called Trump "Your Excellency" and repeatedly commented on how smart the American president was, what a brilliant political mind he had. He said how wonderful it was to work with Mike Pompeo, who had been the director of the CIA then became Trump's secretary of state.

By the end of September, Trump would be saying that he and Kim Jong Un "fell in love."

The negotiations to get to this stage, however, were difficult.

When Pompeo arrived in Pyongyang in April 2018 to follow up on South Korea's conversations, he had directly asked Kim Jong Un if he planned to denuclearize. Kim gave a heartfelt response, although who knows if it was genuine or by design.

"The chairman said that he is a father and husband and he does not want his children to live their lives carrying nuclear weapons on their back," said Andrew Kim, the head of the CIA's Korea Mission Center and Pompeo's translator for the trip.[5]

It seemed auspicious. So both sides sent negotiators to hash out a deal in the months leading up to the summit. They met at the truce village of Panmunjom in the DMZ, but the talks were slow going. The North Koreans had to repeatedly drive the potholed highway back to Pyongyang to get further instructions from their leader.

Even after the two delegations arrived in Singapore, their positions were still so divergent that they were working with two different documents.

The night before the summit, Pompeo said at a press conference that "the only outcome that the United States will accept" was an agreement on "complete and verifiable and irreversible denuclearization of the Korean Peninsula." CVID is a very specific term (the D actually stands for "disarmament") and one that would require international weapons inspectors to have free rein in North Korea.

There was good reason for the American delegation to be skeptical about North Korea's commitment to denuclearization. One way or another, the Kim regime had reneged on every nuclear agreement it had ever signed.

By the end of the summit, Kim Jong Un had the better end of the deal. He got away without making any specific promise to give up his nuclear weapons and ballistic missiles. He simply reiterated the vague agreement he'd made with the South Korean president in April, agreeing to work toward the denuclearization of the Korean Peninsula—not North Korea, *North and South* Korea.

There was no mention of the "complete and verifiable and irreversible denuclearization" that Secretary of State Pompeo had insisted upon the previous night.

Trump had also agreed to suspend the joint exercises that the American and South Korean militaries conduct twice a year, exercises viewed as a crucial part of planning for any sudden change on the Korean Peninsula—like a coup in or an invasion from North Korea.

North Korea considers these exercises provocative and also a drain on its resources, since the country has to conduct its own drills in response.

Sitting off to the side, listening to the talks, two administration officials couldn't believe their ears. They began furiously sending messages to each other to come up with a plan. One called the Japanese national security advisor, and the other got on the phone with the South Korean equivalent. They wanted to give the United States' two military allies a warning of the announcement that was to come, an announcement that would alarm Japan's hawkish government in particular.

Trump's announcement of the suspension of the military drills still caused consternation. At a press conference after the summit, the US president called them "war games"—the North Korean description of the exercises.

Kim had told his American counterparts that although the United States and South Korea claimed that the joint military exercises were defensive in nature, the exercises felt offensive to North Korea.[6]

In another win for Kim Jong Un, Trump also told his counterpart that he would sign a declaration to end the Korean War.[7] It was an idea that Kim Yong Chol, the bearer of the huge envelope, had brought up with Trump during his Oval Office meeting.

Kim Yong Chol said that creating a way to ensure lasting peace on the Korean Peninsula would serve as a sign that the Trump administration was willing to enter into a different relationship with North Korea. Trump said that he was open to making an end of war declaration but that they would still need to work on an actual peace treaty later.

Although keeping the country on a wartime footing has been helpful for creating cohesiveness at home, the Kim regime has long wanted to sign a peace treaty—because then it would be able to insist there was no longer any need for the US military to be stationed in South Korea. But the United States has always balked at any suggestion that it would pull out its troops and hardware from South Korea and potentially leave its ally vulnerable.

Forging a peace treaty would give Kim Jong Un a face-saving way to give up at least some of the nuclear arsenal that he'd spent so much money and effort on obtaining. But by taking the two countries out of a technical state of war, North Korea could also see a way free of the sanctions that were crippling its economy.

For all the disdain in Washington for Trump's tactics, the American president showed surprising perception about what was driving his North Korean counterpart. Again, this was manifested in an unusual way, but in a way that Kim Jong Un could identify with.

During their meeting, Trump got out an iPad and showed the North Koreans a video that his national security staff had made, although the credits said it was made by "Destiny Pictures." He also sent them home with a copy of it.

The video was preposterous, but it was also perfect for Kim Jong Un. It was a vision for a brighter future.

It started with a shot of the crater lake at the top of Mt. Paektu and then zoomed through some of the world's most recognizable construction projects: the pyramids of Egypt, the Colosseum, the Taj Mahal, the skyscrapers of Manhattan, and, of course, Kim Il Sung Square.

It was, the narration said, "a story of opportunity." It was about "two men, two leaders, one destiny." The video repeatedly showed those two men throughout, portraying them as equals.

But, notably, it showed North Korea as one giant development opportunity. The Pyongyang skyline was filled with cranes. It took the famous photo of North Korea at night as seen from space and then turned on the lights to make it look like the black hole had as much electricity as South Korea.

"Think of it from the real estate perspective," Trump told reporters after the summit, imagining "great condos" being built on the "great beaches" of Wonsan. "Boy, look at the view," he said. "You could have the best hotels in the world."

The video featured a shot of a highly developed beach in Florida, where Trump has the Mar-a-Lago resort.

It was, one commentator quipped, not realpolitik but "real estate politik."[8]

To entice Kim Jong Un to give up his nuclear weapons and become a normal member of the international community, Trump tried to give him a sense that he was missing out on a great opportunity.

You are at the bottom of every list that ranks success or human progress, the American president told his North Korean counterpart. But he put a positive spin on it. If you're willing to rethink the premise of what success looks like, we will be there to help you, he told Kim.

He even put forward different models that the Great Successor could follow. He held up the examples of China and Vietnam, which have adopted capitalist economic principles but where the Communist Party retains political control. He even suggested North Korea could be like Japan, the world's third-largest economy and a constitutional monarchy. He suggested that Kim Jong Un could become like the Japanese emperor, occupying the position of revered but ceremonial head of state while the elected government ran the country.[9]

Over the years, the North Korean regime has had plenty of opportunity to embark on Chinese- or Vietnamese-style reforms. They have never wanted to go down that path. And Kim Jong Un certainly would not want to be a mere figurehead like the emperor of Japan—whose father, by the way, had led the brutal occupation of Korea. But there was plenty of room in between their two visions.

So Kim Jong Un had good reason to be feeling relaxed as he sat down for lunch, even if Trump did throw a line to the photographers about making sure they looked "handsome and thin and perfect."

The lunch was as painstakingly negotiated as the talks.

Every item on the menu was subject to much back and forth. In the end, they were served an "East-West nine-course meal" for the working lunch that featured beef short-rib confit, soy-braised codfish with radish and Asian vegetables, and dark-chocolate tartlet ganache.

The North Koreans were hypersensitive about food security, well beyond anything that President Trump's staff had experienced with any other leader. Kim Jong Un's food taster arrived two hours in advance to check the meal for poison.

But the conversation over lunch was light. They talked about basketball and cars. Kim Jong Un told Bolton that he was "famous" in North Korea and suggested the two of them take a photo together. Maybe that would improve his image among regime hard-liners in Pyongyang, Kim suggested, presumably referring to the people who'd called Bolton "human scum" not too many years earlier. The Washington hard-liner laughed in response.[10]

Trump offered to show Kim Jong Un "the Beast," his armored limousine full of high-tech safety features. Watching the two of them walking up to the car and seeing Kim Jong Un heading for the open door, I thought the two of them were going to drive somewhere. But Trump's Secret Service agents stopped the interlude before any North Koreans could get too close to the special vehicle.

Then the two of them strolled in the lush garden of the Capella Hotel together and waved from one of the balconies—a little like the queen of England might do from Buckingham Palace.

Then they repaired to the grand room where they would sign their vague document. A North Korean official wearing white latex gloves inspected and cleaned the pen that had been set on the table for the North Korean leader. But the Great Successor never touched it. His sister handed him a pen—a $1,000 Montblanc—when she gave him the document to sign and then put it back in her purse when he was finished.

And with that, Kim Jong Un had made history. He had defied the predictions that he would not be able to corral the cadres of this anachronistic regime. He had confounded assessments of North Korea's technical capacity to build a hydrogen bomb and a missile that could reach the US mainland.

Now, he had the president of the world's most powerful nation declaring his willingness to work together to achieve his vision.

The tricky part was going to be managing to get the American-led sanctions lifted so that the economy could grow while still keeping hold of his core nuclear and missile capabilities.

Once he got home, his nuclear program still safe and secure, Kim Jong Un turned to part two of his strategy for staying in power: raising living standards around the country.

The hands-off, laissez-faire approach to the economy of his earlier years was over.

In the sweltering heat of July, he went to a textile mill in Sinuiju, on the border with China, where he rebuked factory managers for repeatedly failing to meet their targets and lambasted them over the state of the "decrepit building that looks like a stable."

He also had stern words when he visited a chemical fiber mill nearby; he upbraided the managers for trying to pass the blame about the plant's shortcomings. "I've visited countless units, but I've never seen workers like this," he seethed.

He traveled from the northeast to the southwest, touring textile mills, fish farms, shipyards, a potato-processing plant, power stations, and factories making cookies and backpacks and coal-mining machines. He gave advice on instant noodle packaging.

The same military zeal he had applied to developing the nuclear and missile programs was now being applied to the economy. He encouraged the workers to approach their tasks as if they were involved in "three-dimensional warfare." He called for a construction "blitzkrieg." He even ordered a military regiment to vacate its land to make way for the construction of a large vegetable greenhouse "at lightning speed."

Kim Jong Un was showing that he wanted to boost the market and encourage private consumption as if security of the nation depended on it. The security of his regime certainly did. Having made good on the first part of his "simultaneous push" by acquiring nuclear weapons, he had to approach the second part, the economy, with the same fervor.

He wasn't doing this because he cared about the people and their well-being. His actions over the previous seven years had proven that he couldn't care less about the general population.

No, he cared about his own survival. His grandfather lived to the age of eighty-two, his father to seventy. Kim Jong Un could dream of ruling for thirty or forty or even fifty years to come.

Since taking power at the end of 2011, Kim Jong Un had alternately coddled and terrified the cadres who kept him in power. He'd developed a credible nuclear weapons program. He'd allowed the economy to breathe a little. He'd convinced the leader of the free world that he was a rational counterpart and the skeptical leader of his benefactor, China, that he at least knew how to behave.

Now came his biggest test yet. He had to show the people of North Korea that life was getting better under the Great Successor.

EPILOGUE

THE TRAFFIC WAS TERRIBLE IN BEIJING ON JANUARY 9, 2019, even by the standards of this city of twenty-one million people on the move. The second ring-road was so paralyzed that people were taking the opportunity to do some morning exercises next to their cars. I got out of my taxi to take a photo of the gridlock and see whether I could catch a glimpse of the motorcade.

Kim Jong Un was in town again. President Xi Jinping had thrown a lavish banquet in the Great Hall of the People, the plush ceremonial building on one side of Tiananmen Square, to celebrate Kim Jong Un's thirty-fifth birthday the night before. The following day, Xi hosted his young neighbor for lunch at the state-run Beijing Hotel, a place where Mao Zedong once entertained Kim's grandfather.

After their first five years of enmity, Xi was now pretending that Kim was his prodigal son. Indeed, Kim's visits to China were becoming so commonplace that they were no longer a novelty, just a nuisance for Beijing's commuters.

The Great Successor had pulled off a remarkable transformation. He had managed to convince some of the most powerful people in the world to treat him like the normal leader of a legitimate state.

Indeed, eight days earlier, Kim Jong Un had looked decidedly presidential when he delivered his New Year's Day address.

He did not speak from a podium as in previous years. Instead, as the clock chimed midnight, Kim Jong Un sat in a big leather armchair in a wood-paneled study, portraits of his father and grandfather behind him, leather-bound books filling the shelves.

The echoes were not accidental. One of Kim Jong Un's top aides had been reading a biography of Franklin Delano Roosevelt and had clearly advised his boss to adopt the trappings of the Depression-era American president's famous "fireside chats."

The Great Successor was now seeking to replicate the intimacy with his citizenry that FDR created with Americans in the 1930s and at the same time to reinforce the notion that he was a respectable leader.

The events of 2018 had left an "indelible imprint on history," said Kim Jong Un, dressed in a Western-style suit and just a week away from his thirty-fifth birthday. The coming year, 2019, would be a year "full of hope."

"I want to believe that our relations with the United States will bear good fruit this year, as inter-Korean relations have greeted a great turn, by the efforts of the two sides," he said, reading from a teleprompter and glancing at the notes in his hand.

He referred to the economy thirty-nine times in his speech, and the only time he mentioned his nuclear program was to declare his regime would no longer make, test, use, or proliferate nuclear weapons.

The nuclear weapons were hidden, and the missiles were silent. The assassination of his half brother in Malaysia less than two years earlier had been all but forgotten. The death of American college student Otto Warmbier even more recently had faded from view. President Trump even gave Kim a pass on the incident. "He tells me that he didn't know about it, and I will take him at his word," Trump said after their second meeting, held in Vietnam at the end of February.

But that second summit showed that the diplomatic path would not be smooth.

Trump had concluded that it was his "maximum pressure" campaign that had lured Kim Jong Un out of his nuclear bunker and to the negotiating table.

This was a misreading. Sanctions did have an influence on Kim Jong Un, but they were just one factor. The young North Korean's confidence and the fact that he had a credible nuclear weapons program, together with the pressure of the sanctions, had combined to bring him to talks.

The North Koreans were also having trouble figuring out how Trump operated. They were searching for a logic or a pattern in his decision-making so they could game out his approach.

For clues, one North Korean official had been watching the *West Wing* and *Madame Secretary*, television dramas based on the White House and the State Department. The official asked an American interlocutor: Is this how the White House works? Is it a bottom-up process, where officials send ideas up to the White House? No, the surprised American tried to respond diplomatically, it's the opposite. Donald Trump runs a very top-down operation.

With these misunderstandings hanging over them, Trump went into the Hanoi summit expecting the economy-focused North Korean leader would be desperate to bargain away his nuclear weapons in return for the US-led sanctions being lifted. And Kim Jong Un went in believing that Trump would be making the big decisions and would be looking for a diplomatic victory to tweet about.

When they met for marbled North Korean steaks—rare for Kim, well-done for Trump—that first night in Hanoi, they found that their starting positions were as different as their grilling preferences.

Trump had been willing to lifting the sanctions, with a provision allowing them to be swiftly reimposed if North Korea resumed weapons testing, the North Korean vice foreign minister said after the summit.

But the hardline national security adviser, John Bolton, and secretary of state Mike Pompeo apparently prevailed over their boss, talking him out of easing up on the North Koreans. The American president told his counterpart he needed to give up his entire nuclear program before getting any sanctions relief.

This was essentially the same deal that US presidents had been trying to strike for decades, including during Bolton's time in the Bush administration.

This approach had always failed. It had failed because it overlooked the whole reason why North Korea had pursued nuclear weapons in the first place: the nuclear program is a means to defend North Korea against an American attack.

For the negotiations to succeed, they could not be only about denuclearization. They had to be about transforming a relationship that had been dire for seven decades and convincing Kim Jong Un that he no longer needed his nuclear weapons as protection against an American invasion. Or at least that he no longer needed so many nuclear weapons and the missiles with which to deliver them.

The process required a slow and steady normalization that involved both sides showing good faith. Setting up a liaison office so that the two sides could talk, a precursor to full diplomatic relations, would be a good first step. Working towards a peace treaty would be another. Indeed, they had agreed in Singapore to an incremental and reciprocal approach, and the working-level officials had been discussing this between the summits.

So Kim Jong Un went into the Hanoi talks with an offer to dismantle the Yongbyon nuclear facility—a redundant plant—if Trump lifted the sanctions imposed in 2016 and 2017. That quasi-blockade, designed as punishment for the missile launches and nuclear tests, had cut off seafood, coal, and metals exports.

The Americans were right to be skeptical about the North Korean side being as good as its word. Kim Jong Un's father had made the same offer more than a decade before and had even blown up a cooling tower at Yongbyon. All the while he was pressing ahead with his nuclear program at other facilities.

But Kim Jong Un clearly thought he was making a decent offer, one that warranted at least a temporary end to the sanctions. He would not buckle.

There was no deal. The two leaders walked away.

The silverware and glasses sat untouched on the table where they were supposed to have lunch. The hotel staff ate the foie gras and snow fish that had been prepared for the leaders. The pens lay on a desk set up for a signing ceremony that never happened. While the two men were engaged in their artificial brinkmanship, two countries with nuclear weapons—India and Pakistan—were embroiled in an actual conflict.

The whole tableau would have been ludicrous if it wasn't so deadly serious.

These two unconventional leaders, whose biggest advantages were the facts that they were so different from their predecessors, had fallen prey to conventional thinking.

It would be easy at this point to see the whole effort as doomed, to see Hanoi as evidence that history would repeat itself. The stop-start efforts of the previous quarter century showed that it was prudent to have low expectations about diplomatic engagement with North Korea.

But sitting in Beijing, watching these events unfold, I retained a sense of optimism that this time could be different. I still didn't think for a second that Kim Jong Un would give up the "treasured sword" of his nuclear program. He did not want to become Muammar Gaddafi, giving up his nuclear weapons only to be invaded and overthrown. Nor did I think he would embark on Chinese- or Vietnamese-style economic reforms. He could not become North Korea's Deng Xiaoping, embarking on a version of the "reform and opening" strategy that transformed China into the world's second-largest economy. He could not pursue the kinds of Doi Moi reforms that had allowed Vietnam to flourish.

In both China and Vietnam, the Communist Party has managed to remain firmly in control, even as capitalism has become the motivating ideology for many people. But there was one crucial difference. The Communist Parties in China and Vietnam weren't family dynasties. Their leaders had different surnames. There was at least some internal jockeying for top positions. In North Korea, that kind of leadership contest would not be tolerated.

So even the lure of economic assistance—repeated by the US negotiators in Vietnam, one of the models of reform that Trump had previously held up to Kim—could sound dangerous to the Great Successor.

North Korea has long considered exhortations for reform to be tantamount to calling for regime change, given that the North Korean economy can't just open up and allow a freer flow of information, money, and people without seriously loosening the Kim family's grip on power.

But perhaps there was some middle ground. Kim Jong Un might give up some parts of his nuclear program. And he might inch toward some kind of tentative economic liberalization. Andrei Lankov, a noted scholar of North Korea who once studied at Kim Il Sung University, describes it as "reform without opening."

For, despite the ups and downs, Kim Jong Un's goal remains clear.

He had followed the first part of Deng Xiaoping's maxim: "Let some people get rich first." Now, if he was going to have a shot at staying in power for years to come, he needed to try to follow through on the oft-forgotten second part of that phrase: "And gradually all the people should get rich together."

For that, he needed real, tangible economic development that he, and certainly not any outsider, was directing.

He had a unique window of opportunity to achieve that, one that wouldn't be open for long. The Great Successor, having defied predictions again and again, needed to maintain the momentum that the peace-talks process was giving him in the minds of his North Korean subjects before democracy and disinterest took over.

South Korean president Moon Jae-in, the man whose embrace was instrumental in allowing diplomacy to flourish, would be in office only until 2022 and would be a lame duck for the last couple of years. Moon had been a been an unusually dogged and subtle partner in the negotiations; any successor might be much less invested in the idea of peace between the two Koreas.

Kim's newfound negotiating partner, Donald Trump, would be up for reelection even sooner, at the end of 2020, and his success was far from certain.

The North Koreans were so concerned about Trump's prospects that one of Kim's advisers even consulted a traditional Korean fortune-teller to ask whether he would be reelected. (The answer was yes.)

For his part, Trump also showed a continued appetite for this process. "Relationship very good, let's see what happened!" he tweeted after returning to Washington.

By the end of March, Trump had shown just how willing he was to do a deal with Kim Jong Un, overruling new sanctions that his own Treasury Department had imposed on North Korea just a day before—apparently as a favor to his counterpart in Pyongyang. Asked to explain the extraordinary move, Trump's spokeswoman said: "President Trump likes Chairman Kim, and he doesn't think these sanctions will be necessary."

Kim Jong Un could bet that if Trump lost the election just eighteen months away, the next president would not be as amenable to dealing with him.

Kim didn't have to worry, however, about a change in leadership next door in China. President Xi Jinping had scrapped term limits to allow him to remain in power indefinitely. But that offered little succor. Xi clearly did not think much of the Little Comrade Neighbor and had engaged only when he needed to assert his role in any diplomatic thaw. It would be easy for him to go back to ignoring Kim.

So as Kim Jong Un rolled through China on his train from Hanoi back to Pyongyang, he knew that his window for freeing himself from the sanctions would be open only briefly. Yes, China and Russia had given him some relief already by relaxing the controls on their borders while they pushed at the United Nations for the sanctions to be lifted, noting that Kim no longer needed to be punished for testing. But Kim Jong Un needed more. He wanted the sanctions lifted in principle as well as practice.

And so he left the door open for more talks. "Kim Jong Un expressed his thanks to Trump for making positive efforts for the successful meeting and talks while making a long journey and said goodbye, promising the next meeting," the Korean Central News Agency reported at the end of the failed summit.

It was Kim Jong Un who summed up the prospects for the process best of all. Before the main talks in Hanoi, after their conversation over steak had shown how difficult the day's discussions would be, the Great Successor described the trajectory he saw.

"It's too early to tell, but I wouldn't say I am pessimistic," Kim said when asked by an American journalist how he was feeling. The fact that Kim answered a question from the press at all was unprecedented, and another sign of his willingness to buck convention.

"But," he continued, looking around with a slight smile on his face and Trump at his side, "my gut is feeling that good results will come."

ACKNOWLEDGMENTS

Writing about North Korea is a fascinating, challenging, infuriating, and infinitely interesting enterprise, and one that is never complete since we cannot know all the answers. I am grateful to all those who have shared their insights as I have tried to write about this most impenetrable state and to the friends and family members who have encouraged me as I undertook this book.

I am most thankful to the people who escaped from North Korea and agreed to tell me their stories when they had nothing to gain from doing so. In fact, doing so was risky for themselves and their relatives back home. But dozens of courageous escapees from North Korea spent hours upon hours telling me their difficult stories and patiently answering my endless questions so that I could try to show what life was like in Kim Jong Un's North Korea. I must preserve their anonymity here, but to each and every one of you, thank you. Your stories are so important, and I am very honored to be able to tell them.

To interview North Korean escapees, I needed help from people who have devoted their lives to this work. Their introductions were essential for reporting about life inside North Korea today. I am grateful to Jung Gwang-il of No Chain for North Korea, Park Dae-hyeon and his team at Woorion, Ji Seong-ho of Now Action and Unity for North Korean Human Rights, and Kim In-sung from the North Korea Database for Human Rights.

Thanks to the wonderful Lina Yoon, with whom I've spent many hours talking about the plight of North Korean women in particular. I am indebted to Sokeel Park of Liberty in North Korea, who is not only passionate about helping North Koreans but who also has the sharpest insights into North Korean life today.

Many other experts have shared their time and their thoughts about North Korea with me over the years. For that, I would like to thank the following: Jieun Baek, Joe Bermudez, Bill Brown, Bob Carlin, Adam Cathcart, Victor Cha, Cheong Seong-chang, Choi Jin-wook, Choi Kang, Cho Bong-hyun, Cho Tae-yong, Cho Yoon-jae, Chun Yung-woo, Ralph Cossa, John Delury, Kenneth Dekleva, Christopher Green, Thomas Fisler, Gordon Flake, Rüdiger Frank, Tatiana Gabroussenko, Ken Gause, Bonnie Glaser, Yoji Gomi, Stephan Haggard, Hahm Chai-bong, Melissa Hanham, Peter Hayes, Siegfried Hecker, Aubrey Immelman, Jiro Ishimaru, Frank Jannuzi, David Kang, Kim Byung-yeon, David Kim, Duyeon Kim, Michael Kim, Kim Seok-hyang, Kim Seung-min, Stephanie Kleine-Ahlbrandt, Bruce Klingner, Lee Hark Joon, Hyeon-seo Lee, Steven Levitsky, Jeffrey Lewis, Mark Lippert, Keith Luse, Michael Madden, Alexandre Mansourov, Patrick McEachern, Curtis Melvin, Alastair Morgan, Tony Namkung, Marcus Noland, Chad O'Carroll, Paik Hak-soon, John Park, Kee Park, Dan Pinkston, Ra Jong-yil, Evans Revere, Christopher Richardson, Greg Scarlatoiu, Geoffrey See, Syd Seiler, Gi-wook Shin, Benjamin Katzeff Silberstein, Sheila Smith, Dan Sneider, Scott Snyder, Hannah Song, Kathy Stephens, Torkel Stiernlöf, David Straub, Sue Mi Terry, Thae Yong-ho, Michael Vatikiotis, Wang Son-taek, Grayson Walker, and Joe Yun.

There are others who have shared their insights with me but have asked not to be named here because they continue to travel to North Korea. They know who they are and that I am grateful to them.

Special mention to Andrei Lankov, who has been an endless font of knowledge and shrewd perception since I first arrived in Seoul in 2004.

In Switzerland, Titus Plattner shared much of his own reporting with me as I was writing this book, and Christina Stucky came with me to the Köniz municipal offices at a moment's notice and helped me understand Swiss discretion. Deepest thanks to Imogen O'Neil, who was kind enough to share her insights into the Kim family and who very generously let me use parts of her unpublished book.

I was very lucky in 2014 to join the *Washington Post*, a paper where I instantly felt I belonged. My editors allowed me to devote a lot of time and resources to covering North Korea and trusted my instincts as I went off on reporting trips without knowing what I would find. Parts of this book draw on reporting I did for the *Post* during my four years covering Japan and the Koreas.

I was very fortunate to have as my editor Will Englund, who always made my stories better and provided invaluable counsel on how to deal with the tricky situations I sometimes found myself in. Emily Rauhala was a source of constant encouragement and an excellent sounding board. Gerry Shih covered for me in the final weeks. Thank you to Doug Jehl and Tracy Grant for being supportive of this project, and for being so generous in allowing me time to finish it.

In Seoul and on difficult reporting trips in China and Thailand, I was fortunate to work with Yoonjung Seo. She was the best colleague and reporting partner I could have hoped for. She arranged many of my interviews with escapees, and her gentle manner put them at ease when I arrived with my questions.

While writing this book, I had invaluable research and translation help from Shinhee Kang, Min Joo Kim, Yeonji Ghim, Min Jung Kim, and Yuki Oda. Min Joo rallied with last minute translations and answers.

My long-suffering Korean teacher Lee Un-kyung patiently allowed me to divert lessons from grammar to North Korea jargon.

A number of people read parts of the manuscript once it was complete and offered helpful feedback. Sincere thanks to Patrick McEachern, Titus Plattner, Imogen O'Neil, Jonathan Pollack, and Shea Cotton. Toby Manhire ran his sharp editor's eye over the almost-finished book and improved it immensely with his suggestions.

The impressive Fyodor Tertiskiy conducted a close read and made many helpful suggestions and corrections. Any errors that remain are, of course, mine alone.

My agent, Flip Brophy, believed in this project from the outset and found me a wonderful editor at PublicAffairs, Clive Priddle, who has been a delight to work with.

I am lucky to have found encouraging mentors at just the right times in my career: Ann Marie Lipinski took me into the Nieman Foundation for Journalism at Harvard, fortified me, and sent me back out into the world raring to go. David Rothkopf convinced me that I had insights and experiences that I should share in a book. Chung Min Lee spurred me on when I thought I couldn't do it.

I have benefited enormously from working on Japan and the Koreas alongside Sarah Birke, Emma Chantlett-Avery, Danielle Demetriou, Elise Hu, Jennifer Lind, and Motoko Rich and enjoyed their friendship at the same time. I spent many hours writing side by side in Tokyo with Sandra Fahy, whose academic work on North Korean human rights is unparalleled. In Beijing, Kathy Long and Yvonne Murray cheered me down the home stretch.

In Tokyo, I was fortunate to have friends who provided encouragement, entertainment, and childcare during missile launches and nuclear tests. Thank you to Tomoko Sugiyama Wilson and Tom Wilson, Rika Beppu and Taito Okiura, Sarah Birke and Philip Blue, and Adam Day and Wendy MacClinchy.

I would also like to thank friends who've supported me from afar: Emily Anderton, Natalia Antelava, Susie Banikarim, Soung-ah Choi, Emma Jacobs, Lucy Kebbell, Stephanie Kirchgaessner, Flavia Krause-Jackson, Maggie Kymn, Toby Manhire, Leonie Marinovich, and Andrew North.

When I arrived in South Korea on my first foreign posting, I had the good fortune to become friends with an exceptional journalist named Barbara Demick, who of course went on to write *Nothing to Envy,* the gold standard for books about North Korea. Barbara, you have been a generous friend and mentor, and I've learned so much from you.

I have my father, Brian, to thank for my love of reading and also my love of travel and other cultures. Once I became a foreign correspondent, he flinched only slightly when I told him I was off to Baghdad or Tehran or Pyongyang. Thank you for always believing in me, Dad. And thank you for your steady support too, Janine.

When I was offered the job of moving to Japan for the *Washington Post,* my mother, Christine, left her comfortable life in New Zealand to move overseas for the first time. Through four years in Tokyo, she took loving care of my son, enabling me to travel extensively and write at all hours. Mum, I couldn't have done this without you.

Thank you most of all to my son, Jude, who endured my absences while I went off to collect more pieces of this puzzle and my distraction while I was present. May the children of North Korea soon be able to speak as freely, explore as widely, and watch as much Netflix as you.

Anna Fifield
Beijing
March 2019

NOTES

CHAPTER 1: THE BEGINNING

1 *Korean Pictorial*, January 1986 issue.

2 Lee U Hong, *Angu na kyowakoku: Kita Chosen kogyo no kikai* (Tokyo: Aki shobo, 1990), 20.

3 Descriptions of seeds and agricultural methods from Lee, 32, 118, 168.

4 Yi Han-yong, *Taedong River Royal Family: My 14 Years Incognito in Seoul* (Seoul: Dong-a Ilbo, 1996).

5 Ju-min Park and James Pearson, "In Kim Jong Un's Summer Retreat, Fun Meets Guns," Reuters, October 10, 2017.

6 Kim Il Sung, *With the Century*, vol. 2 (Pyongyang: Foreign Languages Publishing House, 1992), 54.

7 Details about Stalin's plans for Kim Il Sung, Cho Man Sik, and Kim Il Sung's banquets come from Blaine Harden, *The Great Leader and the Fighter Pilot* (New York: Penguin Books, 2015), 64–66.

8 Details about Kim Il Sung's return to North Korea and the Soviet view of him come from Bradley K. Martin, *Under the Loving Care of the Fatherly Leader: North Korea and the Kim Dynasty* (New York: Griffin, 2006), 46–52.

9 Details about Kim Il Sung's reception at the rally come from Harden, 67.

10 Martin, *Under the Loving Care*, 52–53; Andrei Lankov, *The Real North Korea: Life and Politics in the Failed Stalinist Utopia* (Oxford: Oxford University Press, 2014), 6.

11 Baik Bong, *Kim Il Sung*, vol. 2 (Tokyo: Miraisha Publishing, 1970), 55–56.

12 Martin, *Under the Loving Care*, 67.

13 Bruce Cumings, *The Korean War: A History* (New York: Modern Library Edition, 2010), 152.

14 Blaine Harden, "The US War Crime North Korea Won't Forget," *Washington Post*, March 24, 2015.

15 *Strategic Air Warfare: An Interview with Generals Curtis E. LeMay, Leon W. Johnson, David A. Burchinal, and Jack J. Catton*, edited and with an introduction by Richard H. Kohn and Joseph P. Harahan (Office of Air Force History, US Air Force, 1988), 88.

16 "Record of a Conversation with Illarion Dmitriyevich Pak, Chairman of the Jagang Provincial People's Committee," April 13, 1955, History and Public Policy Program Digital Archive, RGANI fond 5, opis 28, delo 314. Translated for NKIDP by Gary Goldberg. https://digitalarchive .wilsoncenter.org/document/116308.

17 Suh Dae-sook, *Kim Il Sung: The North Korean Leader* (New York: Columbia University Press, 1988), 302.

18 Don Oberdorfer, *The Two Koreas: A Contemporary History* (New York: Little, Brown and Company, 1998), 347.

19 "GDR Ambassador Pyongyang to Ministry for Foreign Affairs, Berlin," April 14, 1975, History and Public Policy Program Digital Archive, Political Archive of the Foreign Office, Ministry of Foreign Affairs (PA AA, MfAA), C 6862.

20 Kim Hakjoon, *Dynasty: The Hereditary Succession Politics of North Korea* (Stanford, CA: Shorenstein Asia-Pacific Research Center, 2017), 87.

21 Kim Jong Il, *Brief History* (Pyongyang: Foreign Languages Publishing House, 1998).

22 Oberdorfer, *The Two Koreas*, 341.

23 David Sanger, "Kim Il Sung Dead at 82," *New York Times*, July 9, 1994.

24 Anna Fifield, "Selling to Survive," *Financial Times*, November 20, 2007.

25 Kim Hakjoon, *Dynasty*, 131.

26 Ri Nam Ok, Kim Jong Nam's cousin, thought that Ko Yong Hui was behind this move. From Imogen O'Neil's unpublished book, *The Golden Cage: Life with Kim Jong Il, a Daughter's Story*.

27 O'Neil, *The Golden Cage*.

28 Kim Hakjoon, *Dynasty*, 153.

29 Kenji Fujimoto, *I Was Kim Jong-il's Cook* (Tokyo: Fusosha Publishing, 2003).

CHAPTER 2: LIVING WITH THE IMPERIALISTS

1 *Immortal Anti-Japanese Revolutionary, Teacher Kim Hyong Jik* (Pyongyang: Publishing House of the Workers' Party of Korea, 1968), 93–94.

2 Yi Han-yong, *Taedong River Royal Family: My 14 Years Incognito in Seoul* (Seoul: Dong-a Ilbo, 1996).

3 David Halberstam. *The Coldest Winter: America and the Korean War* (New York: Hachette Books, 2007), 80.

4 Robert S. Boynton, *The Invitation-Only Zone: The True Story of North Korea's Abduction Project* (New York: Farrar, Straus and Giroux, 2016), 33.

5 Yoji Gomi, *Three Generations of Women in North Korea's Kim Dynasty* (Tokyo: Bunshun Shinso, 2016).

6 Ko Yong-gi, "A Curious Blood Line Connecting Kim Jong Un and Osaka," *Daily North Korea*, December 14, 2015.

7 Sin Yong Hui's memoir, cited in the South Korean media, including by investigative journalist Cho Gab-je in a post on chogabje.com on June 26, 2012.

8 *Anecdotes of Kim Jong Un's Life* (Pyongyang: Foreign Languages Publishing House, 2017), 49.

9 Details about the houses and provisions come from Imogen O'Neil's unpublished book *The Golden Cage: Life with Kim Jong Il, a Daughter's Story.*

CHAPTER 3: ANONYMOUS IN SWITZERLAND

1 According to an author interview with Thomas Bach, former president of the International Olympic Committee.

2 Guy Faulconbridge, "North Korean Leaders Used Brazilian Passports to Apply for Western Visas," Reuters, February 28, 2018.

3 Evan Thomas, "North Korea's First Family," *Newsweek*, July 17, 2009.

4 Andrew Higgins, "Who Will Succeed Kim Jong Il?" *Washington Post*, July 16, 2009.

5 Mira Mayrhofer and Gunther Müller, "Nordkorea: Kim Jong-un Wird auf die Machtübernahme Vorbereitet," *Profil* (Austria), September 21, 2010.

6 According to an unpublished interview conducted by Swiss journalist Bernhard Odehnal.

7 "Kim Jung-un mochte Nike Air-Turnschuhe, aber keine Mädchen," *Berner Zeitung*, October 6, 2010.

8 Higgins, "Who Will Succeed."

9 Interview with Odehnal.

10 Information from Simon Lutstorf about Kim Jong Un's basketball games at the high school comes from Titus Plattner, Daniel Glaus, and Julian Schmidli, *In Buglen und Kochen eine 4*, SonntagsZeitung, April 1, 2012.

11 "Revealed: Kim Jong-un the Schoolboy," Al Jazeera English, November 7, 2010.

12   Atika Shubert, "Swiss Man Remembers School with Son of North Korean Leader," CNN, Sept. 29, 2010.

13   Higgins, "Who Will Succeed."

14   Colin Freeman and Philip Sherwell, "North Korea Leadership: 'My Happy Days at School with North Korea's Future Leader,'" *Daily Telegraph*, September 26, 2010.

15   "Kim Jong-Un Mochte Nike Air-Turnschuhe, Aber Keine Mädchen," *Berner Zeitung*, October 6, 2010.

16   Interview with Odehnal.

CHAPTER 4: DICTATORSHIP 101

1   Details about songs on the airwaves and speculation in the South Korean press come from Kim Hakjoon, *Dynasty: The Hereditary Succession Politics of North Korea* (Stanford, CA: Shorenstein Asia-Pacific Research Center, 2017), 156–158.

2   *Anecdotes of Kim Jong Un's Life* (Pyongyang: Foreign Languages Publishing House, 2017), 4.

3   "Kim Jong Il's Doctor Opens Up on '08 Stroke," Associated Press, December 19, 2011.

4   Jamy Keaten and Catherine Gaschka, "French Doctor Confirms Kim Had Stroke in 2008," Associated Press, December 19, 2011.

5   Lee Yung-jong, *Successor Kim Jong Un* (Seoul: NP Plus, 2010).

6   Thae Yong-ho, *Password from the Third-Floor Secretariat* (Seoul: Giparang, 2018), 280.

7   According to Cheong Seong-chang of the Sejong Institute.

8   "'Mother of Military-first Chosun' Made Public," *Daily NK*, July 12, 2012.

9   Cho Jong Ik, "'Great Mother' Revealed to the World," *Daily NK*, June 30, 2012.

10   Christopher Richardson, "North Korea's Kim Dynasty: The Making of a Personality Cult," *Guardian*, February 16, 2015.

11   Barbara Demick, "Nothing Left," *New Yorker*, July 12, 2010.

12   Demick, "Nothing Left."

13   Stephan Haggard and Marcus Noland, *Witness to Transformation: Refugee Insights into North Korea* (Washington, DC: Peterson Institute for International Economics, 2010).

14   "N. Korean Technocrat Executed for Bungled Currency Reform," Yonhap News Agency, March 18, 2010.

15 Kim Hakjoon, *Dynasty*, 176.

16 "Kim Jong Il Issues Order on Promoting Military Ranks," Korean Central News Agency, September 27, 2010.

CHAPTER 5: A THIRD KIM AT THE HELM

1 Ken Gause, "North Korean Leadership Dynamics and Decision-Making under Kim Jong-un: A Second-Year Assessment," CNA, March 2014, 2.

2 Gause, "North Korean Leadership Dynamics," 110.

3 Gause, "North Korean Leadership Dynamics," 3.

CHAPTER 6: NO MORE BELT TIGHTENING

1 Stephan Haggard and Marcus Noland, *Famine in North Korea: Markets, Aid, and Reform* (New York: Columbia University Press, 2009), 187.

2 According to Curtis Melvin, a researcher at the US-Korea Institute at Johns Hopkins University in the United States.

3 Benjamin Katzeff Silberstein, *Growth and Geography of Markets in North Korea: New Evidence from Satellite Imagery* (US-Korea Institute at the Johns Hopkins School of Advanced International Studies, October 2015), 29–36.

4 Kang Mi-jin, "Stall Transfers Yield Big Profits at the Market," *Daily NK*, May 14, 2015.

5 Cha Moon-seok, *Information about North Korea's Market: Focusing on Current Status of Its Official Market* (Seoul: Korean Institute for National Unification, 2016).

6 Kim Byung-ro, "North Korea's Marketization and Changes in the Class Structure," from *The Economy and Society in the Kim Jong-Un Era: New Relationship between the State and Market*, edited by Yang Moon-soo (Paju: Haneul Academy, 2014).

7 Yonho Kim, *North Korea's Mobile Telecommunications and Private Transport Services in Kim Jong Un Era* (US-Korea Institute at SAIS, 2018).

8 Yonho Kim, *North Korea's Mobile Telecommunications*.

CHAPTER 7: BETTER TO BE FEARED THAN LOVED

1 "N. Korea Requires Students to Take 81-hour Course on Kim Jong-un," KBS, November 25, 2014.

2   Helen-Louise Hunter, "The Society and Its Environment," in *North Korea: A Country Study*, edited by Robert L. Worden, 79–86 (Federal Research Office, Library of Congress, 2008), 85–86.

3   James Pearson, "The $50 Device That Symbolizes a Shift in North Korea," Reuters, March 26, 2015.

4   Greg Scarlatoiu, preface to *Coercion, Control, Surveillance, and Punishment: An Examination of the North Korean Police State* (Washington: Committee for Human Rights in North Korea, 2012), 5.

5   Hunter, "The Society and Its Environment," 79–80.

6   Andrei Lankov, "The Evolution of North Korea's 'Inminban,'" NK News, April 28, 2015.

7   Andrei Lankov, "Daily Life in North Korea," Al Jazeera, May 21, 2014.

8   Kang Dong-wan, *Hallyu Phenomenon in North Korea: Meaning and Impact* (Institute for Unification Education of South Korea), 73–74.

9   David Hawk, *Parallel Gulag* (Washington: Committee for Human Rights in North Korea, 2017), 21.

10   David Hawk, *The Hidden Gulag: The Lives and Voices of "Those Who Are Sent to the Mountains"* (Washington: Committee for Human Rights in North Korea, 2012), 4.

11   Hawk, *Parallel Gulag*, 11.

12   All descriptions of torture are from the Commission of Inquiry on Human Rights in the Democratic People's Republic of Korea Report of Detailed Findings, 2014, 235.

13   Commission of Inquiry report, 2014, 124.

14   Hawk, *Parallel Gulag*, 31.

15   Anna Fifield, "North Korea's Prisons Are as Bad as Nazi Camps, Says Judge Who Survived Auschwitz," *Washington Post*, December 11, 2017.

CHAPTER 8: GOODBYE, UNCLE

1   Milan W. Svolik, *The Politics of Authoritarian Rule* (UK: Cambridge Studies in Comparative Politics, 2012), 5.

2   Ju-min Park and James Pearson, "North Korea Executes Defence Chief with an Anti-Aircraft Gun: South Korea Agency," Reuters, May 13, 2015.

3   Ra Jong-yil, *Jang Song Thaek's Path: A Rebellious Outsider* (Seoul: ALMA, 2016).

4   Ra, *Jang Song Thaek's Path*, 145.

5   Ra, *Jang Song Thaek's Path*, 167.

6 "Kim's Niece Kills Herself in Paris," *JoongAng Daily*, September 18, 2006.

7 Andray Abrahamian, *The ABCs of North Korea's SEZs* (US-Korea Institute at SAIS, 2014).

8 Ra, *Jang Song Thaek's Path*, 254.

9 Thae Yong-ho, *Password from the Third-Floor Secretariat* (Seoul: Giparang, 2018), 328.

10 Alexandre Mansourov, "North Korea: The Dramatic Fall of Jang Song Thaek," *38 North*, December 9, 2013.

11 Mansourov, "North Korea."

12 "Traitor Jang Song Thaek Executed," Korean Central News Agency, December 13, 2013.

CHAPTER 9: THE ELITES OF PYONGHATTAN

1 Park In Ho, *The Creation of the North Korean Market System* (Seoul: Daily NK, 2017).

2 "The Complex Ties Interlinking Cadres and the Donju," *Daily NK*, July 8, 2016.

3 Jonathan Corrado, "Will Marketization Bring Down the North Korean Regime?" *The Diplomat*, April 18, 2017.

CHAPTER 10: MILLENNIALS AND MODERNITY

1 "Rungna People's Pleasure Ground Opens in Presence of Marshal Kim Jong Un," Korean Central News Agency, July 25, 2012.

2 Thae Yong-ho, *Password from the Third-Floor Secretariat* (Seoul: Giparang, 2018), 307.

3 Yoji Gomi, *Three Generations of Women in North Korea's Kim Dynasty* (Tokyo: Bunshun Shinso, 2016).

4 Anna Fifield, "What Did the Korean Leaders Talk About on Those Park Benches? Trump, Mainly," *Washington Post*, May 2, 2018.

CHAPTER 11: PLAYING BALL WITH THE "JACKALS"

1 Dennis Rodman, speaking at the Modern War Institute in West Point, New York, March 3, 2017.

2 Shane Smith in *VICE on HBO Season One: The Hermit Kingdom* (Episode 10), February 23, 2014.

3 Dennis Rodman to Megyn Kelly on NBC, June 19, 2018.

4 Jason Mojica, "In Dealing with North Korea, Fake It 'til You Make It," *Medium*, February 26, 2018.

5 Dennis Rodman in *Dennis Rodman's Big Bang in Pyongyang* (2015).

6 Vice film.

7 Vice film.

8 Darren Prince in *Dennis Rodman's Big Bang in Pyongyang*.

9 Dennis Rodman in *Dennis Rodman's Big Bang in Pyongyang*.

CHAPTER 12: PARTY TIME

1 Timothy W. Martin, "How North Korea's Hackers Became Dangerously Good," *Wall Street Journal*, April 19, 2018.

2 Curtis M. Scaparrotti to House Committee on Armed Services, April 2, 2014.

3 Ellen Nakashima and Devlin Barrett, "U.S. Charges North Korean Operative in Conspiracy to Hack Sony Pictures, Banks," *Washington Post*, September 6, 2018.

4 Patrick Winn, "How North Korean Hackers Became the World's Greatest Bank Robbers," *Global Post Investigations*, May 16, 2018.

5 Martin, "How North Korea's Hackers Became Dangerously Good."

6 Ju-min Park, James Pearson, and Timothy Martin, "In North Korea, Hackers Are a Handpicked, Pampered Elite," Reuters, December 5, 2014.

7 Sam Kim, "Inside North Korea's Hacker Army," *Bloomberg Businessweek*, February 7, 2018.

8 Joshua Hunt, "Holiday at the Dictator's Guesthouse," *The Atavist Magazine*, no. 54, November 2015.

CHAPTER 13: THE UNWANTED BROTHER

1 Bruce Bueno de Mesquita and Alastair Smith, *The Dictator's Handbook: Why Bad Behavior Is Almost Always Good Politics* (New York: PublicAffairs, 2011), 30.

2 "Jong-nam Kept Antidote to Poison in Sling Bag, Court Told," Bernama News Agency (Malaysia), November 29, 2017.

3 According to Ri Nam Ok, as told to Imogen O'Neil.

4 Song Hye Rang, *Wisteria House: The Autobiography of Song Hye-rang* (Seoul: Chisiknara, 2000).

5   Song Hye Rang, *Wisteria House.*

6   According to Ri Nam Ok, as told to Imogen O'Neil.

7   Yi Han-yong, *Taedong River Royal Family: My 14 Years Incognito in Seoul* (Seoul: Donga Ilbo, 1996).

8   According to Ri Nam Ok, as told to Imogen O'Neil.

9   Yi Han-yong, *Taedong River Royal Family.*

10   According to Ri Nam Ok, as told to Imogen O'Neil.

11   Ju-min Park and A. Ananthalakshmi, "Malaysia Detains Woman, Seeks Others in Connection with North Korean's Death," Reuters, February 15, 2017.

12   Based on an interview with someone with knowledge of the intelligence who spoke on condition of anonymity.

13   According to Mark.

14   Kim Jong Nam to Japan's TV Asahi, interview aired October 12, 2010.

15   "Kim Jong-il's Grandson Feels Sorry for Starving Compatriots," *Chosun Ilbo*, October 4, 2011.

16   Alastair Gale, "Kim Jong Un's Nephew Was in Danger After Father's Killing, North Korean Group Says," *Wall Street Journal*, October 1, 2017.

17   "Kim Jong-un's Brother Visits London to Watch Eric Clapton," BBC News, May 22, 2015.

CHAPTER 14: THE TREASURED SWORD

1   Anna Fifield, "After Six Tests, the Mountain Hosting North Korea's Nuclear Blasts May Be Exhausted," *Washington Post*, October 20, 2017.

2   Kim Jong Un to central committee meeting of the Workers' Party, as reported by KCNA, April 21, 2018.

3   Translation from Christopher Green, *Daily NK.*

4   Joseph S. Bermudez, *North Korea's Development of a Nuclear Weapons Strategy* (The US-Korea Institute at SAIS, 2015), 8.

5   James Person and Atsuhito Isozaki, "Want to Be a Successful Dictator? Copy North Korea," *The National Interest*, March 9, 2017.

6   Alexandre Y. Mansourov, "The Origins, Evolution, and Current Politics of the North Korean Nuclear Program," *The Nonproliferation Review* 2, no. 3 (Spring–Summer 1995): 25–38.

7   Mansourov, "The Origins, Evolution, and Current Politics."

8   Jonathan D. Pollack, *No Exit: North Korea, Nuclear Weapons and International Security* (The International Institute for Strategic Studies, 2014), chapter 3.

9   Scott Douglas Sagan and Jeremi Suri, "The Madman Nuclear Alert: Secrecy, Signaling, and Safety in October 1969," *International Security* 27, no. 4 (2003): 150–183.

10 H. R. Haldeman with Joseph DiMona, *The Ends of Power* (New York: Times Books, 1978), 83.

11 Mercy A. Kuo, "Kim Jong-un's Political Psychology Profile: Insights from Ken Dekleva," *The Diplomat*, October 17, 2017.

12 H. R. McMaster in interview on MSNBC, August 5, 2017.

CHAPTER 15: THE CHARM OFFENSIVE

1   From Imogen O'Neil's book *Inside the Golden Cage*.

2   According to sushi chef Kenji Fujimoto and Konstantin Pulikovsky, Russia's envoy to the Far East who visited North Korea frequently during the Kim Jong Il era.

3   According to Michael Madden of North Korea Leadership Watch.

4   Author interview with Lim Jae-cheon, a Kim family expert at Korea University in Seoul.

5   Anna Fifield, "What Did the Korean Leaders Talk About on Those Park Benches? Trump, Mainly," *Washington Post*, May 2, 2018.

6   Anna Fifield, "Did You Hear the One about the North Korean Leader, the $100 Bill and the Trump Card?" *Washington Post*, April 30, 2018.

CHAPTER 16: TALKING WITH THE "JACKALS"

1   Eric Talmadge, "Economist: N. Korea Eying Swiss, Singaporean-Style Success," Associated Press, October 29, 2018.

2   Lee Seok Young, "Successor Looks Set for Own Escort," *Daily NK*, August 26, 2011, citing Lee Yeong Guk, author of the book *I Was Kim Jong Il's Bodyguard*.

3   According to Kenji Fujimoto.

4   John Bolton, "The Legal Case for Striking North Korea First," *Wall Street Journal*, February 28, 2018.

5   Andrew Kim, "North Korea Denuclearization and U.S.-DPRK Diplomacy," speech given at Stanford University on February 25, 2019.

6   Andrew Kim, "North Korea Denuclearization."

7 First reported by Alex Ward, "Exclusive: Trump Promised Kim Jong Un He'd Sign an Agreement to End the Korean War," Vox, August 29, 2018. Confirmed through my own reporting.

8 Freddy Gray, "Donald Trump's Real-Estate Politik Is Working," *The Spectator*, June 12, 2018.

9 Based on author interviews with sources who spoke on condition of anonymity.

10 Karen DeYoung, Greg Jaffe, John Hudson, and Josh Dawsey, "John Bolton Puts His Singular Stamp on Trump's National Security Council," *Washington Post*, March 4, 2019.

INDEX

Anna Fifield is the Beijing bureau chief for the *Washington Post*. She previously spent eight years reporting on North Korea, first for the *Financial Times* and then for the *Post*, and has visited North Korea a dozen times. She was a Nieman journalism fellow at Harvard University, studying how change happens in closed societies, and received the Shorenstein journalism award from Stanford University in 2018 for her outstanding reporting on Asia.

From Byron, Austen and Darwin

to some of the most acclaimed and original
contemporary writing, John Murray takes pride in
bringing you powerful, prizewinning, absorbing
and provocative books that will entertain you
today and become the classics of tomorrow.

We put a lot of time and passion into what we
publish and how we publish it, and we'd like to
hear what you think.

Be part of John Murray – share your views with us at:

www.johnmurray.co.uk

 johnmurraybooks

 @johnmurrays

 johnmurraybooks